For my good friends
and generous supporters
at The Graduate College.

Jerry Plunkett

1/21/04

THE
VONNEGUT
EFFECT

THE
VONNEGUT
EFFECT

JEROME KLINKOWITZ

University of South Carolina Press

© 2004 University of South Carolina

Published in Columbia, South Carolina, by the
University of South Carolina Press

Manufactured in the United States of America

08 07 06 05 04   5 4 3 2 1

Library of Congress Cataloging-in-Publication Data

Klinkowitz, Jerome.
  The Vonnegut effect / Jerome Klinkowitz.
    p. cm.
  Includes bibliographical references (p.) and index.
    ISBN 1-57003-520-2 (cloth : alk. paper)
    1. Vonnegut, Kurt—Criticism and interpretation. 2. Postmodernism (Literature)—
  United States. I. Title.

PS3572.O5 Z746 2004
813'.54—dc22   2003017061

For Peter Reed, master plane spotter and critic

CONTENTS

PREFACE

THE VONNEGUT EFFECT is a chronological investigation of Kurt Vonnegut's writing as reflected by the social and critical contexts in which it has developed. The "effect" of his work has been unique in that he is the single American author to have won and sustained a great popular acceptance while embracing the more radical forms and themes of postmodern literature. Postmodernism, with its challenge to narrative authority, exposure of previously unquestioned assumptions, and rejection of traditional fiction's conventions (including the reader's willing suspension of disbelief), has certainly expressed the tenor of recent times. But novelists in the postmodern mode, such as John Barth, Thomas Pynchon, Kathy Acker, Ishmael Reed, and Ronald Sukenick, have for the most part found their most loyal audiences among academics, theorists, and critics. Kurt Vonnegut's fiction is highly regarded in these quarters as well but is especially noteworthy because of its popularity with general readers. Studying its effect, then, involves watching his innovations emerge from the very heart of his era's culture and noting how that culture has in turn accepted such work as a reliable index of its social and aesthetic values.

How Kurt Vonnegut's writing achieves its effect can be measured by examining how his themes and techniques stay a close but crucial step ahead of issues developing in American culture during the half century in which he has been publishing. At a time when highbrow tastes were favoring a harshly satiric acidity and lowbrow inclinations tended toward sentimentality, Vonnegut's work found ways to include both, one feature not so much balancing the other as showing how both attitudes were just that: perspectives that could be adjusted at will. Overriding the variable matters of taste were more enduring qualities of simple human decency, understanding, and compassion. As human traits, they attracted readers; but as tested against the challenges of modern life and shown to be ultimately bankable in a world where so much else had been devalued, these characteristics helped make Kurt Vonnegut the type of writer to which readers returned again and again, attracting new generations along the way.

In finding a way to develop such attitudes into a form for postmodern fiction, Vonnegut benefited from his three areas of professional training: biochemistry, anthropology, and journalism. In an age when many serious writers learned their art at universities, Kurt Vonnegut escaped the English department almost entirely. His two and one-half years of undergraduate work in the sciences (before military service intervened) gave him a solidly mechanical sense of how things function, and his postwar graduate studies in anthropology reenforced his personal beliefs in the flip side of science: that when it comes to human beings, cultural relativism (rather than scientific absolutism) is the most useful key to understanding why things are as they are. How these notions get expressed in writing was something to be learned the hard way but also a way grounded in day-to-day living: as a journalist. Both Shortridge High School in Indianapolis and Cornell University let student reporters and editors work in professional circumstances, turning out products that addressed in a serious manner the serious issues of the day, including the approach of World War II. Yet college humor was also part of the job, and in his work on the *Shortridge Echo* and the *Cornell Sun,* Vonnegut got solid experience in reporting hard news from the freshness of a young person's viewpoint.

The world Kurt Vonnegut inherited in the years following World War II was remarkably different from the one into which he had been born. Because it was different for almost everyone else in his generation, making sense of it would be not just an artistic fancy but also a great public service. Throughout the next half century this writer would confront increasingly daunting challenges by judging them in the context of his own experience. That experience—as a midwesterner whose family took a big financial hit in the Great Depression but kept their heads above water in the economic middle class, as a young man who studied science and then saw what such wizardry could accomplish in destroying the treasures of civilization during World War II, as an American starting a family and his career within the new corporate structure of the 1940s and 1950s, and as a person cutting free of that structure not so much to become a literary artist as to set up and run his own short-story business—was shared by a great number of his fellow citizens. As such it was the lifestyle of an age. And in using it to sort out the new conditions of existence the author was speaking in commonly accessible terms. The difference was that he wanted to question things, doing so in a thoroughly open-minded manner.

Hence readers, beginning with his first stories for *Collier's* magazine in 1950, were exposed to a style of writing whose effect was not at all in the manner of what they had learned at school. Wonders of modern science were in this man's work no longer received with reverence; instead they were tested against the most common terms of simple living. These same middle-class values, empowered by means of a convincingly vernacular voice and attitude, were put up against both historical outrages and seemingly supernatural threats—and in Vonnegut's work they came out of it not only still standing but also with a new sense of worthfulness. He could make jokes against logic, using logic's own terms to break the bonds of its confinement. What appeared in his texts was new but no more threatening than the spectacle of its author, as familiar as the guy next door, fooling around with some new contraption (and vowing that he, and not it, would be the master).

Kurt Vonnegut's own heroes, during a childhood that had seen the conditions of his family's life turned upside down by financial abstractions transpiring half a continent away on Wall Street, were the film comedians Laurel and Hardy. In dedicating his novel *Slapstick* to their memory he recalled how they "never failed to bargain in good faith with their destinies, and were screamingly adorable and funny on that account." The author, typical American that he is, has made the same bargain, negotiating his destiny with the materials available. That so many of them are common property of his age makes the effect of his work successful.

ACKNOWLEDGMENTS

WORKING ON KURT VONNEGUT has been an especially pleasurable task, thanks to all the good company. In an era when the subject contemporary studies too often involves battles of the books, the mood surrounding Vonnegut has been consistently cheerful. Chiefly responsible for this is the author himself, whose life and writings serve as good examples of how community support is essential for anyone getting anything done. From John Somer, with whom I began working on Vonnegut more than a third of a century ago, to Kevin Boon and David Andrews, Vonnegut scholars younger than my children with whom I have cooperated, studying fiction by the "Grand Old Man" (as we have come to call him) has brought me in contact with some of the nicest people in the business. Loree Rackstraw, Asa Pieratt, Bob Weide, André Eckenrode—life would dull without them. Peter Reed, who published the first book on Vonnegut back in 1972, has shared other interests with me as well, including his experience as a Royal Air Force officer fascinated by the narratology of air combat memoirs from World War II. It is one of the many ironies of our times that as he was being bombed by the Luftwaffe in Britain the RAF was bombing Vonnegut in Dresden. There is no need to say "so it goes" because each survived. It is to Peter, just now winding up a long and brilliant career as a teacher, scholar, and administrator at the University of Minnesota, that this book is dedicated.

Extended families start at home. My wife, Julie Huffman-klinkowitz, is a co-author (along with Asa B. Pieratt Jr. and me) of *Kurt Vonnegut: A Comprehensive Bibliography* (1987) and has helped research new items while keeping our Vonnegut archive professionally organized. My children, Jonathan and Nina, now well into their adulthood careers in journalism and law, often spot news media references before I do and have made Vonnegut's writings part of their own lives. At the University of Northern Iowa, where I have taught since 1972, colleagues are always a great help, as is the university's Graduate College, which underwrote a semester's "Professional Development Leave" that made my work on this book possible.

Kurt Vonnegut has been progressively tolerant, amused, and cooperative with all of our work on his canon. In the preface to his 1974 essay collection, *Wampeters, Foma & Granfalloons,* he described John Somer and me as "two nice young college professors" whose "intentions were friendly" but who nevertheless seemed to be performing "therapeutic vivisection" on him. Thankfully he survived, and over the years he has become a friend to all of us, making us characters in a concluding scene in his novel *Timequake* and completing the cycle of critical and creative intervention.

Quotations from Vonnegut's works are used with his permission. They are indicated with page numbers and abbreviated titles. Full citations appear in the bibliography.

A KEY TO ABBREVIATIONS

BB	*Bluebeard*
BC	*Breakfast of Champions*
BSB	*Bagombo Snuff Box*
BTT	*Between Time and Timbuktu*
CC	*Cat's Cradle*
D	*Deadeye Dick*
F	*Fates Worse Than Death*
G	*Galápagos*
GB	*God Bless You, Mr. Rosewater*
HBWJ	*Happy Birthday, Wanda June*
HP	*Hocus Pocus*
J	*Jailbird*
MN	*Mother Night*
PP	*Player Piano*
PS	*Palm Sunday*
S	*Slapstick*
SF	*Slaughterhouse-Five*
ST	*The Sirens of Titan*
T	*Timequake*
WFG	*Wampeters, Foma & Granfalloons*
WMH	*Welcome to the Monkey House*

THE
VONNEGUT
EFFECT

INTRODUCTION

Vonnegut in America

IN 1957 KURT VONNEGUT was living in West Barnstable, Massachusetts, in a colonial-style frame house on Scudder's Lane, a picturesquely named but quite functional address on the business side of Cape Cod. Kurt would tell people wondering where he lived to picture the cape as an arm flexed to make a muscle. His home was not at the fingertips, Provincetown, though he and his wife Jane had tried that location out after leaving Schenectady and his job as a publicist for the General Electric Research Laboratory (GE Lab) when his first novel, *Player Piano* (1952), was published. Nor was it in fashionable Hyannis Port, site of the already famous Kennedy compound. Hyannis and all such trappings of the better life were just seven miles away but on the opposite side of Cape Cod's narrow land mass, looking outward to the sea. West Barnstable was right where the biceps would be, facing the salt marshes that ringed Cape Cod Bay.

Though the town was not muscular it did serve as home to people who worked—some for the Kennedy family, as did Vonnegut's friend Frank Wirtanen, who skippered their yacht, and others in the various trades of welding, carpentry, boat repair, insurance sales, and the like. Vonnegut, after his brief flirtation with the artist colony life out at the tip, had found West Barnstable to be a better place to raise a family and write fiction about similar homely themes salable to *Collier's* and the *Saturday Evening Post*. *Player Piano,* futuristic as it was, had not delivered much promise for the strictly artistic life. Although well reviewed, it sold less than half of its first printing of seventy-six hundred copies—most of those, Vonnegut would joke, in Albany, Schenectady, and Troy, the company-town residences of folks curious to see how their old neighbor had dystopianized the world of GE. Vonnegut was by now head of an eight-person family, with three children of his own and another three adopted when his sister and brother-in-law died within days of each other. If his writing were to pay the bills it had to be more remunerative than the small sum (for two years of hard labor) his novel had earned. So it was on short stories that the author relied to earn his living: stories for the great family weeklies of the American midcentury to which a single sale would bring in never less than seven hundred dollars and sometimes as much as twenty-five hundred dollars. Do two or three a year for the high-paying *Post* plus a couple more for outlets such as *Argosy* and *Cosmopolitan* and you had enough income to live responsibly by your own workmanship—like the skippers, boat repairers, carpenters, and welders Kurt had for neighbors in West Barnstable, all of them living out the American dream.

Not that there were not occasional rude awakenings. Sometimes it seemed nothing would sell. At other times writer's block (as when the author's father died) interfered. But then, like anyone else whose business was in a temporary slump, he filled in part-time with something else. At one point Vonnegut called on his expertise as a publicist to write copy for a Boston agency, whose client—a major foundry—intrigued the author with the delicacy of its castings. Another time, willing as were so many other socially conscientious persons of his generation, he taught for a while in a school for emotionally disturbed children. Or, as happened in 1957 when just two stories were sold and 1958 looked to be only half as good, he could take advantage of some neighborly connections and just out-and-out fake it, this time as a sculptor. Why not? The college training he had was as a biochemist, with some unfinished graduate work in anthropology. Writing was something he had picked up on his own, an academic extracurricular that put him on the staff of both his high school and university student newspapers. Could the plastic arts be that much harder?

If this sounds like a joke, it is exactly how his stint as a sculptor started. At a neighborhood party Vonnegut got talking with a friend who worked for the Sheraton Corporation taking contract work to furnish and decorate the Logan International Motel being built near the Boston airport. The guy was stumped at how to handle a long blank wall twelve feet high and about forty feet long in the motel's restaurant. That was indeed a lot of space, Vonnegut agreed, and not the easiest shape to work with. But he had an idea and for the fun of it sketched it out: a comet traveling across the nighttime sky. He even gave it a title: "New England Enters the Space Age." As he does now when retelling the story, Vonnegut laughed. The space race, with Russia's triumphant Sputnik outclassing any number of American launch failures, was on everyone's mind that autumn. Putting a comet on display in the dining room at Logan International was wry humor. "I was kidding," the author has ever since claimed.

But a month later something good showed up in the mail: not an acceptance from *Cosmo* or the *Post,* but a contract offering to pay eleven hundred dollars for the proposed sculpture to be built according to Vonnegut's design and installed on the restaurant wall. There was a delivery date, but the amateur sculptor, to this point strictly a conceptualist, accepted it. He needed the money.

Recalling the events, as he is prone to do when visiting friends, Kurt reprises both the methods and the materials of his short fiction from the 1950s and of his best novels since then. Although it is a generally human trait—for instance, French workers good at it are called *bricoleurs*—in this country it is taken as a sign of American ingenuity: the ability to get the job done with whatever materials happen to be available. Some practitioners of the art view it as a comic talent, constructing elaborate Rube Goldberg machines to accomplish simple ends with flamboyantly elaborate machinery. Kurt Vonnegut knows machines; his World War II army training was as a mechanical engineer doing field assemblies of the mighty 240-millimeter howitzers, putting them together the right way quickly and effectively. As a story writer in postwar America he was also working under field conditions as effectively as he could to get a saleable piece written.

For the goal at hand a self-admiring contraption was not the answer. Instead he had to gather available resources and turn them to his end of making a piece of fiction that was worthwhile to read, with at least one character whose desire readers could cheer on through adversity, and with enough information so that these same readers could not only follow along but complete the story themselves if required. For this balance of discovery and delight Vonnegut would use what his world provided. In the fall of 1957 that world had given him Sputnik orbiting above, an oddly shaped blank wall in the motel restaurant at Logan International, and some neighbors who could help him earn eleven hundred dollars—if not for stories or novels, then for something else equally artful.

Step one was to see if he could learn welding, for the design he had sketched involved assembling steel rods to simulate a comet tail's elaborate display. A local blacksmith was glad to teach him, but the intricacies of his first lesson convinced Vonnegut that he would be smarter to just hire the welder to fabricate the design. In terms of the artistic concept this was no different than the second stage, which involved representing the comet's head with a ball of granite such as the author had seen decorating grave-stones. But a visit to the appropriate funereal stone yard brought bad news: these granite balls, so common in the nineteenth century, had been carved on lathes made for cannonballs—and had not been made since such cannons were retired from the U.S. arsenal half a century before. "I was aghast," Vonnegut recalls. "To finish my sculpture and collect my commission, would I have to sneak out at night and rob a graveyard?" But as fits the luck of bricoleurs in France, improvisers in America, and handy-men everywhere, circumstances came to the rescue. When the old man running the stone yard learned why the granite ball was needed, he laughed, saying a manufacturer's second would do, and he led the author out to a disused field where dozens of such rejects from a century ago rested in the weeds.

Listeners to this tale, like readers of a Vonnegut story, have thus had their time entertainingly engaged; they have met a character whose goals they can root for, who has in an informative way faced some adversity and solved it, and who is on his way to accomplishing what the reader has hoped for: getting the sculpture done in a novel but not incredible way. All that remains is to wind things up, with improvisation and ingenuity serving well to the end. A carpenter builds a platform for transporting the finished work, while Vonnegut glues the granite ball to the welded-steel tail and draws a template of the assemblage showing where and how it is to be fixed to the restaurant's wall. The finished work is hauled to Boston by Vonnegut and another friend who, as a boatyard owner, has a large trailer. And although the motel's builders have allowed zero tolerance, the sculpture fits into the template's specified holes. The job is done! The sculptor collects his fee, and all is well.

So well, in fact, that the originally skeptical motel builders ask Kurt if he has some ideas for other blank walls that need decoration. Oh, he has ideas aplenty but keeps them to himself. Designing the comet had been fun—a joke, in fact. But in making it come true he has failed as a welder, contemplated robbing a cemetery, and had his heart stop in the moments it took to see if the template's specifications and the construction workers' engineering would match up with his sculpture's mounting points. De-spite the fact that the restaurant artwork hung there for twenty years—from the time of Vonnegut's almost utter anonymity in 1957 to the heights of his fame throughout the 1970s—and was even depicted on the restau-rant's menu and on the motel's stationery, it would remain forever an unsigned, unacknowledged work. No wonder, then, that during a re-modeling the restaurant was gutted and all its fixtures thrown out, the sculpture being scrapped for its steel. New England, after all, was by now well beyond its entrance into the space age; no one even used that term anymore. But for two decades the piece had done its work, filling a blank space with something imaginatively interesting. And nearly fifty years later his story about making it would be one of Vonnegut's favorite entertainments—along with other odd endeavors such as being the country's second Saab automobile dealer for a brief, hilarious period around the same time, another story that reflects just who this person was back then and what he did to devise various ways of making a living.

The Saab story is something Vonnegut has talked about and has written down, in part, in his introduction to *Bagombo Snuff Box* (1999), an assemblage of early short fiction passed over for previous collections. The details of the story are wonderful: seeing a truckload of these odd little cars, colored and shaped like Easter eggs, coming out of Boston; asking the driver what on earth they were and being told franchise dealerships were available; setting up Saab Cape Cod and undertaking to sell not just foreign cars to a skeptical domestic public (who scarcely knew about even Volkswagens at this point in the 1950s) but ridiculous vehicles whose doors opened backward into the wind, whose identification plates on the inside of their glove boxes described the Saab company as the proud manufacturers of Messerschmitt and Focke-Wulf fighters to the German Luftwaffe, whose engines demanded a mixture of gasoline and oil, which if allowed to settle created clouds of black smoke and if neglected would reduce the engine "to the ore state" (*BSB*, 9). Worst (and most un-American) of all, Saab published its price list; buyers knew exactly what Vonnegut had paid and the margin they were expected to add; in other words, no dickering. Very few sold. But, as with the sculpture experience, it gave Vonnegut not just more material for a good story but great experience working with a useful storehouse of amusing, instructive materials.

This introduction to *Bagombo Snuff Box* also contains Vonnegut's rules for creative writing, and needless to say they parallel his experiences with selling both sculpture and Saabs. Realize that your audience consists of strangers who owe you nothing and do not want their time wasted. Give them at least one character they can root for—characters who want something, whose wants are revealed in sentences that carry forth this action, who face problems in achieving their desires (and hence can show what they are made of), and whose story begins as close to the end as possible. Above all, "Give your readers as much information as possible, as soon as possible" (*BSB,* 10). As far as mysteries of narrative development, "To heck with suspense. Readers should have such complete understanding of what is going on, where and why, that they could finish the story themselves, should cockroaches eat the last pages." It has been no surprise that the Saabs did not sell (how could they?), nor would it be fair that after all his ingenuity in getting the sculpture fabricated his own template for the mountings would be off (not that he will ever risk such a project again!). But look at all the interesting information picked up along the way, things about persons, places, and things that have posed challenges to the narrator as he advances his desire. And in the process of advancement, he has been quite the handyman, quite the bricoleur, making things work—no matter what.

Using materials at hand to get the job done, even if those materials were designed for something else, is the distinguishing feature of American ingenuity, French *bricolage,* and Kurt Vonnegut's literary art. His life follows this pattern of ingenious improvisation and is employed as a helpful device to anchor his writing: almost every one of his novels and short-story collections begins with an autobiographical preface, and his three books of essays use experiences from his life as their bases for understanding and judgment.

And so the story is well known. Vonnegut's ancestors on both sides of his family were emigrants from the failed German revolution of 1848 to America. Like the "free thinkers" who flocked to Milwaukee, Cincinnati, and other budding midwestern metropolises to build the ideal of a social democracy on the foundation of business, science, education, and the arts, Kurt's people came to Indianapolis and helped establish the city's cultural integrity—not so much civilizing a wilderness as constructing a social world on humane ideals. By the century's turn they were among the city's first families, among them the leading architect, the owner of the biggest and finest hardware store, and the best brewer. All of it, so rich and so wonderful, was made from nothing there on the Indiana plain in a city improvised from a new land's raw materials and the old country's failed ideals. Born in 1922, the author could take this for granted, at the same time admiring its improvisatory spirit:

Such provincial capitals, which is what they would have been called in Europe, were charmingly self-sufficient with respect to the fine arts. We sometimes had the director of the Indianapolis Symphony Orchestra to supper, or writers and painters, or architects like my father, of local renown.

I studied clarinet under the first-chair clarinetist of our symphony orchestra. I remember the orchestra's performance of Tchaikovsky's *1812 Overture,* in which the cannons' roars were supplied by a policeman firing blank cartridges into an empty garbage can. I knew the policeman. He sometimes guarded street crossings used by students on their way to or from School 43, my school, the *James Whitcomb Riley School.* (*BSB,* 293–94)

Taken from his collection's "Coda to My Career as a Writer for Periodicals," these thoughts reflect both Vonnegut's materials and the special use he has made of them. In the Indianapolis of his childhood the police force could equally protect children in crosswalks and fill in for Napoleon's cannons at the symphony—either was easily improvised from the main task of catching criminals and maintaining public order. That such an ideal world might not last, that its founding families' wealth could be dissipated and the richly supportive cultural network be dispersed, did not mean the end of things for young Kurt. When his grandfather's remarriage deprived the family of what would have been his mother's inheritance and when the Great Depression brought an end to his father's architectural commissions, Kurt adapted well, turning misfortune to advantage. Having to leave the grand house his father had designed (so large that it required servants to maintain the household) and move into a simple bungalow made it easier for Kurt to be friends with middle-class kids. Public schools, still among the country's best, were his paradise; Kurt hoped that his parents would not make good on their dream to send him back to the private schooling his older brother and sister had enjoyed. To do so would mean giving up friends, hobbies, curious interests, and fascination with life as lived—losing his entire world just as he had remade it.

As for schooling, that would also have to be a remaking, this time at his father's insistence. Because the arts had proven to be an unreliable moneymaker Kurt Vonnegut Sr. insisted that his sons not follow him as third-generation architects in Indianapolis. Science was a far better prospect, and so Bernard, nine years older than Kurt, was sent off to the Massachusetts Institute of Technology for a doctorate in physics and a career—most of it to be pursued at the General Electric Research Laboratory in Schenectady, New York—as an atmospheric physicist, studying clouds and devising seeding techniques to make it rain. A younger brother should benefit from this example, and so Kurt was prepped for undergraduate training in chemistry and biology at Cornell University in Ithaca, New York. This was a long way from Indiana, Kurt noted, and without the prospect of returning home that his uncles, aunts, and older cousins, also educated out east, had enjoyed. But there were ways of adapting to this strange new educational life. As a surrogate for the comforts of his supportive extended family back home, the new freshman immediately pledged a fraternity for the most literal of reasons: to be surrounded by "brothers" so far from Indianapolis. Plus he signed on at the student paper, working more seriously at what had been the extracurricular activity he had enjoyed most in high school. Here he built his own bridge to the real world, as he recalls in a speech delivered at the paper's banquet forty years later and collected with other essays, addresses, letters, and commentaries in *Palm Sunday: An Autobiographical Collage* (1981). Thinking back to those long nights required to put out a morning edition, Vonnegut recalled the pleasure of walking back to his room across campus "after having put the *Sun*," as the paper was called, "to bed":

> All the other university people, teachers and students alike, were asleep. They had been playing games all day long with what was known about real life. They had been repeating famous arguments and experiments, and asking one another the sorts of hard questions real life would be asking by and by.
>
> We on the *Sun* were already in the midst of real life. By God, if we weren't! We had just designed and written and caused to be manufactured yet another morning newspaper for a highly intelligent American community of respectable size—yes, and not during the Harding administration, either, but during 1940, '41, and '42, with the Great Depression ending, and with World War Two well begun.
>
> I am an agnostic, as some of you may have gleaned from my writings. But I have to tell you that, as I trudged up the hill so late at night and all alone, I knew that God Almighty approved of me. (*PS*, 66–67)

Yet Kurt Vonnegut was not to spend his life as a newspaperman either. World War II intervened. Without it, he is fond of saying, his friend Joseph Heller may well have had a career in the dry-cleaning business, while Vonnegut, as the fiftieth anniversary of D-day was celebrated, could just as easily have been retiring as garden editor of the *Indianapolis Times*. But being a draft-age American in 1943 meant that options were limited;

having lost his current semester's credits because of a long bout with pneumonia, Kurt withdrew from school and enlisted in a special plan the military had devised for bright young college men: the Army Specialized Training Program (ASTP). Here was something novel indeed, the chance to continue one's higher education as a serviceman with the promise of being able to select one's military specialty as a member of the best and the brightest of this greatest generation to be.

For the next year Kurt Vonnegut continued his schooling at Carnegie Tech, the University of Tennessee, and other institutions of higher learning where the army used short courses to qualify its recruits in various proficiencies. There is little doubt that this program was social engineering, a way to channel bright young college men into occupations that would benefit America's new role as a leader in the postwar economy. Then came the Normandy invasion, which commenced on 6 June 1944. Casualties were horrific, and once the breakout began late in July the prospects were for a long advance across the European continent that would be expensive in terms of men and material. General Eisenhower made an insistent call for more men—for so many that regular combat reserves could not even begin to fill the need. General Marshall, chairman of the Joint Chiefs of Staff, had never liked the presumed elitism of the ASTP, and in anticipation of Ike's great crusade he had arranged to cancel the program. Suddenly Vonnegut and 120,000 young men like him were pulled from their studies and given a quick course in infantry training. By late November of 1944 he was in Europe, his poorly prepared division replacing the D-day troops who in the past half year had pushed the front all the way from Normandy's beaches to Belgium's southern countryside near Bastogne. Kurt's arrival was just in time for the greatest test of American infantry in World War II: the Battle of the Bulge.

Talk about improvisation: Private Vonnegut had spent most of his service career at one college or another studying mechanical engineering. When finally given field training, it was in the assembly of the 240-mm howitzer, a much larger piece of artillery than could be accessed, let alone effectively used, in the fluid, near chaotic conditions resulting when the German Wehrmacht's Runstead offensive overran American lines. As part of the 106th Infantry Division he was assigned as battalion scout, with the ultimate test coming several days into the battle when his unit was disoriented and lost. He says in *Palm Sunday,* "My last mission as a scout was to find our own artillery. Usually, scouts go out and look for enemy stuff. Things got so bad that we were finally looking for our own stuff. If I'd found our own battalion commander, everybody would have thought that was pretty swell" (*PS*, 87).

With the five soldiers from his scouting unit and about fifty others he had never seen before, Vonnegut found himself hiding in a gully as a German unit took up a position above them. His group fixed bayonets to defend themselves. No Germans came in after them; instead barrages of 88-mm shells were sent into the trees above followed by a repeat of the Wehrmacht's instructions to surrender. Kurt recalls, "We didn't yell 'nuts' or anything like that. We said, 'Okay,' and 'Take it easy,' and so on" (*PS*, 88).

The balance of Vonnegut's war was spent in a prison camp the Germans had improvised from a slaughterhouse in Dresden. This was far from both the eastern and western fronts and, by virtue of its architectural treasures and art museums, was considered an open city, neither defended nor assaulted and definitely not used for any contributions to the war effort. The author first described his experiences there in the 1966 introduction to the hardcover edition of *Mother Night*, his third novel, which had originally appeared as a paperback in 1962. "There were about a hundred of us in our particular work group," Vonnegut writes, "and we were put out as contract labor to a factory that was making a vitamin-enriched malt syrup for pregnant women. It tasted like thin honey laced with hickory smoke. It was good. I wish I had some right now" (*MN*, vi). Sneaking spoonfuls of this syrup was how he survived the near-starvation conditions as Russian troops advanced and Germany began reeling toward collapse.

Mother Night would be set in wartime Berlin and postwar New York (with a few scenes transpiring in an Israeli prison for war criminals two decades later, coincidental with the Adolf Eichmann trial). Vonnegut had let his paperback original appear without any introductory autobiographical material. But in 1966 he was at work on another novel, to be called *Slaughterhouse-Five; or, The Children's Crusade* (1969), and so to clarify his "personal experience with the Nazi monkey business" (*MN*, v) he offered a quick sketch of what would be the defining event of his work in progress. It had happened on the night of 13 February 1945 about halfway through his tenure as a prisoner of war. That was the night Dresden was bombed for the first time in a war that was well into its sixth year, by which point most other German cities had been reduced to rubble. The Dresden attack would be unique, an application of all the techniques the British Royal Air Force had learned so far. The first wave of heavy aircraft from Bomber Command dropped high explosives. Vonnegut writes, "There were no particular targets for the bombs. The hope was that they would create a lot of kindling and drive firemen underground" (vi). Next came an assault with incendiaries "scattered over the kindling, like seeds on freshly turned loam." Then there were more explosives to keep the firemen away while all the fires across Dresden grew, joined together, and "became one apocalyptic flame. Hey presto: fire storm. It was the largest massacre in European history."

People numbering 135,000, nearly all of them civilians, died that night; the city's normal population of 70,000 had been doubled by its reputation as a refuge for children, old people, and families fleeing the Russian army advancing from the east. Of course, there were greater losses elsewhere in the war and much greater atrocities. But the definition of a massacre is that all the killing happens at once, in a single place, which is how Dresden won its dubious place in the record books.

Vonnegut admits, "We didn't get to see the firestorm. We were in a cool meat-locker under a slaughterhouse with our six guards and ranks and ranks of dressed cadavers of cattle, pigs, horses, and sheep" (*MN*, vi). Here, three stories underground, survival was possible—uniquely so because everyone else in Dresden was sheltering in shallow basements. The author could only imagine what was happening:

> We heard the bombs walking around up there. Now and then there would be a gentle shower of calcimine. If we had gone above to take a look, we would have been turned into artifacts characteristic of fire storms: seeming pieces of charred firewood two or three feet long— ridiculously small human beings, or jumbo fried grasshoppers, if you will.
>
> The malt syrup factory was gone. Everything was gone but the cellars where 135,000 Hansels and Gretels had been baked like gingerbread men. So we were put to work as corpse miners, breaking into shelters, bringing bodies out. And I got to see many German types of all ages as death had found them, usually with valuables in their laps. Sometimes relatives would come to watch us dig. They were interesting, too. (vi–vii)

John Somer, one of the first scholars to work on Kurt Vonnegut, finds this Dresden experience to be a key to all the author's fiction through *Slaughterhouse-Five,* his sixth novel. In *The Vonnegut Statement* (1973) Somer (coeditor with Klinkowitz) argues a thesis much like Philip Young's wound theory for Ernest Hemingway's writing: that the Dresden fire-bombing was the central and most deeply traumatic event of Kurt Vonnegut's life—and that he would spend twenty years coming to terms with it, treating its horror in oblique ways through his first five novels before facing it directly in what nearly all critics now acknowledge as his masterpiece. "When I got home from the Second World War twenty-three years ago," Vonnegut writes in the first chapter of *Slaughterhouse-Five*, "I thought it would be easy for me to write about the destruction of Dresden, since all I would have to do would be to report what I had seen" (*SF*, 2). In conversation today he will deny that the event was traumatic—just an adventure, he insists. But then Hemingway argued vehemently against the basis (if not the application) of Philip Young's interpretation. There is no debating the fact that Vonnegut struggled to find a way to articulate the event, for as he admits, "there is nothing intelligent to say about a massacre. Everybody is supposed to be dead, to never say anything or want anything ever again" (17). Suffice it to say, as the author does at this novel's beginning, "Over the years, people I've met have often asked me what I'm working on, and I've usually replied that the main thing was a book about Dresden" (3).

Slaughterhouse-Five now stands as just the eighth contribution to what would become by the turn of the new century a twenty-two-book canon, fourteen of which are novels; *Slaughterhouse-Five* is far from the last word. For that matter the Dresden firebombing was not the end of his POW experiences. V-E Day would not come until nearly three months later, and the war's final weeks presented the author with scenes he would draw on for both autobiography and fiction. In *Bluebeard* (1987), for example, Vonnegut's protagonist is a man who in later life would graduate from an apprenticeship in literal illustration to a career as an abstract expressionist artist, using paints and gestures as their own subject matter, bypassing the need for verbal articulation. One of his experiences between being an illustrator and triumphing as a painter is serving in World War II. For the most part his service career is quite different, with a second lieutenant's commission and participation in successful campaigns in North Africa and Sicily and across postinvasion France. The two similarities are that Karabekian and Vonnegut are each captured by the Germans and made prisoners, and that as V-E Day approaches, their guards simply vanish, leaving the Americans and POWs from other Allied nations to greet the morning on what Karabekian describes as "the rim of a great green valley on what is now the border between East Germany and Czechoslovakia" (*BB*, 208). The scene is breathtaking, one that stays with the artist so that he is able to paint it nearly half a century later. "There may have been as many as ten thousand people below us—concentration camp survivors, slave laborers, lunatics released from asylums and ordinary criminals released from jails and prisons, captured officers and enlisted men from every Army which had fought the Germans." Remnants of the Wehrmacht, "their uniforms in tatters but their killing machines still in working order, were also there."

In the closing pages of his 1991 memoir, *Fates Worse Than Death: An Autobiographical Collage of the 1980s,* Kurt Vonnegut describes the scene as he witnessed it, accompanied by a photograph a fellow POW had taken with a loaded camera found among the detritus of war, developed and saved all these years and given to the author when this book was in preparation. Kurt writes, "We are somewhere in rural southeastern Germany, near the border with Czechoslovakia. Our guards have marched us from a suburb of Dresden into this wilderness and suddenly disappeared, leaving us on our own in a wholly ungoverned area which would not be occupied by the Red Army for about a week" (*F,* 217). The valley just behind them "is being stripped of everything edible, as though by a locust plague, by liberated prisoners of war like ourselves, by convicts, by lunatics, concentration camp victims, and slave laborers, and by armed German soldiers." Here at war's end, just as he had done in his first and only battle six months before, Private Vonnegut and his comrades are looking for their own forces. "We are hoping to find the American Army, so that we can eat and then go home. That Army is on the west bank of the Elbe River, which is far away."

Not having the photograph until May 1990 did not keep Vonnegut from recasting this end-of-the-war scene clearly in *Bluebeard;* nor does it prevent that novel's protagonist from painting it, so many years later, as a demonstration of how even literal figuration can, by virtue of massive scale, overpower a viewer's ability to completely comprehend it. These are the lessons Vonnegut presumably brought home from World War II: that experience can indeed outstrip conventional abilities to recapture it for art, but also that new artistic conventions can be devised to suggest that same difficulty. As the first chapter of *Slaughterhouse-Five* describes, other uses of the Aristotelian unities of time, space, and action would have to be devised. It would take an experienced fiction writer to do that, a true handyman adept with the materials of character, plot, and theme. True, in 1945 he was sitting with the makings of a great story. But for the next two decades he would not yet have the knack for putting it together the uniquely effective way its nature demanded. All Vonnegut knew was that the usual ways of assembling a best-seller, with a conventionally plotted beginning, middle, and end that provided a scope of action for recognizable heroes (such as could be played in a movie version by Frank Sinatra and John Wayne), would not work for what he had packed up in his army kit bag.

One part of a soldier's paraphernalia might be of help: a benefit of the GI Bill offering support for postwar higher education. But in the summer of 1945 there were more personal matters to attend to: marrying his childhood sweetheart, Jane Cox, and enjoying a honeymoon on the shores of Lake Maxincuckee in northern Indiana. He said good-bye to the Vonnegut cabin (which was just then being sold) and took leave of his big extended family in Indianapolis, among whom he would never live again.

A dispersal of sorts had already begun. His brother, Bernard, was now in upstate New York working as an atmospheric physicist at the General Electric Laboratory, the state-of-the-art facility for its day. His father had built a home outside the city in suburban Williams Creek and had been living there as a widower since 14 May 1944, when Kurt's mother, long afflicted with depression and taking barbiturates by prescription, had died of a possibly suicidal overdose. Alice, middle child of the three siblings, would marry and raise her family in the East. By the time Vonnegut wrote his eighth novel, *Slapstick; or, Lonesome No More!* (1976), his last immediate Indianapolis relative had died; the book's prologue describes a trip with his brother to the funeral in a city sundered from them in terms of any current personal intimacy. The author realized, "We didn't belong anywhere in particular any more. We were interchangeable parts in the American machine" (*S*, 7). Realization of all that this loss entailed informs *Slapstick* in both theme and technique, but by September 1945 the process was already under way. In *Fates Worse Than Death,* Vonnegut recounts the last chapter of his life back home in Indiana, reprising motifs of family life and childhood memories in an essay about summer vacations and an eventual honeymoon at the lake: "If I were ever to write a novel or a play about Maxincuckee, it would be Chekhovian, since what I saw were the consequences of several siblings' inheriting and trying to share a single beloved property, and with their own children, once grown, moving to other parts of the world, never to return, and on and on" (*F,* 51). Transiency is thus a key element, balanced by the lake's continued life in memory, a device that insures the author's serenity. The honeymoon, readers learn, also had its literary element: Kurt's bride used part of their time to read him what she considered the greatest of all novels, *The Brothers*

Karamazov. Did this reading have an influence on his subsequent work? Over fifty years later he could still remember its last word: "Hurrah!" (53).

In December 1945 Kurt moved with his new wife to Chicago, where in a few weeks his graduate studies in anthropology would begin. Between his years at Cornell and the various army Specialized Training Program courses, he had had a good undergraduate preparation. Should he round out the requirements and take a bachelor's degree? That would be a waste of time, his advisers told him; go straight for a master's, for once he had that degree a B.A. would be superfluous. His GI Bill benefits were generous but not infinite, so they should be used most effectively.

For the next year and a half Vonnegut took courses at the University of Chicago and worked as a pool reporter for the City News Bureau. The government paid for his educational expenses, but with a child on the way Kurt needed at least the approximation of a family income, and so his extracurricular talents as a journalist once again (and not for the last time) were of use. Following the police beat may have given him a better training in anthropology than he was getting at school. In the opening chapter of *Slaughterhouse-Five* he describes the first story he had to cover, phoning in details to one of the tough-as-nails women who had taken over the newspaper trade during World War II. From the accident scene Vonnegut reports all the ghastly details of how a young veteran whose first day on the job as an elevator operator had turned to tragedy, thanks to the first-floor elevator door's elaborate design of ornamental iron lace: "This veteran decided to take his car into the basement, and he closed the door and started down, but his wedding ring was caught in all the ornaments. So he was hoisted into the air and the floor of the car went down, dropped out from under him, and the top of the car squashed him. So it goes" (*SF,* 8).

End of story? Not in the brave new world of harsh details and naked emotions that was characterizing American life as toughened up by four years of war effort. Kurt's copy editor wants to know what the victim's wife said. The young reporter replies that she does not know yet. He is told to call her up and say he is Captain Finn from the police department and write down what she says. Vonnegut does, gets the story (including news that there is a baby), and completes his report. But there is still a bit more about human nature to be learned:

> When I got back to the office, the woman writer asked me, just for her own information, what the squashed guy had looked like when he was squashed.

I told her.

"Did it bother you?" she said. She was eating a Three Musketeers Candy Bar.

"Heck no, Nancy," I said. "I've seen lots worse than that in the war." (*SF,* 8–9)

The styles of human nature that this same young man was studying at the University of Chicago were, to his dismay, a segregated affair, with primitive peoples considered quite apart from civilized societies. That was a shame, he believed. Wouldn't it be more interesting to see how certain traits of human behavior compared between the two? The topic on which Vonnegut wished to improvise was an interesting one: just what did it take, he wondered, to produce a truly revolutionary movement in human affairs? Was there a constant, a key number, a critical mass of individuals and ideas that had to be in place for a revolution in values to happen?

His proposal was to compare two such groups who were doing their work about the same time, at the end of the nineteenth century and beginning of the twentieth century, but a world apart from each other both in geography and sophistication: the Cubist painters in Paris and the Plains Indians of the Ghost Dance movement in North America. Getting nowhere with the project, he tried another idea for a master's thesis: the fluctuation between good and evil in simple tales. Here he delighted himself by finding that there was a recognizable footprint for a story, depending upon the culture, even microculture, that devised it. An Eskimo narrative would proceed one way, a *Saturday Evening Post* short story another, with equally dramatic idiosyncrasies for other stories in other magazines. Graphing the changes between good and evil yielded a chart by which the tale's place of origin could be identified. *New Yorker* stories had one distinctive pattern, *Redbook* stories another; just do the graph and Vonnegut could tell you in all likelihood where the piece had been published.

Today comparative studies of primitive and civilized cultures are encouraged. In 1947 they were not, and Vonnegut's improvisation with the professional standards of anthropology was not encouraged, except by one faculty member whose disaffinity with his colleagues had him on the way out. With his course work completed and time for submitting a thesis coming due, Kurt's GI Bill eligibility would be lapsing. Before 1947 ended he had left the program without a degree and was seeking work elsewhere. His insights into the Ghost Dance movement would find expression later in his first novel, *Player Piano*, while the fluctuations between good and evil in simple tales made for an interesting chalk talk he could give decades later when literary fame had made him a lecture-circuit celebrity. The valid piece of anthropological training he took with him from the university involved learning, from Professor Robert Redfield, how humans seem best organized into folk societies of about two hundred people each, big enough for mutual support but sufficiently small so that there could be unique and necessary roles for everyone. This too would become a theme in his fiction.

On 11 November 1947 Kurt Vonnegut celebrated his twenty-fifth birthday; he was a husband, a father, and possessor of five years' higher education and more than two years of military service—but with no degree and no professional qualifications, save that of the journalism he had done on high school and college papers and supporting himself as a graduate student. The City News Bureau in Chicago was a dead-end job, and across the country no newspapers were hiring: journalists had come back from the army to reclaim old assignments, and the women who had filled in for them were not about to give up theirs, so there was a surplus among those trained to do the only work Vonnegut knew. But given the circumstances, there was something he could put together. He knew how to write, he knew about science, and he had a brother who was making headlines as an atmospheric physicist at the General Electric Research Laboratory in Schenectady, New York. Combining these ingredients gave him what he needed: a job as publicist for the GE Lab.

There were happy aspects of the job. The laboratory practiced pure rather than applied science: geniuses were turned loose to pursue their own research, with the company making a safe gamble that whatever they came up with would produce patents worth many times the expense. Moreover, pure research was good image. GE's corporate motto from this era did not make reference to its toasters, mixers, or jet engines, even though each of these objects was a field leader. Instead the message was "At General Electric, Progress Is Our Most Important Product." Kurt Vonnegut was hired to help spread this news. Writing copy was only part of his work; the most important thing he had to do was look in on the scientists, see what they were doing, learn about and share their enthusiasms, and then translate all that into something an average American could read about and appreciate. There were much worse livings to be earned.

The problem for Kurt was the manner of making this living. Working for a huge corporation was a fact of postwar American life, and millions of other veterans were in the same circumstance. However, this corporate ideal included a sociology of employment, something William H. Whyte, Vance Packard, and David Reisman began describing in such books as, respectively, *The Organization Man, The Hidden Persuaders,* and *The Lonely Crowd*. Vonnegut would wind up writing about it in the next decades, when as a book reviewer he would interpret current events in terms of what he had suffered when working for GE. "Peer review" was one of these sociological practices he and his coworkers had to endure in the public relations office. Another was "self-criticism," agonizing sessions of which Vonnegut describes in a piece titled "Money Talks to the New Man," his review of Goffredo Parise's novel *The Boss* from the *New York Times Book Review* of 2 October 1966 (p. 4).

In Parise's book the employer is a monster whose peculiar style of corporate "new-think" has his workers tying themselves into emotional pretzels. Vonnegut's real-life experiences at General Electric can top that, he advises readers. His own boss was a man named Griffin who would insist that his staff submit to regular counseling sessions that probed well beyond matters of the office's business. At the firm Parise satirizes, the boss expects his people to behave like happy idiots. "Griffin was something else again," Vonnegut avers, implying the worst. In the novel under review the employer forces one of his men to marry a Mongolian idiot and submit to painful vitamin injections ("Griffin and I had our troubles, but nothing like that"). But there are comparisons so close that they collapse the distances between fiction and fact, between Parise's Italian office world and Vonnegut's own—how workers resent such treatment, for example, and how their only recourse is gossip: "We used to dish the dirt like that all the time up in Schenectady," Vonnegut recalls. "It is the kind of talk you hear around water coolers in every corner of the world."

To escape it the writer of publicity copy brought his typewriter home at night and over weekends to begin drafting something else: short stories. Half a generation earlier, in similarly depressing conditions, his mother had tried the same thing. By writing fiction for the famous (and well-paying) family magazines of the time she would recover the family wealth she had lost through her father's remarriage and the new century's changing economic times. At her new vocation she failed, unable (her son has always insisted) to construct the homely, even vulgar fantasies a middle-class readership demanded for its entertainment; according to Kurt, she was just too well mannered, the squalid little secrets of life and their pathetically common antidotes unknown to her. But thanks to that same loss of family wealth, her son knew them all too well. And it was to them he turned as a way of writing himself out of the corporate life at GE.

Off his stories went to the best-paying markets, including *Collier's* and the *Saturday Evening Post*. Back they came, not with outright rejections like his mother's but with words from a sympathetic editor, Knox Burger, at the first journal who wondered if the writer were the same Kurt Vonnegut he had known as a fellow college journalist. Get an agent, Burger advised, one who could tell him how to make these stories more sellable. Vonnegut did, and the rest is history. The first to be published, "Report on the Barnhouse Effect," appeared in *Collier's* for 11 February 1950. The young man announced this impending event to his father, whose pride shows through in a letter he saved and made into a commemorative plaque the author now has hanging in his workroom and quotes (in *Palm Sunday*) as the pledge he made back in 1949:

"Dear Pop:

"I sold my first story to *Collier's*. Received my check ($750 minus a 10% agent's commission) yesterday noon. It now appears that two more of my works have a good chance of being sold in the near future.

"I think I'm on my way. I've deposited my first check in a savings account and, as and if I sell more, will continue to do so until I have the equivalent of one year's pay at GE. Four more stories will do it nicely, with cash to spare (something we never had before). I will then quit this goddamn nightmare job, and never take another one so long as I live, so help me God.

"I'm happier than I've been for a good many years.

"Love."

The letter is signed with my first initial, which is what he called me. It is no milestone in literature, but it looms like Stonehenge beside my own little footpath from birth to death. The date is October 28, 1949.

Father glued a message from himself on the back of that piece of masonite. It is a quotation from *The Merchant of Venice* in his own lovely hand:

An oath, an oath, I have an oath in Heaven: Shall I lay perjury on my soul? (*PS*, 26)

Chapter One

COMING TO TERMS WITH THEME

Early Stories and *Player Piano*

WHEN IN 1951 KURT VONNEGUT quit General Electric and moved his growing family to Cape Cod (the Cape), Massachusetts, and a hoped-for career of full-time writing, the materials he took with him spoke much for his education in the sciences and experiences with the researchers at GE. Of his half dozen short stories published so far (all of them with *Collier's*), four were on themes of futuristic technology; the other two, "All the King's Horses" and "Mnemonics," concerned the corporate-style psychology he had suffered through in the same office whose business it was to tell the world how progress was the company's most important product. He had started a novel as well, *Player Piano,* to be published in 1952 and set in a hypothetical future but in every respect reflecting the philosophy of General Electric and the lives of its employees in present-day upstate New York.

From the satiric, sometimes dystopian tone of these works Vonnegut would seem happy to have left the world that bred them. After a first try at living the unfettered artist's life in Provincetown, at the Cape's farthest reach, he moved back to common society, as it were, eventually settling his family in a big house just outside West Barnstable, still on the Cape but halfway back to Boston. Here he would write stories on more typically domestic issues, making his way into the high-paying *Saturday Evening Post* (whose $2,500 per story far outclassed the $750 he had first earned from *Collier's*). Matters of corporate science and sociology would figure in some of these works, but the emphasis was on life as lived by average Americans, just the people who were reading these magazines. If something exotic appeared, be it scientific, economic, or psychological, that deviation from the mean would by story's end be resolved in a way that reaffirmed the middle-class values underwriting both subscriptions and advertising sales. Though always interested in the humor of an affair, Kurt

Vonnegut—liberated from the corporate world and happily running his own short-story business—seemed comfortably at home.

Those who insist that this man is a science-fiction writer should consider the narrative voice he chose for this first material. It is not the "Barnhouse Effect" itself that Vonnegut foregrounds for *Collier's* issue of 11 February 1950; instead, as his title indicates, it is a "Report on the Barnhouse Effect" that is being presented, with an emphasis from the start on the nature of the person telling it. "Let me begin by saying that I don't know any more about where Professor Arthur Barnhouse is hiding than anyone else does" (*WMH*, 156), the story begins—a terrible admission for someone being evaluated as a laboratory's publicist, but it is supportive of the narrative style its author (still working for GE at the time) finds necessary for telling this type of story. Nor can this narrator tell how to replicate the Barnhouse Effect, which is his second up-front admission. So he scarcely qualifies as a scientist either. Nor is he. In this first story Kurt Vonnegut's narrator is a psychology instructor who has done his academic research under the professor's direction, in the process learning that the so-called Barnhouse Effect existed—not how or why because its inventor never revealed the knowledge behind it. Now, expected to report on the phenomenon, he can only look back on his experiences with the great man and see what they add up to. In other words, all he can do is tell a story.

Any scientist and any scientific publicist would shudder at the narrator's result. "It's all anecdotal," they would charge. "But that's the beauty of the thing," this laboratory publicist who was trying to write his way out of the corporation might say in response, for that is precisely the point of "Report on the Barnhouse Effect." It tells the story of a researcher who discovers a power all out of proportion to his own meagre stature and humble methods. The man's work does not even begin in a laboratory, for he has discovered the principle of "dynamopsychism" (a fancy term for the force of a mind) while shooting dice in an army barracks craps game. The world's first recognition of this technique does not come as any formal acknowledgment from the scientific community but rather in the amazed encouragement from a fellow soldier, who exclaims, "You're hotter'n a two-dollar pistol, Pop" (*WMH*, 159).

Throughout the story Vonnegut's narrator maintains a straight-faced but essentially comic pose, mixing the language of theoretical physics with the homely manner in which Professor Barnhouse develops his psychic effect. But if the reader of this report is puzzled by this contrast, so is its writer. As the narrator tries to get a thesis under way with the man (remember Vonnegut's own struggles to write an anthropology thesis for a professor on the outs with his department), he becomes increasingly puzzled by the distractions that keep interfering with their work, specifically concerns with destruction wrought during the recently concluded World War II and the threat of more war and destruction to come. Concern for such matters has made Professor Barnhouse an odd duck at his university, but slowly the young narrator is drawn into his confidence. Over time the narrator is converted: not to the man's brand of science, which remains forever a mystery, but to his ethic of pacifism. By the report's end it turns out that there will be no report at all, only the narrator's advice that he is about to go underground with the professor's secret, keeping it safe from both commercial and military exploitation and potent only as a threat to militarism.

That scientists should be responsible for the uses of their discoveries had been part of Kurt Vonnegut's personal ethic since before the war, when as a Depression-era grade school and high school student he had also been taught the elementary civics lesson that a democracy such as America needed a standing army no larger than was demanded for defense. Much of what he had seen at General Electric charmed him, but the amorality of some of its scientists did not, particularly those who became lost in the abstractions of their work. The firestorm he had seen manufactured at Dresden, for example, was a hideous example of what scientific brilliance and military planning could produce when two such ends-in-themselves were united. "Report on the Barnhouse Effect" speaks out against these tendencies so common to the postwar years, making Kurt Vonnegut a protest writer from the start, albeit one closely involved with his popular culture.

"Thanasphere," "EPICAC," and "The Euphio Question" draw even more on science and technology of the day but always with the readers of *Collier's* (and not *Popular Mechanics*, let alone *Scientific American*) in mind. As Peter J. Reed establishes in *The Short Fiction of Kurt Vonnegut* (1997), the author's motivation is not "science fictional" but "sociological. It comes not from a fascination with speculations about technology but from a desire to show the moral and practical consequences of patterns of behavior" (5).

The patterns are evident in all three of these "scientific" stories, which were first published in *Collier's* for 2 September 1950, 25 November 1950, and 12 May 1951, respectively. In "Thanasphere" the science goes right: an observation station is launched into orbit around the earth, from which doings in the Soviet Union could be monitored—precisely the mission so many Cold War airmen undertook, although in spy planes rather than from space. What fails is the human element, as the officer on board gets distracted by a different kind of intelligence: messages from people in the afterworld who are anxious to send word to the living. These voices soon become more than distracting; they are more interesting than what military forces may or may not be doing. Simple gossip about people one has known counts more than science and technology, especially when technology has inadvertently spiced things up by presenting gossip from the dead. Here is Kurt Vonnegut's definition of humanism, refined many years later for a lecture presented to the American Physical Society and collected in *Wampeters, Foma & Granfalloons: Opinions* (1974). Humanists, he says there and demonstrates in this story, are simply creatures who are more interested in human beings than in anything else. In the story it is military science that loses out, as the air force's spy in the sky cares only for the gossipy messages he is intercepting (at one point even seducing the project scientist with a warning from his long-dead mother). In the essay the losers are the zoo animals that Kurt has taken his pet dog to see; he has assumed that the animal will show great interest in all these fellow carnivores, but instead all the dog cares about are people visiting the zoo, qualifying him as a humanist. Who wins? Kurt Vonnegut and his belief that humans fulfilling their own natural purposes are superior to the cold facts of science. Of course, scientists have to disguise this fact, and that is how "Thanasphere" ends, with all those voices from the afterlife kept secret. People still want to know, and as the story concludes, a reporter asks how soon an exploratory rocket will be sent into space. The scientist replies, "You people read too many comic books. Come back in twenty years, and maybe I'll have a story for you" (*BSB*, 27). For the record, Vonnegut did, attending the Apollo XI moon launch with credentials from the *New York Times* and CBS Television News. His report of the occasion appears in *Wampeters, Foma & Granfalloons*, where the sentiments expressed are much the same as in his short story from two decades earlier. The view expressed in this early work remains consistent throughout the author's career, from anonymity to fame and from popular magazines of the 1950s through novels of the postmodern age.

"EPICAC" and "The Euphio Question" have even more technology in them than do Vonnegut's stories about the thanasphere and Professor

Barnhouse's invention—and the sociological interest is proportionately greater. From a computer programmed to write love letters (and which then falls in love with the young woman who receives these missives) to the hilariously narcotic effect of radio waves captured from outer space, the author is much more interested in people's behavior. It is no accident that the behavior this futuristic technology provokes is anything but futuristic: Vonnegut's characters react to intoxicating radio waves just about the way they would handle too much alcohol, and when his computer is programmed to perform a human function it is not surprising that the machine starts acting like a human being—a hopelessly lovesick one at that. Even the author's most thoroughly science-fictionish novel, *The Sirens of Titan* (1959), maintains an interest in people *as people;* this point is made in the narrative when a pair of figures share a drink and amuse the bartender, who finds them familiar from both his trade and his leisure reading: "they were simply two *Saturday Evening Post* characters at the end of the road" (*ST,* 86–87).

By the time Vonnegut wrote those lines his career with the family weeklies was coming to an end, largely because television had stolen their advertising, and before closing shop entirely such journals trimmed back the amount of fiction they could publish. But in 1951 Kurt Vonnegut's glory years with *Collier's* and the *Saturday Evening Post* were still ahead of him. Following their initial publications his stories went through four cullings: for *Canary in a Cat House* in 1961, when Vonnegut had no literary reputation except as a regular contributor to the magazines; for *Welcome to the Monkey House* in 1968, when publisher Seymour Lawrence was relaunching the author's career with Delacorte Press; for *Wampeters, Foma & Granfalloons* in 1974, when in the face of sudden fame he elected not to include the passed-over stories in a collection of his shorter work; and finally in 1999, when at the urging of scholar Peter J. Reed he let the early short stories thought unsuitable for the previous collections take their places in his established canon via the volume *Bagombo Snuff Box. Welcome to the Monkey House* reassembles all the stories from *Canary in a Cat House* (a little-noticed paperback original) but one: "Hal Irwin's Magic Lamp," a *Cosmopolitan* story from June 1957 that had appeared in the first collection with its last line dropped and which Vonnegut rewrote before letting Reed include it in the final gathering. Given that *Monkey House* received reviewers' attention in its hardcover edition and has remained in print as a Dell paperback alongside Vonnegut's first twelve novels throughout his tenure as a major American writer, the nature of its selection is instructive.

"Report on the Barnhouse Effect," "EPICAC," "All the King's Horses," "The Euphio Question," "The Foster Portfolio," "More Stately Mansions," "Tom Edison's Shaggy Dog," "Unready to Wear," "D. P.," "Tomorrow and Tomorrow and Tomorrow," "Adam," "Deer in the Works," "Next Door," "The Kid Nobody Could Handle," "Miss Temptation," and "The Manned Missiles"—here stand the stories of Kurt Vonnegut's 1950s that are his first choice to accompany his best-selling and most widely studied novels into literary history. Most are from *Collier's* and the *Saturday Evening Post,* though *Cosmopolitan* and the *Ladies' Home Journal* are also represented, making for good coverage of the era's popular culture. "Deer in the Works" comes from *Esquire,* a well-paying market the author must have appreciated; "Unready to Wear" and "Tomorrow and Tomorrow and Tomorrow" are reprinted from *Galaxy Science Fiction* but are no more sci-fi stories than are Vonnegut's science-related pieces from *Collier's* and the *Post*—they were only offered to the dime-a-word sci-fi journals after the family weeklies (which paid twice to seven times that much) had rejected them. Throughout these narratives the writer returns to familiar themes, and the familiarity spans such variables as scientific innovation and the day-to-day doings in middle-class American lives. Indeed, for Kurt Vonnegut it does not matter if the action is taking place in the present or in the future; nor does it make a difference if the setting is outer space or at the neighbors' house next door. To the eye of this humanist, people are the most interesting subject, and underlying his vision is the theme that people are likely to act in predictable ways—often charmingly so, with a winsome innocence the author encourages his readers to appreciate, but predictable all the same. The art of his work consists in how far he can stretch the occasion to make this predictability serve as a clever solution to the story's problem, as an insight into the nature of the characters involved—in other words, as a surprise.

Consider two of the most apparently diverse of these short stories, "Unready to Wear" and "The Foster Portfolio." The former, as noted, was published in the trendiest of science fiction journals, while the latter appeared in *Collier's,* homeliest of the family weeklies with the least-pretentious-toward-brainy content. Each story seems to fit the specific market's needs, with "Unready to Wear" telling about a new world in which folks have learned how to be "amphibious" (borrowing bodies to inhabit as casually as people now wear clothes) and "The Foster Portfolio" describing a poor working stiff's chance to remake his life a much more practical way, by cashing in some investments. The pioneer amphibian tells his own story, while Herbert Foster's is narrated by the man who manages this client's financial portfolio. But readers soon learn that each story's theme is conveyed not so much in the objects and issues involved as by the manner of the telling—and in both "The Foster Portfolio" and "Unready to Wear" that manner is much the same.

"I'm a salesman of good advice for rich people," the narrator of the Foster piece begins. "It's a living," he allows, "but not a whale of a one" (*WMH*, 53), an important distinction because much of the story evolves around the surprising contrast this storyteller discovers. His clients are people much better off than he is, usually so rich that they make his job seem like being a hungry delivery boy for a candy store. Herbert Foster, however, appears just the opposite, looking and acting like the first investor to be worse off—far worse off—than the man paid to do his bidding. For several pages Foster is portrayed as seeming to have no business asking for financial advice at all. His income looks to be well below what is needed for active shopping among stocks and bonds; as an anthropologist might note, his home has all the hallmarks of wage-slave struggle, being "a jerry-built postwar colonial with expansion attic," furnished on time payment with "three rooms of furniture, including ashtrays, a humidor, and pictures for the wall, all for $199.99" (56). Foster has a wife, and she too submits to the anthropologist's measure: "A skinny, shrewish-looking woman smiled at me vacuously. She wore a faded housecoat figured with a fox-hunting scene. The print was at war with the slipcover of the chair, and I had to squint to separate her features from the clash about her. 'A pleasure, Mrs. Foster,' I said. She was surrounded by underwear and socks to be mended, and Herbert said her name was Alma, which seemed entirely possible" (54).

The narrator's snide comment about her name establishes both the Fosters' typicality and his own presumed superiority to it. This posture survives the story's first surprise, that a supposed cog in the wheels of America's lower-middle-class economy is in fact holding a portfolio of stocks worth three quarters of a million dollars, a substantial sum at any time but for a reader of *Collier's* magazine in 1951 a truly astronomical figure. "My client, Herbert Foster, hadn't had a new suit in three years," the narrator notes in response to this news, and "he had never owned more than one pair of shoes at a time" (*WMH*, 57). His secondhand car still has worrisome payments pending, he carries a bag lunch (with a tuna and cheese sandwich instead of meat), and so forth—"the Fosters were going through hell" trying to live within a limited budget, and their adviser admits that "God knows it's no disgrace to live that way." Of course not, because most readers of *Collier's* were in similar (if not quite so tight) circumstances. Kurt Vonnegut was too—remember that letter to his father. Therefore the fact that Herbert Foster does not want to draw on earnings from his portfolio, inherited just recently from his grandfather, plunges Vonnegut, his narrator, and all the *Collier's* readers into an even more anthropologically curious examination of his way of life. Why would someone want to continue this meanly frugal existence when simply drawing interest on one's capital would propel him and his family into the privileged classes of the country's economy?

The answer is probably too simple, as confirmed by the author's worry with some of the stories he kept out of his canon until *Bagombo Snuff Box*, pieces weaker than "The Foster Portfolio," stories in which "the premise and the characters of each were so promising, and the denouement so asinine, that I virtually rewrote the denouement" before letting them appear in the collection (*BSB*, 289). Herbert Foster's denouement is that he does not want to use investments to better his living because the economically tough times he has been enduring allow him the pleasure of slipping away to earn a few extra dollars at a second job. And what a second job it is, playing jazz piano in a honky-tonk dive so refreshingly different from his family life that the contrast is literally intoxicating.

This second piece of news is something the narrator can accept with more ready understanding. Throughout "The Foster Portfolio" he has shown himself to be a highly qualified assessor of middle-class American habits, ways of behavior that are all the more prominent for the tenuous hold the Fosters have on that life—their house is jerry-built, their furniture from a discount mart, their car secondhand, its tires retreads, their brownbag-lunch sandwiches made with the less expensive spread. As he has said, it is no disgrace to live that way; millions of Americans are doing it right now, he knows. Why do they do it? In hopes of someday having something better. Well, Herbert Foster has something better now, the delights of a secret life he can enjoy at will, with the excuse that such outré behavior is underwriting a quest for the same American dream.

No critic would think of calling "The Foster Portfolio" a science-fiction story, but all the elements of Vonnegut's allegedly sci-fi work are there. The Fosters' homely life is described with the precision employed by a visitor to another planet; the glitch in Herbert Foster's behavior—not wanting to use the great amounts of money he has—is as curious a departure from normality as anything encountered in an alien world; and the sudden great amount of money might just as well have come from outer space, so distinct is it from the man's normal existence. But is his existence really so normal? It is human, to be sure, but in a way that violates certain commonly accepted norms—all of which goes to say that these norms may not be so reliable after all.

As for "Unready to Wear," set in a technologically innovative future and involving the adoption of various other bodies as one's own, Vonnegut's thematic orientation remains much the same as in his stories of 1950s middle-class life. The narrator here shares the roles Herbert Foster and his investments counselor performed in the earlier tale. "I don't suppose the oldsters, those of us who weren't born into it, will ever feel quite at home being amphibious—amphibious in the new sense of the word," he begins, because this new capability has made redundant "what used to be my business. After all, I spent thirty years building the thing up from scratch, and now the equipment is rusting and getting clogged with dirt" (*WMH*, 229). This spokesperson for the action is thus both in and out of it, experiencing the change but mindful of how things were beforehand. The joy of this story is the offhand way the narrator handles the exposition, running through information that should be flabbergasting but which in his telling seems as familiar as the analogs to behavior more appropriate to *Collier's* than to *Galaxy Science Fiction*:

> Well, after we'd learned to be amphibious, and after we'd built the storage centers and laid in body supplies and opened them to the public, Madge [his wife] went hog wild. She borrowed a platinum blonde body that had been donated by a burlesque queen, and I didn't think we'd ever get her out of it. As I say, it did wonders for her self-confidence.
>
> I'm like most men and don't care particularly what body I get. Just the strong, good-looking, healthy bodies were put in storage, so one is as good as the next one. Sometimes, when Madge and I take out bodies for old times' sake, I let her pick out one for me to match whatever she's got on. It's a funny thing how she always picks a blond, tall one for me. (230–31)

After this introduction the narrator presents some stabilizing history, explaining how a scientist named Ellis Konigswasser had devised the method of doing all this by adjusting one's mental attitude. The steps were simple. First, Dr. Konigswasser taught, you had to understand what a dictator the body was, how it made all sorts of parasitical demands. Separate yourself from those demands and you would be halfway toward being free of it. "Then, by concentrating on what you wanted, and ignoring as much as possible what the body wanted beyond plain maintenance, you made your psyche demand its right and become self-sufficient" (*WMH*, 234).

If this sounds less like scientific technology than the self-help philosophies being promoted by such family magazine regulars as Dale Carnegie and Norman Vincent Peale, one should remember that it was *Collier's* and the *Saturday Evening Post* that Vonnegut thought of (and not *Galaxy Science Fiction*) when putting his blank sheet of paper into the typewriter. And once the premise is accepted, results are obvious. People are more efficient without bodies; only when inhabiting them do they take up space, need food, catch colds and get sick, and find themselves influenced by chemicals that precipitate such states as anger, depression, and fear. What gives the story a slight science-fiction flavor is its denouement, always the riskiest part of a Vonnegut narrative from the 1950s, when he was relying more on theme than on technique. The last piece of news is that not all humans have become amphibians; those who have resisted declare war on those who have succumbed (or, as the traditionalists insist, deserted their bodies), and by using the same gender-specific bait described earlier they manage to trap the narrator's wife in an attractive body (this is, after all, the woman who would try on three or more before deciding which one was right for the evening). On trial for his beliefs, our amphibian narrator is given the forum that science-fiction stories provide: the chance to justify himself and his position. His approach is clever but goes no farther than does Dr. Konigswasser's theory in scoring narrative points: our bodies, he tells his adversaries and reminds readers, are the only points of power enemies hold, for it is only our bodies that can be hurt. Then, to make capital of this for his own needs, he bluffs the probody forces by claiming that amphibians (invisible, of course) surround them. In sci-fi fashion he wins the logical point and with it the war.

The resolution is both as surprising and as simple as Herbert Foster's denouement in the earlier tale, with the thematic message being much the same. People can be prisoners of their habits or they can use these very limitations to get what they really want. Whether for *Collier's* or for *Galaxy Science Fiction*, the homely nature of the author's vision is consistent. Why, then, was "Unready to Wear" not placed in the better-paying *Collier's* or *Saturday Evening Post*? The reason may be the reference by which Vonnegut bookends the tale. At its start his narrator had mentioned all the hard work invested in building up his business, an enterprise now gone obsolete. Its specific nature remains undescribed, but as the nature of amphibious life is explained, readers can presume that the commercial affair had something to do with physical aspects of life now long passed. But for the story's end, following a denouement that Vonnegut probably suspects has not been the strongest, the narrator mentions his single regret, about having to abandon "the pay-toilet business it took me thirty years to build" (*WMH*, 243).

This little vulgar bit shows the irreverence Kurt Vonnegut was displaying in even his earliest work. Pushing the limits of taste rather than stretching the imaginative properties of science was what kept some of his material out of the conservative family weeklies. But even within their formats he could work a certain magic, based on turning some of these magazines' favorite themes back upon themselves. After all, the author was a trained anthropologist who could identify a story's published source simply by studying a graph of its fluctuations between good and evil. For *Collier's* and the *Saturday Evening Post* those fluctuations measure the alternating successes and failures of economics; for the *Ladies' Home Journal* the variables concern romance, while for *Cosmopolitan* (at least during the 1950s) good and evil fluctuate in tune with somewhat more sophisticated elements of both economics and love. Were Vonnegut to have stuck to the graphs themselves, he could have assured himself a certain level of income from these journals. But as with his work at the University of Chicago, this student of human manners was not content to exploit the obvious. Instead he no sooner found a market for his fiction than he began experimenting with it, seeing how far one type of magazine's theme could be pushed before it spilled over into the world of another.

Those that turned out to be the strongest stories on their own terms made it into *Canary in a Cat House* and *Welcome to the Monkey House*. The ones Vonnegut liked less survived only because some libraries, usually public rather than university ones, preserved bound volumes of these journals. He saved none of them. "These stories," he recalls, "printed in magazines fat with fiction and advertising, magazines now in most cases defunct, were expected to be among the living as long as individual lightning bugs" (*BSB*, 2). But for that very reason they are valuable today, as an index to the American 1950s and Kurt Vonnegut's writerly activities during that age. It is by reading them all together that one gets a sense of the person, the times, and how he interacts with them.

"Unpaid Consultant" (from *Cosmopolitan* of March 1955) and "Custom-Made Bride" (from the *Saturday Evening Post* for 27 March 1954) are among the twenty-three stories passed over thrice before being collected in

Bagombo Snuff Box. In an age when the country was enjoying the full fruits of postwar economic recovery, Vonnegut's narratives put certain notions about these good times to the test. The former piece features the same investments counselor from "The Foster Portfolio," this time calling on someone who admits to being rich: his old girlfriend, now a highly paid TV star. Her peculiarity is that she is married to (and still dotes on) her high school sweetheart, a simple garage mechanic. To complement her fame her husband felt obliged to fuel her fancy by becoming a world-class expert, supposedly working as a highly sought-after industrial consultant on his speciality. What is it? Catsup. The narrator can hardly believe it— that the husband has become a celebrity himself in such a field, let alone that such expertise should even be needed—and is equally taken aback by the wife's pleasure in her husband's having "found himself" (*BSB,* 174). All of this seems silly because it takes just a few minutes on the side to learn that the man has never been lost. It has been his wife's fame that made him feel he needed an appropriately glamorous profession of his own; once the narrative exposes that quest as a needless sham he can go back to being happy for what he is, an honest mechanic on whom the world depends. "Not half an hour ago," he boasts, "a man with a broken fuel pump thanked God for me" (181). A similar irreverence toward expertise informs "Custom-Made Bride," in which a fantastically success-ful high-tech designer finds himself unhappy because the recrafting of his simple, middle-class wife has brought him nothing but trouble. The reso-lution is brought about by the same narrator, who as an investment counselor is uniquely poised to appreciate both ends of the economic spectrum. Traditionally his role would be to guide clients from the low end toward the high. But in this case, as with the others, he helps the char-acters see into another dimension of value, this time actually named: the "soul" (121).

What better role for someone who views his job as "a little like being a hungry delivery boy for a candy store" (*WMH,* 54). In this character's hands Vonnegut can trust that the narrative will turn out OK—that wealth, in other words, will be neither panacea nor curse but rather just something that common sense can put safely in its place. Readers of the *Saturday Evening Post* and *Cosmopolitan* might well dream of money and glamor, but chances are that the amounts of each they could hope to acquire would be only modest improvements over what they already have. As a writer of short stories Kurt Vonnegut is in much the same business as his investments man, guiding folks toward better use of their imaginative capital. That he is not rich, either in dollars or in unbridled fancy, makes his service all the more helpful and ultimately reliable.

If there is a major difference between the stories Vonnegut preserved and those he did not (until *Bagombo Snuff Box* and some last-minute rewriting saved them for the canon), it may involve a delayed appreciation of the domestic element. Although some such stories make it into *Welcome to the Monkey House,* more do not, including these early pieces appearing in Vonnegut's best market, the *Saturday Evening Post:* "The No-Talent Kid," "Ambitious Sophomore," "The Boy Who Hated Girls," and "This Son of Mine . . ."—all products of the 1952–56 period when the author was appearing most regularly in this journal he considered his best means of support. What Vonnegut was doing during these years is closer to their topics than those of some other stories: supporting himself and his family, raising three kids in what he strove to make a conventional middle-class environment. These conditions were not without a test, for the author was always living by his wits, sometimes at the end of them. At times like these he would improvise, as any responsible husband and father would, trying his hand at selling Saab autos or designing a sculpture for the new Boston airport motel. These exploits would themselves generate stories, but the greatest challenge was one that prompted a book years later by his wife. Family stories for a family magazine, tales of improvising some fill-in work to keep the wolf from the door, a family memoir of having one's brood double overnight when three orphaned nephews were adopted—these are texts that deserve being read together.

In mid-September 1958 within thirty-six hours Kurt's brother-in-law and sister died, he in a bizarre accident when a commuter train ran off an open drawbridge and she of cancer, the two of them leaving four young sons. Kurt and Jane collected the older boys and made them at once members of their family. In 1987, after the Vonneguts had separated and divorced and he had married photographer Jill Krementz and Jane was wed to editor Adam Yarmolinsky, Jane, as Jane Vonnegut Yarmolinsky, published a memoir of those years with Kurt and the six children, *Angels without Wings.*

There is a certain distance in Jane's narrative. She had toyed with it for years, keeping notes in an old file from one of Kurt's rejected stories. Separation and divorce increased the gap. The onset of a long but fatal disease brought her back to the narrative, which would appear ten months after her death. In it the principals are renamed: Kurt becomes Carl; their children Mark, Edith, and Nanette are renamed Matt, Amy, and Nelly, though their ages correspond with the action's start on 15 September 1958—twelve, eight, and four respectively. The scene Jane describes is as healthily domestic as anything in her husband's family magazine fiction being written at this time:

> It was Monday morning, and even the old house seemed to know the summer was over. It takes until two weeks past Labor Day for summer to truly end on Cape Cod, before the last weekend guests pack their bags and go away, before the fun lovers stop swarming in the west end of Hyannis, and before you have become accustomed to the school bus collecting the children from under the horse chestnut tree on the corner at 8:05. The old house seemed to sigh with me as it disgorged the children through the rarely used front door, just barely in time. Was it a sigh for the spent summer? Or for lost youth? Or was it just a breeze coming through the house from a different direction? Or what? My oldest child, Matt, mounting the school bus steps, looked back quizzically, as if he wondered, too. (Yarmolinsky, *Angels,* 3)

Upstairs, Kurt (called Carl) is working, resuming his productive pace from the spring that had been interrupted for the family delights of summer on the Cape. Though selling his material has always been a struggle, Jane has faith in him—more than faith, for it was because of her belief in the importance of his writing, "prophetic and true, bordering on genius" (Yarmolinsky, *Angels,* 6), that she had fallen in love with him. This optimism kept Jane happy: "Some of it even rubbed off on him, although he never would have admitted it. Cheerfulness in the face of adversity was not his mode. He preferred a kind of ironic desperation, blended with fits of manic mirth. Which is what kept *him* going" (6–7). Whatever the source for motivation, the Vonnegut family needed it, for at this time their life was not much richer than that of the fictive Fosters. "As soon as I paid the mortgage, the excess water bill, the electric bill, and the life insurance premium, there wouldn't be enough left over for food, much less a new typewriter. Unless something sold" (7). Like the loyal wives in so many Vonnegut stories of the 1950s, Jane has even turned adversity to talent; while others sew clothes and reupholster furniture from the same bargain bolt and make new soap bars by sticking together the slivers of others, she papers a wastebasket with rejection slips. Into this economically tight but still barely sustainable world come Kurt and Jane's four nephews, made orphans by their parents' almost simultaneous deaths. The decision is not even discussed. "If it's as bad as we think," Jane tells Kurt as he is leaving for his sister's deathbed, "bring them back." No alternative is considered. "That was all that was said. But it was decided" (12).

Throughout *Angels without Wings* there are many references to what would become the Vonnegut canon. But in all cases they are not literary but purely autobiographical from the life this soon-to-be-extended family experiences together. *Bluebeard* would appear the same year, 1987, as *Angels without Wings,* and in it the narrator describes the valley outside Dresden where prisoners of war, concentration camp survivors, inmates set free from asylums, and soldiers detached from the various warring countries' armies wander aimlessly, removed from the conflict that has defined their lives for the past half decade and more, yet unable to find direction to the future. Closing her eyes on the day she becomes a mother of seven instead of just three, Jane Vonnegut dreams a similar scene, quite close to the one her husband would describe many years later in the conclusion to *Fates Worse Than Death.* There had been a cataclysm, filling the world with refugees, and some of them were seeking her help, coming to her for shelter. This is not the first time she has had this dream; earlier that summer she had responded to one like it by searching the barn and attic for all these homeless, countryless people in need. She vows to fix up the barn as a place to live in, an act the painter who narrates *Bluebeard* duplicates near the end of that novel as he paints his masterpiece of the scene he (and the actual Kurt Vonnegut) experienced and which Jane has dreamed.

Such a correspondence of images is not rare for married couples, particularly those who are thoughtful, articulate, and in love with each other's minds as well as bodies and souls. What is remarkable is the different nature of the stimulus: for Kurt the war, but for Jane the ongoing struggle of domestic life, the family experience her husband would digest and write about years before putting his first memories of the war to paper. Only after having raised a family and worked hard at sustaining its life would these scenes from the German countryside of 1945 seem less a military adventure than a glimpse into the human condition.

"Armageddon in Retrospect"—so reads the envelope in which Jane keeps her narrative materials. Although the working title fits, it is not hers but rather just one of many stories Kurt had worked on for a time and then discarded, saving the envelopes for future use. That first fall the school-day routine more than doubles, as now four new children must be readied for ninth, sixth, and fourth grades, plus nursery school. "And so the new amalgamated family life began," Jane writes. "The tone of the new creation was firmly set within the first week. The big old house on the curving corner became a mecca for children and animals of all ages. Occasionally an intrepid stray adult would wander by," but for the time being Kurt and Jane would lose contact with their older friends. "We almost forgot how to communicate with them. We made up our own language" (Yarmolinsky, *Angels*, 72).

As the narrative of *Angels without Wings* proceeds, themes from many of Kurt's stories from the period emerge. His oldest nephew, for example, could not help but be a rival head of family—as indeed he was, albeit at the age of fourteen. "It was important for him always to be in confrontation with whoever had, or threatened to have, more authority than he" (81), Jane notes, a situation Kurt had already written about in more than one story and would so again, all the more ruefully, given his new experience with the first of his children to be difficult. But this difficulty is balanced by the next-to-eldest adoptee's behavior, which is happy and successful in taking Kurt as a model and ideal. The fourth grader is an equal delight, but problems come with the toddler, twenty-one months old when his parents died.

From this last nephew comes a life lesson that Vonnegut would use seven years later in *God Bless You, Mr. Rosewater; or, Pearls before Swine* (1965) and in many other works that followed: the simple trauma of being born and having to make one's way on earth. The child's infant years had been anything but easy, his life "in the hands of a sick mother, a harassed father, older brothers primarily interested in shaping their own identities, and a series of babysitters" (Yarmolinsky, *Angels*, 108). And then the adoption: "So what did he do when he arrived on Cape Cod with only part of his familial constellation intact, greeted by yet more strange faces and alien arms, an unfamiliar crib in a foreign room in some unknown place? He cried, naturally. He screamed. He shrieked. He sobbed. He banged his head and screamed again from the self-inflicted pain. After all, he had only recently arrived on the planet anyway, and life had been chaotic from the very beginning. How was he to know it wasn't to go on like this forever?" (108–9). Nine months later he is gone, but in a way even more unhappy than his coming, in circumstances "so traumatic," Jane confesses, "that I still can't talk about them without crying" (111). A cousin in Alabama with a childless marriage has from the start lobbied for adopting the youngest; other relatives take her side. Kurt and Jane resist, having vowed from the start to keep what was left of the boys' family together—even the family dogs. "For it was abundantly plain that the solidarity of the brothers was the single healthiest aspect of the new family montage," Jane notes. Kurt, who was present when news of his sister's (their mother's) death was brought to them less than a day after they had begun adjusting to the idea of being fatherless, was impressed with how the three eldest had held a meeting just for themselves and come out of it with the vow that they would remain together. Now, nine months into the new conditions, Jane can see how "they might be adjusting in different ways, and maturing at uneven rates, but one thing above all else stood out about them, and that was their brotherhood. If that could be maintained," Kurt and Jane guessed, "they would emerge from the trauma strong and healthy. If not, they might collapse" (113). Or they might not—who knew? But it was above all a question of values in making the judgment, and the emerging Vonnegut family values were at odds with those of the relatives down south.

An argument develops, disturbing emotions and distracting Kurt to the point that he cannot write. Money, already short, becomes a critical issue, giving the relatives who have by now turned into adversaries an additional argument for taking the youngest boy. As conditions further unravel, it becomes obvious that the child will go to a new home; the decision is what Jane calls "the most difficult I've ever had to make" (Yarmolinsky, *Angels*, 131). Family life continues; but thanks to the trauma, Kurt and Jane's marriage is never the same.

When taking perspective on his family life Kurt Vonnegut almost always adds the tag line that all his kids turned out OK. Jane Vonnegut Yarmolinsky shares the same view, concluding *Angels without Wings* with chapters on each of their children and how they are doing, which is fine. At least eight of the stories Kurt wrote in the 1950s have strictly domestic themes, two appearing in *Welcome to the Monkey House* and six in *Bagombo Snuff Box*—in neither case enough to characterize the volume, but when read together and combined with the other half dozen focused on husband and wives they are sufficient to give a coherent picture of the author's ideas of family life. It is not surprising that they are much like Jane's in *Angels without Wings*: certainly not that of the smiling couple with their sanitized children cozying up in front of the TV while dinner simmers automatically in an all-electric kitchen, but rather of a group who has bucked the rules in favor of imaginative freedom while maintaining the essential decency that this same freedom ultimately serves.

In the stories any way a family can be artificially extended helps. Surrogate parents also fill the bill—more than one piece features George

Helmholtz, the high school band instructor who guides his artificial family of student musicians through emotional as well as musical scores. In similar manner the stories of couples falling in and out of love and always back in again show people benefiting from a certain amount of role-playing. In his preface to *Welcome to the Monkey House,* Vonnegut admits how one of the collection's stories, "Long Walk to Forever," quite truthfully "describes an afternoon I spent with my wife-to-be. Shame, shame, to have lived scenes from a woman's magazine" (*WMH,* xv).

Such scenes are not limited to Vonnegut's stories in the *Ladies' Home Journal, Redbook,* and *Cosmopolitan.* They appear in his futuristic stories such as "EPICAC" and "The Euphio Question" and even motivate the action in his first two novels, the most science-fiction-like of his oeuvre: *Player Piano* and *The Sirens of Titan.* Especially in the first, as thematic a work as any of the stories written for his magazine market of the 1950s, the narrative's dystopian ideas of an unhappy future are played against recurring scenes where characters strive for domestic happiness. Because of the book's history—as a hardcover pitched to futurologists with its dust jacket promising a picture of "America in the Coming Age of Electronics," as a specially printed edition for the Doubleday Science Fiction Book Club, and as a garishly presented paperback retitled *Utopia-14* (1954)— *Player Piano* would always be considered less central to the Vonnegut canon, not in the least because its sci-fi aspects are considered seriously while in *The Sirens of Titan* similar elements are given a satiric send-up. But this first novel is central to the themes Vonnegut was developing in the 1950s, with the corollaries to Kurt's favorite domestic scenes providing the key technique for moving the action along.

"Ilium, New York, is divided into three parts": the novel's first line about a distant future invokes the past, paraphrasing the opening of Caesar's *Conquest of Gaul.* Readers of the younger author's day, many of them new college graduates from the GI Bill who had been taught "Great Books" courses in mass sections scaled up for their enrollment, would recognize the line and know Caesar's strategy behind it: divide and conquer. Triumph of the new technological ideal is assured, they would know, because of the situation Vonnegut describes:

> In the northwest are the managers and engineers and civil servants and a few professional people; in the northeast are the machines; and in the south, across the Iroquois River, is the area known as Homestead, where almost all of the people live.

If the bridge across the Iroquois were dynamited, few daily routines would be disturbed. Not many people on either side have reasons other than curiosity for crossing. (*PP,* 1)

The separation is sociological, with the roots for it understandable as anthropology. In the cataclysmic world war that precedes this novel's action, the managers and engineers who ran the factories had adapted to the absence of the workers, sent off to fight as they were. Not that these soldiers won the war; know-how did, the brilliant improvisation that allowed production with minimal manpower. Now, with the war over for ten years, the improvised conditions of wartime have endured an initial postwar protest and have become the norm. The managers and engineers live here; the machines, which scarcely need to be tended as everything has become automatized, are over there; and shoved off to the side are the people who have no defining identity at all—they used to be the workers, but in the new society this role no longer exists.

At the center of this world is the book's protagonist, Dr. Paul Proteus, manager of the Ilium Works at the young age of thirty-five. He is brilliant, important, and absolutely central to the plant's successful operation. But as introduced, he seems as homely a figure as any in Kurt Vonnegut's family stories for *Collier's* or the *Post*. His biggest concern this minute? Making sure the house cat he is introducing to the factory is comfortable, acting for all the world like the most familiar of pet fanciers, cooing to the animal with kitty-kitty-kitty sounds and making sure she will be set to do the job she has been recruited for: catching the mice that have chewed through the wires and put a set of buildings temporarily out of commission. Here is an example of the patented know-how that won the war, and at base it is no more sophisticated than the simplest act in having a pest-free household.

This cat carries Vonnegut's thematic action right through the first chapter of narrative. Proteus asks an engineer to devise a sensing device so that the cat will know in which of the many buildings to hunt mice, and just asking is as good as having the job done: "As Paul walked out to his car in the pale March sunlight, he realized that Bud Calhoun *would* have a mouse alarm designed—one a cat could understand—by the time he got back to the office. Paul sometimes wondered if he wouldn't have been more content in another period of history, but the rightness of Bud's being alive now was beyond question. Bud's mentality was one that had been remarked upon as being particularly American since the nation had been born—the restless, erratic insight and imagination of a gadgeteer. This was the climax, or close to it, of generations of Bud Calhouns, with almost all of American industry integrated into one stupendous Rube Goldberg machine" (*PP*, 4).

Calhoun the tinkerer is not much different than Kurt Vonnegut the handyman, and the world they inhabit, though many decades apart in the projective scheme of things, is still an America of *Collier's* and *Saturday Evening Post* proclivities. The Ilium Works of General Forge and Foundry occupying three parts of the metroplex is similar to that of General Electric, with its machinery located in Schenectady, its engineering brainpower trained and residing in Troy, and its workforce recruited from Albany. That the industry of this future world is programmed by artificial intelligence does not remove it from Vonnegut's 1950s, for the master computer has the same name, EPICAC (*PP*, 8), that the author gave it in his *Collier's* magazine story of 25 November 1950. And when Paul's mouse-hunting cat runs afoul of the plant's automated sweeper, the result is much the same as that in another Vonnegut story, "Deer in the Works," from *Esquire* of 1955.

From the start of *Player Piano*, then, Vonnegut's tone for expectations is set: actions transpire that are compatible with the world of 1950s magazine fiction, the world that would be supporting this author throughout the decade. These are the conditions at work—and at home as well. Complementing the professional worlds of "EPICAC" and "Deer in the Works" is the domestic scene to which Paul returns at the first chapter's end. If Kurt Vonnegut could feel shame for living stories from a women's magazine, Paul's wife experiences no such qualms. Her mantric statements "I love you, Paul" are delivered on cue to each appropriate circumstance, answered as if by rote with Paul's antiphonal response, "I love you too, Anita," as regular and predictable as the dialogue expected in any *Redbook, Cosmopolitan,* or *Ladies' Home Journal* story.

Indeed, whether by the canon of these short stories or by the patterns of life that generate such narratives, she has been carefully taught. "Anita had the mechanics of marriage down pat," we are told, "even to the subtlest conventions. If her approach was disturbingly rational, systematic, she was thorough enough to turn out a creditable counterfeit of warmth. Paul could only suspect that her feelings were shallow" (*PP*, 16), which means that he has begun to read her as easily as a magazine—perhaps even determining the regular fluctuations between good and evil that distinguish the dramaturgy she projects.

Paul's growing dismay with the qualities of both his family life and his professional work is played against the contrasting insights of a visitor. Like so many of Kurt Vonnegut's short stories, this novel benefits from an alternative perspective, as someone from the outside drops in to assess the situation in startlingly fresh ways. *Player Piano*'s outsider is decidedly exotic: the Shah of Bratpuhr, spiritual leader of a presumably Hindu sect who visits Ilium on a State Department tour, replete with a diplomat to dress up appearances and a translator to slice right through the propaganda. "*Citizens*," the State Department host keeps calling the welfare state workers reclaimed from economic redundancy; "*slaves*," the Shah relabels them according to his own values, free as they are from the corporate-speak this new America has adopted and from the love-speak women such as Anita use to mimic a family life appropriate to such a world.

Thus there are narrative dimensions to Kurt Vonnegut's first novel, but they are strongly thematic in nature. Both at home and at work Paul Proteus enjoys a smooth mastery of environment that is nonetheless unsatisfying. The Shah's perspective offers comically ironic commentary, and via several excursions of his own Paul gets to test various other points of view. One of his destinations—by necessity secret from both his wife and his employer—is Homewood, the part of Ilium where the laid-off workers live. His reason for traveling there is reminiscent of another Vonnegut story, "Unpaid Consultant," for only in Homewood can be found the expert every owner of an old car treasures most highly: a good, honest mechanic. Other episodes broaden Paul's view even more, such as matching wits with a robotic checker-playing machine, seeing how locals prefer the humanly appealing imperfections of an old-time tavern to a technologically ideal but antiseptic new one, and learning how his friend Lafferty has cured his own malaise and beat the system by doing something heretofore considered unthinkable: quitting it.

Quitting this insistently perfect world is a revolutionary idea, but it is no more radical than Paul's admission to himself that he feels happier in grungy Homewood than either at work among the technologically perfect machines or at home with his state-of-the-art wife. Homewood is a world that is quite familiar, with its people and places as comfortably appealing as those in any of the author's magazine pieces. The folks in this part of town are kind and decent; their foibles are amusing, not hurtful or threatening, much like the actions in a typical Vonnegut short story. Their only wish is to be of use, to have something to do—the theme of "Unpaid Consultant" and many other Vonnegut fictions. Their only crime is that the times have left them behind, the same fate that magazine fiction about this world was about to suffer.

In time Paul comes to diagnose his lethargy by contrasting himself with those doing better in the new scheme of things. Unlike these celebrants of technology, he feels no "sense of spiritual importance" that makes such work a veritable religion. Nor does he have "the ability to be moved emotionally, almost like a lover, by the great omnipresent and omniscient spook, the corporate personality" (*PP,* 55) that sublimates the happy desires of marriage; in short, he lacks "the capacity to really give a damn," meaning that the brave new world of science has done its sterilizing work on the bug of his human enthusiasm.

Everything in *Player Piano* so far has been handled in terms of theme. The little plot reversals and parallel actions are nothing a short story from the family magazines could not handle, and the novel's overall message is very much in tune with the writing Vonnegut had been doing in formats designed for *Collier's* and the *Saturday Evening Post.* But because his major turn of events is thematic as well, Vonnegut introduces a spokesman for the ideas so important that they dare not be cloaked in the short-story mechanics that had worked so well for the modest, homely truths of "EPI-CAC" and "Report on the Barnhouse Effect." Carrying the message here might tax the strength of Vonnegut the family magazine storyteller. Better to bring on a more extensively qualified authority: Kurt Vonnegut the anthropologist.

For characterization's sake, call him James J. Lasher. For his specializations in the new society, rate him R-127 with an SS-55 background. These are codings for a Protestant minister with a master's degree in anthropology. Vonnegut was still working on his thesis for the latter, and as a well-paid regular contributor to *Collier's* he certainly felt that he had been preaching to the choir of American secular success. Like Vonnegut with his cautionary tales for the family market, Lasher can understand a once upwardly mobile economic culture that has come to question itself. "For generations," Lasher says of people struggling with the new scientific times, "they've been built up to worship competition and the market, productivity and economic usefulness, and the envy of their fellow men—and boom! it's all yanked out from under them" (*PP,* 78). The result does make sense anthropologically, for "They can't participate, can't be useful any more. Their whole culture has been shot to hell."

Paul Proteus responds to this lesson with ideas of his own. He is able to appreciate how a sense of worth can be conveyed by something as sophisticated as a religion or as vulgar as the hocus pocus of lodge membership. Just belonging to a group imparts at least some worth. It is among these plain people that he feels his own dignity returning. His exuberance anticipates the love Vonnegut's protagonist feels for common folk in *God Bless You, Mr. Rosewater,* based as it is on the doctrine of usefulness the author will expound in *The Sirens of Titan.* But at the heart of *Player Piano* lies an essentially domestic situation, as clear-cut yet freshly instructive as any in Vonnegut's short stories. For as much as Paul is dissatisfied with corporate life, Anita feasts on it. When he is offered the promotion to head of the company's Pittsburgh Works, he finds it meaningless—so different from his wife's reaction. While he tosses restlessly, "Anita slept— utterly satisfied, not so much by Paul as by the social orgasm of, after years of the system's love play, being offered Pittsburgh" (*PP,* 116). As if in a typical *Cosmopolitan* story, the two exist in a strange symbiosis, Paul being physically sustained by his wife's "sexual genius" (117) while Anita's drive is fueled exclusively by his career success.

To sustain *Player Piano*'s theme Vonnegut becomes a novelist of manners. Here his anthropological talents are of help, particularly in the set-piece narrative about General Forge and Foundry's corporate retreat, a boys' summer camp for grown men held annually on an island called the Meadows. Based on a General Electric institution that must have given Vonnegut, direct from the University of Chicago's program, mordant delight, it combines games of individual achievement with activities reinforcing group identity. How clever, then, for the revolutionary elements in this society to sabotage the games themselves, undermining the corporate image by subverting the very program meant to enhance it, a program that has mythically suppressed radical thoughts.

The revolution comes as described by Reverend Lasher, who argues the same anthropological thesis that Vonnegut had proposed at the University of Chicago a few years before. It takes just a relatively small critical number of innovatively inclined souls to get a revolutionary movement going, particularly when social conditions create a need for one. Like Vonnegut in his thesis work, Lasher argues analogically, pegging the imminent revolution against technological mastery to the same Ghost Dance movement of Plains Indians back in the 1890s. After more than a quarter century of warfare against them Native Americans were demoralized, Lasher explains. Treaties had been broken and lands surrendered for promises of peace and security that guaranteed even more land to be turned over in the future.

Means of supporting and defending themselves were gone, along with "all the things they used to take pride in doing, all the things that had made them feel important, all the things that used to gain them prestige, all the ways in which they used to justify their existence" (*PP,* 249). Old religious beliefs no longer held true; old styles of warfare seemed useless. In desperation new myths had to be devised and tried—such as the Ghost Shirt, a garment making wearers immune to the cavalry's previously omnipotent bullets. A new religion systematized this myth. Hence was born the Ghost Shirt Society and the accompanying Ghost Dance religion.

Mimicking the comparison of primitive and civilized groups that had landed Vonnegut in hot water at the University of Chicago, Lasher finds similar conditions prevailing among the dispossessed workers of contemporary Ilium: "'All right,' said Lasher, his voice low. 'In the past, in a situation like this, if Messiahs showed up with credible, dramatic messages of hope, they often set off powerful physical and spiritual revolutions in the face of terrific odds. If a Messiah shows up now with a good, solid, startling message, and if he keeps out of the hands of the police, he can set off a revolution—maybe one big enough to take the world away from the machines, Doctor, and give it back to the people'" (*PP,* 252).

In the closing pages of *Player Piano,* Lasher's revolution happens, led by the disaffected characters Vonnegut has introduced, among them Dr. Paul Proteus. But is there any hope that this revolt, just one of many in human events, can be permanently effective? The Ghost Dance movement was, after all, a pitiful failure. But insisting that a revolution be practically effective is a matter of contradictory thinking, for as anthropologists such as Vonnegut and his spokesman Lasher know, revolutions are by definition reactions against set order. Replace that order with a new one—which is, after all, not a good in itself but just another cultural description—and the conditions for a future revolt are put in place.

There is a way that *Player Piano* conveys this sense of flux. When near the end readers are given a catalog of all the machines destroyed, a page-long alphabetical litany running from air conditioners, amplidynes, analyzers, and arc welders to water heaters, wheels, X-ray spectrogoniometers, and zymometers, we get the sense that the author is once again lulling us into the same mindless comfort we have derived from listening to the rhythmic burble-burb of Anita's electric washer, the whirlings and spinnings of an automated industry's machines, or the lovely sounding but reductively translated sounds of the Shah's exotic language. The implication is that life itself simply burbles and gurgles along, an organism propelled by its own momentum, to no end other than its own continuing existence, as self-defeating as that life may seem when subjected to cultural analysis.

Thus Anita strives to artificialize everything, taking the primitive farmhouse Paul has found for them and thwarting its back-to-basics ethic by trivializing everything into cozy little decorative touches. Even the worker revolutionaries cannot refrain from artifice, the desire to tinker with a broken vending machine overcoming their better knowledge of how such automation has put them into such a sorry state to begin with. Yet this closing scene does not suggest that the novel has been a testament to futility. Instead, *Player Piano* documents the joy of life's endearing episodes, one after another providing the family magazine entertainment that makes human existence so palatable even when things go wrong. The humor of it all is telling, yet never overly harsh, with plenty of room for all-too-true stories. Vonnegut cannot let the novel end without including several of them. There is the tale of a man given welfare work and finding out that it is just like being back in the army, mindless discipline and all. A corporate functionary has his credentials lifted until he completes the agony of a physical education course that a check of his college transcript shows is missing. There is even a private joke, in which a woman is found working as a prostitute rather than letting her husband sustain his writer's career by drafting public relations copy. Much of this is pure *Collier's* material, the type of narrative situation created by anyone's nagging nightmare of military service or overlooked education requirements. Such, this novel tells us, without losing its sense of humor, is life. And life itself is as self-propulsive as the monologue a barber delivers as if on automatic pilot to an uncomprehending but tolerant Shah of Bratpuhr, who is getting his ears lowered in the barber chair.

Any of these items could have generated a short story for *Collier's* or the *Saturday Evening Post*. Their presence in *Player Piano* helps define the novel's world of familiar, middle-class manners—manners that can be either people's salvation or their undoing. The question that the Shah asks as his concluding take on American life is a simple one: "what are people for?" (*PP,* 277). By addressing it to the computer EPICAC he reveals his own typically human fallibility. How should a computer know, for it is just a fabrication by people. But there lies Vonnegut's answer: human beings exist to make things, to be of use or produce something useful, thereby expressing a reason for being.

In this particular novel the human reason for being has turned back on itself, as human invention for a time robs people of their purpose. Yes, a revolution can be mounted against such a condition, but any act of revolt contains the same potential of leaving people once more prisoners of their own talents for artifice. "What people are for" may well consist of wondering what people are for. In later novels such as *Cat's Cradle* (1963) and *Slapstick* (1976) Vonnegut will posit this state as the ultimate human condition. He also asks the question as his story writer's career ends with the title piece for *Welcome to the Monkey House,* having his collected short fiction and first novel neatly bookend the genesis of his writer's career.

No description of the human condition, whether in *Player Piano* or elsewhere, should be considered final. "This isn't the end, you know," a character states on the novel's last page. "Nothing ever is, nothing ever will be—not even Judgment Day." All the better, Vonnegut's anthropologist spokesman responds, and he announces cheerfully, as the book's last line: "Forward March."

Chapter Two

COMING TO TERMS WITH TECHNIQUE

The Sirens of Titan, Mother Night, Cat's Cradle,
and *God Bless You, Mr. Rosewater*

AS LONG AS THE FAMILY MAGAZINE market for short fiction existed, Kurt Vonnegut need not be bothered with purely technical concerns. There was an accepted form for such material, and his anthropologist's training had helped him discern how there was an identifiable pattern for each type of narrative according to its publication in *Collier's* or *Cosmopolitan* or *Esquire*. Readers of such journals were not eager or even equipped for technical experiment. And even when one of the author's offerings would be passed over by the better-paying venues and wind up in a science-fiction publication, the sci-fi world had made it clear that ideas and not literary stylings were what counted there.

In *God Bless You, Mr. Rosewater* the protagonist addresses a convention of science-fiction writers; and while admitting that none of them could write worth beans, he praises their work as valuable to the extent that they really care about people. Kurt Vonnegut was certainly one of them, both in that he cared about people and in how he rated this concern above purely literary matters. But the interests of everyday folks were also central to stories saleable to the great family magazines, in which theme usually carried the day. And so for as long as this market lasted, Vonnegut made it his main commercial resort.

Yet as television grew through the 1950s and drew off the family magazines' advertising revenue, issues of *Collier's* and the *Saturday Evening Post* got thinner, doing just a single story instead of the usual five, and finally went out of business altogether. Short-story writers such as Vonnegut lost their jobs, but so did editors such as Knox Burger, the author's old friend from college newspaper days. Burger found work acquiring paperback originals and invited Vonnegut to try his hand at one of these. Did Kurt have a plot in mind? You bet he did, even if it involved cooking it up on the spot. Theme, however, was not enough to satisfy the reader of a paperback original. Unlike the weightier matters of concern that found their place in hardcover fiction, the attractiveness of this cheaper, hybrid format was that it could entertain and not just instruct. Within its pages had to be the variety and delight of an entire issue of *Collier's*, for such was the product it was replacing on the newsstands. By necessity Kurt Vonnegut would have to start playing with technique.

Between 1959 and 1965 four novels were produced with this new market in mind. *The Sirens of Titan* and *Mother Night* actually appeared this way, dressed out as space opera and World War II thriller stuff respectively. *Cat's Cradle* and *God Bless You, Mr. Rosewater* might well have accompanied them onto the newsstand and bus station reading racks, had not the man who produced them for the Western Printing Company, Samuel Stewart, moved to a new job with Holt, Rinehart and Winston, where novels were published in hardcover editions. As narratives of apocalyptic destruction and prince-and-the-pauper reversals, these last two could have been drugstore fare as well. But in choosing such popular formats for his new novels Vonnegut had proven himself equally adept at transforming subgeneric formats as he had been in vitalizing the themes of popular magazine fiction. Even though critical acclaim and best-sellerdom were still a big step away, his career as a novelist was finally under way.

"Everyone knows how to find the meaning of life within himself" (*ST*, 7): so begins *The Sirens of Titan*, in the offhand manner of "The Euphio Question" and "Unready to Wear" but with implications well beyond the confines of such short stories. Theme alone could not handle such a responsibility, even at a novel's length of three hundred pages as provided here, unless the author were a Jean-Paul Sartre capable of philosophizing all that time. *The Sirens of Titan* is anything but philosophical, though plenty of philosophies course their way through its complex action. Certainly not dull or plodding, the action jumps almost constantly through the multidimensionality of time and space, thanks to the clever device known as a "chrono-synclastic infundibulum," a slice of space in which all time exists in perfect simultaneity. All Vonnegut needs is this simple premise to enable narrative coverage of exceptionally vast range, with an almost entirely fluid point of view encompassing the doings of characters on Earth, Mars, Mercury, and a moon of Saturn, the "Titan" of this novel's title. Characters are also diverse, from the old-money aristocracy of Winston Niles Rumfoord (who is in several respects modeled on Franklin Delano Roosevelt) to the vulgar riches of Malachi Constant, a dissolute playboy compounded from the worst elements of contemporary glitz.

How Rumfoord's wife Beatrice moves from companionship with the first man to the second constitutes the clearest line of plot. Throughout his novelist's career Vonnegut would often rely on such basic structures, all the simpler for the great amount of complexity to be kept track of. But if this love interest (actually more of a sex interest, as love is quite slow to develop in these circumstances) is the bare skeleton of *The Sirens of Titan*—the simplest of recurrent melodies, so to say—then all else that happens are the inventive and sometimes magical improvisations on this theme, improvisations that soon become a form in themselves. As a premise, the chrono-synclastic infundibulum that gets things under way is sufficient to propel an entire novel's action, just as the similar device of time travel will allow such a universe of effects in *Slaughterhouse-Five*. Here is Vonnegut's great, if simple step beyond the confines of popular magazine fiction and the thematics of *Player Piano:* no longer must the premise of his writing be a variation on some social concern. In *The Sirens of Titan* the tinkerings are with time and space themselves.

The thematic statement of this novel is essentially a technical one: that in answering specific questions about the future and the one big general one about the purpose of life, an entirely new interpretation of temporal and spatial reality is presented. Again, the interpretation makes sense most easily as a literary device. Beatrice must leave her husband Winston and father a child with Malachi so that the son, Chrono, can pick up a good-luck piece. Meanwhile an extraterrestrial named Salo from the intergalactic world of Tralfamadore is traveling across the universe with a sealed message; when his space craft breaks down he spends the equivalent of 155,000 Earth years marooned on Titan waiting for a spare part. Only at the novel's end do readers learn that the spare part is Chrono's lucky piece. *This* has been the entire point of human history! But whereas as theme a notion like this might have filled a short story at best, when expressed as a literary device it makes for a full novel's worth of good reading. Consider how the nature of human events is changed simply by altering the temporal and spatial perspectives. From Titan, Salo has a telescopic view of Earth, and one of his hobbies becomes watching what transpires on this planet:

> It was through this viewer that he got his first reply from Tralfamadore. The reply was written on Earth in huge stones on a plain in what is now England. The ruins of the reply still stand, and are known as Stonehenge. The meaning of Stonehenge in Tralfamadorian, when viewed

from above, is: *"Replacement part being rushed with all possible speed."*

Stonehenge wasn't the only message old Salo had received.

There had been four others, all of them written on Earth.

The Great Wall of China means in Tralfamadorian, when viewed from above: *"Be patient. We haven't forgotten about you."*

The Golden House of the Roman Emperor Nero meant: *"We are doing the best we can."*

The meaning of the Moscow Kremlin when it was first walled was: *"You will be on your way before you know it."*

The meaning of the Palace of the League of Nations in Geneva, Switzerland, is: *"Pack up your things and be ready to leave on short notice."* (*ST,* 271–72)

The language is intentionally banal, reminiscent of the unaffected way Vonnegut's characters had spoken to one another in his magazine stories, particularly those that dealt with the future of euphio waves and EPICAC computers in the offhand language of conversations around the water cooler. This very banality highlights the temporal wonder of so much human effort—the entire course of world civilization, in fact—serving a purpose no grander than cheery little messages from a slow-as-molasses repair shop. Have a nice day; the check is in the mail; I love you, Paul; I love you too, Anita. The appraisal of human meaning is familiar by now, but the literary technique to express it is an innovation.

Beatrice moves from Winston to Malachi, and Salo travels from one edge of the universe to the other: from these axes the entire novel's action can be plotted, an action that otherwise defies understanding, as conventional measures are of little use in comprehending Vonnegut's complex plot. Much of this may have gone right over the heads of this paperback original's purchasers. Like the sirens pictured on its cover, the space opera trappings are a come-on, offering no satisfaction in themselves but opening the way to narrative situations beyond the reach of conventional exposition. But if the real answer lies in all those insipid messages to Salo, what has conventional exposition ever achieved? Human history has always seemed "a nightmare of meaninglessness without end" (*ST,* 8) because explanations had been sought from some external source. Only something standing above and beyond such effort could explain it, ran the reasoning. With Salo's breakdown Vonnegut provides the ultimate external authority for the doings of mankind—and look what this gets you, he implies. Not that Salo's message is any more inspiring. At novel's end, when a friendship has developed and Salo moves to cement it by going against orders and uncovering the message's great secret content, the revelation is even more deflating than the history of the world: just the single word "Greetings."

Looking outward, then, is a guarantee of ultimate futility. Only superficially about space, *The Sirens of Titan* actually takes its readers inward, to examine aspects of mind and matter, heart and soul for which conventional thematics would lack scope. In terms of technique, it is important to remember that in the microcosmic scheme of things the novel's action commences only because of Winston Niles Rumfoord's determination to do what his country's space program has backed off from: sailing straight into a chrono-synclastic infundibulum and thereby getting a final answer to things. It is here that Rumfoord's affinities with Franklin D. Roosevelt contribute to the literary technique. Like other Americans of his generation, Kurt Vonnegut grew up regarding FDR as a virtual president for life. Elected when Kurt was just nine years old, the man was still in office when the author was twenty-two and a veteran of World War II. Roosevelt had not only presided over this greatest war in world history but had guided the country through a similarly (if more peacefully) transformative event, the Great Depression. Between 1932 and 1945 the United States would undergo as much radical change as was ever experienced in its history, and at the head of that process, as the seeming agent of that change, was Franklin D. Roosevelt. It is no accident that Rumfoord is introduced "almost singing his greeting in a glottal Groton tenor" (*ST,* 20), cocks his cigarette at a jaunty angle in "a long, bone cigarette holder" (25), and is identified as a member of the old-money, old-family aristocracy that has supplied so many presidents. For what Rumfoord plans to do is akin to Roosevelt's transformation of values (and thereby the quality of life). How weak *The Sirens of Titan* would be if its substance were rooted in the claptrap of space opera. Instead, Vonnegut makes the materials of his science fiction so obviously ridiculous (the space aliens from Tralfamadore, for instance, look like plumbers' helpers) that no one in his right mind would seek seriousness there. Instead, the reader's intelligence is directed somewhere more familiar and much more reliable: to FDR, who, as Rumfoord seeks to do, actually created a new and quite workable secular mythology for an America paralyzed by the Great Depression.

As Winston Niles Rumfoord plays a generational role in the evolving structure of American culture, so does Malachi Constant. If the wealthy interstellar explorer and his dog (named, with ridiculous intent, "Kazak, the Hound of Space") are in fact equivalents of FDR and Falla, it should be no trouble to digest the apparent exoticisms of Malachi Constant and find their own correspondences in the social world of modern times. His background and adventures reflect the lives of many people Vonnegut's age: an adolescence in a civic paradise, military service to preserve this way of life (as Malachi's experiences on Mars prove to be), followed by the heroic attempt to found a family and keep it together in the face of life's competing forces. What is bad in outer space—the temptation to despair in the face of meaninglessness—is equally bad on Earth; and what is good, such as the redeeming warmth of friendship, is good everywhere.

What solves the malaise of purposelessness besetting the world of *The Sirens of Titan* is the same combination that got American society back on its feet after World War I had destroyed the securities of old values: an economic depression and a major war. Financial collapse is important for Malachi to seek priorities elsewhere and to create a general need for new values. Then, as it did in 1942–45, a major war sweeps the economic doldrums away and in the process gives the culture at large something better to believe in, which is commonality of purpose. What happens in *The Sirens of Titan* is greater because it involves a third force, that of religion. As FDR provided the New Deal for material concerns, Winston Niles Rumfoord offers the Church of God the Utterly Indifferent as an antidote to the type of ontological thinking that has created humankind's problems. An external source for meaning, this new faith teaches, does not exist; thinking that one does is what makes life so troublesome. "Puny man can do nothing at all to help or please God Almighty," Rumfoord proclaims, "and Luck is not the hand of God" (*ST,* 180). Is this nihilism? Far from it, for as members of this new church proclaim, "Oh, Mankind, rejoice in the apathy of our Creator, for it makes us free and truthful and dignified at last" (215). Drawing again on his anthropologist's disposition, Vonnegut uses these adherents to demonstrate how truth is self-invented, meaning fabricated not by superior authorities but by people within their own cultural contexts, according to their specific needs. When Malachi, nicknamed "Unk" during his military training on Mars, keeps a secret journal in an attempt to make sense of things, he is in fact fashioning a text of this new faith. "It was literature in the finest sense," the narrative says of his creation, "since it made Unk courageous, watchful, and secretly free. It made him his own hero in very trying times" (132).

In fabricating this new philosophy for human existence, one thing is shared by the narrative's many actors: by being used, they all contribute to the plot's solution. Beyond any theme, this service to structural technique is what unites them. That they are individually so different and play so many distinct roles in other parts of life contributes to the novel's impact, and this itself suggests a theme: that, as Beatrice Rumfoord suggests, "The worst thing that could possibly happen to anybody . . . would be not to be used for anything by anybody" (*ST,* 310).

Mother Night presents a classic story of someone being used, that of Howard W. Campbell, Jr., who through no will of his own has served the purposes of practically every country involved in international politics. Recruited in the late 1930s by his native America to infiltrate the Nazi establishment in the Germany where he lives and works as a playwright, Campbell broadcasts coded information he cannot understand, under the guise of fascist propaganda he finds too ridiculous to believe. After the war America formally disclaims him, the Soviet Union uses his example for further propaganda, and the state of Israel kidnaps him for trial as a war criminal.

What is the truth of Campbell's story? As a paperback original, the 1961 edition (released to newsstands in February 1962) gives no clue to being a novel at all. "An American Traitor's Astonishing Confession," reads the cover blurb. Inside, following a noncommital title page, the book begins with an "Editor's Note" signed by Vonnegut and describing how "this, the American edition of the confessions of Howard W. Campbell, Jr." (*MN,* ix) has been prepared—as if Vonnegut were presenting a historical text, not writing fiction. A fresh half title follows: "The Confessions of Howard W. Campbell, Jr.," succeeded in turn by a full-dress, display-type page reading the same. A third page, with Campbell's dedication, concludes the apparatus.

Unraveling the truth is the substance of *Mother Night,* and fictive technique is the key to that unraveling. In its various levels of textuality the novel is Kurt Vonnegut's first metafictive work, and a very sophisticated one at that. When read in its preferred 1966 edition, the hardcover first that adds an additional layer of textuality with Vonnegut's introduction signed from Iowa City (where he was in residence at the University of Iowa Writers' Workshop, teaching fiction and working on the first draft of *Slaughterhouse-Five*), *Mother Night* becomes as complex as any of the self-reflexive fictions published later in the decade by writers such as Donald Barthelme, Ronald Sukenick, and John Barth. At the very least, all this enfolding apparatus makes for a very personal narrative: from one perspective Campbell's; from another Vonnegut's own, given the autobiographical shadings the text adopts in 1966 (and maintains through the author's fame with his second novel dealing with World War II, *Slaughterhouse-Five*). At the same time, any sense of this being a "true story" is undone by the artificial nature of this same enfolding; if Campbell feels he is being used by the intelligence and propaganda interests of various countries, readers can see all the more so how he is being manipulated as a fictive creation. All this lends credence to the depth of Campbell's despair. "That's how I feel right now," he complains to the American agent who has guided his actions through the war and afterward, "like a pig that's been taken apart, who's had experts find a use for every part. By God—I think they even found a use for my squeal!" (*MN*, 155–56).

There have been despairing comments like this in *The Sirens of Titan* and also compensating answers, such as Beatrice Rumfoord's advice that it is far worse *not* to be of use to anyone. But Campbell, who feels as rendered as a stockyard pig, finds that his own process has been more thorough: "The part of me that wanted to tell the truth got turned into an expert liar! The lover in me got turned into a pornographer! The artist in me got turned into ugliness such as the world has rarely seen before" (*MN*, 156). Whereas *The Sirens of Titan* uses structural experiments with space and time to explore the dimensions of human meaning, *Mother Night* plays with the time and space of printed narrative—to suggest what the very idea of representation can do to a human being. Who is Howard Campbell? Is he a heroic counterspy sacrificing his life for his country? Or is he, as the "Kurt Vonnegut, Jr." who signs the editor's note describes him, "a man who served evil too openly and good too secretly, the crime of his times" (ii)?

Vonnegut's second novel had demonstrated the flaw in philosophical thinking that insists on external authority for human worth. Here in his third novel the author examines a more specific problem relating to the artifice his earlier work had offered as a counter to conventional religious belief. As a moral it becomes clear to him in 1966, when he writes the Iowa City introduction: "We are what we pretend to be, so we must be careful about what we pretend to be" (*MN*, v). Much of Howard Campbell's life involves fabrication. At the action's start he is a playwright, and an especially imaginative one at that; his dramas are best described as light escapism, their only values based on a solipsistic romanticism to which during the Nazi years he and his wife can retreat as "a nation of two" (27). When an American agent visits Berlin and recruits him to smuggle secret information out of Hitler's Reich, Campbell agrees only because the role appeals to him as a romantic, letting his outside life be sacrificed to an inner truth just he knows. There is a parallel, then, between his prewar and wartime lives; each shares a similar basis, and each is perverted into something else—the love story from a nation of two being turned into foul pornography, his propaganda broadcasts becoming so ludicrous that they cross the line from satire into the stuff a desperate people will believe.

Mother Night abounds in texts, and the readings of these texts are complicated by shifts in time and space. Meanings will be different according to who reads the material and when. The narrative structure is Vonnegut's most complex so far, with as much time travel to it as will happen in *Slaughterhouse-Five* and with a geography as various as any in his novels. There are Campbell's prewar years in the fantasy world of German theater, his experiences as a broadcaster within the wartime Nazi hierarchy (from its ascendancy to its collapse), his postwar life in the anonymity of Greenwich Village, his simultaneous rediscovery in the late 1950s by Soviet agents and American neo-Nazi enthusiasts, and his capture and imprisonment by Israel, where in preparation for his war crimes trial he is told to write this memoir. Throughout the novel there are incessant shifts of time and place; in 202 pages there are no fewer than forty-five chapters, their jumps in time and space accentuated with such intentionally distracting titles as "Tiglath-pileser the Third," "The Answer to Communism," and "St. George and the Dragon." Vonnegut will use this same technique of many short chapters with oddly diverting titles in *Cat's Cradle*—where, in telling a grandly apocalyptic story replete with various exoticisms of manner and locale, such a style seems appropriate. But the story *Mother Night* tells in 1961 is supposedly one everyone knows: how the Nazis rose to power in the 1930s, started a war that they for a time dominated, then collapsed in a Götterdämmerung that scrambled personal lives and national identities for a generation afterward. By making his narrative such a necessarily mixed-up affair Vonnegut is defamiliarizing the material, making it impossible for readers to proceed as if they already know the story. By turning things upside down and inside out within each chapter, and from jumping constantly in time and space from one chapter to the next, he keeps readerly attention fresh and, most importantly, receptive to new and surprising ideas.

The question then becomes: How does an author hold such a diverse structure together? One way, of course, is by relying on the subject's nature: as the major international event of the twentieth century, the war's history is generally known. But there is another device that unifies the book at the same time that it works against the easy acquiescence of familiarity. Here Vonnegut makes a major technical breakthrough, again anticipating the way he will unify *Slaughterhouse-Five*. His raw materials for this innovation are those common to black-humor novelists of the 1950s such as Terry Southern and Bruce Jay Friedman: shock-value surprises made from combining radically unalike associations, such as showing the masterminds of Nazi terror enjoying themselves in an intramural Ping-Pong tournament or revealing that Adolf Hitler is an emotive fan of Lincoln's *Gettysburg Address*. The author of *Mother Night* writes two such scenes. By themselves they could have appeared in anything by Southern or Friedman, or perhaps have been used in their developed form by the most artistic of the black humorists, Stanley Elkin. But Vonnegut's purpose is different. Unlike the black humorists—who, like the science-fiction writers of the period, were more interested in theme than in technique—he looks well beyond shock value as a thing in itself to use it in combination with other surprises in order to create a subliminal structure that holds his narrative together.

Consider the nature of these otherwise thematic surprises. During the war Campbell has a close friend in the German propaganda ministry named Heinz Schnildknecht; this in itself is part of the author's plan for showing the human side of what readers would know otherwise only as a monstrosity, because Schnildknecht is quite personally characterized by his love for his motorcycle, something having nothing to do with Nazi propaganda. How ironic, then, that when Campbell makes his escape from crumbling Berlin he does it by stealing Schnildknecht's prized possession. This wartime experience is recalled when the man shows up years later as a gardener in Ireland, courting fame as an authority on the death of Hitler; Campbell notes the irony in his own memoir, saying "Hello out there, Heinz. . . . What were you doing in Hitler's bunker—looking for your motorcycle and your best friend?" (*MN,* 89). But this is not the end of *Mother Night*'s use of Heinz Schnildknecht, for near the novel's close it is revealed that he has never really been a Nazi propagandist or a gardener in Ireland at all—these have been simply covers for his true role as an Israeli agent, working for Campbell's conviction.

Three times and places—three Heinz Schnildknechts. But one novel. To reenforce the method, Vonnegut fills *Mother Night* not just with absurdities but with absurdities that rebound to the third degree. Near the end of Campbell's secret life in New York, when he has become a propaganda pawn of socialist and neo-fascist forces, his notoriety attracts the American

Legion, a third force that demonstrates its judgment against him by leaving a hangman's noose in his vandalized apartment. The noose is tossed in the garbage, but not to stay there or be carted off to a landfill; instead a garbageman named Lazlo Szombathy finds it and seizes the chance to hang himself. So far, black humor. But Vonnegut raises this absurdity to the third power by looking into the reason for Szombathy's suicidal behavior: it turns out that he was despondent because as a refugee he could not practice the veterinary science in which he had been trained and during which he discovered a cure for cancer. Like billiard balls rebounding off a table's sides or pinballs ricocheting among the bumpers and levers of an amusement game, no person, place, or thing can make an appearance in *Mother Night*'s narrative without being knocked around three times—and in the replications of these triplets the novel's readers begin sensing, perhaps subconsciously, that somehow all this disconnected action is holding together. This is how Campbell's "nation of two" text is turned into pornography: a looting Russian soldier picks up the playwright's manuscripts from the rubble of Berlin, pirates the literary material, and turns the romantic stuff into the *Fanny Hill* of the postwar Soviet Union. But that is just two points of action; the third is that the soldier is caught and punished, but not for plagiarism; his crime against the state has been his efforts at originality, complementing the stolen Campbell canon with anti-Soviet satire of his own.

Hardly can a character appear in this novel without gaining three distinct identities. Take Arndt Klopfer: in Germany, Campbell has known him as the official Reich chancellery portrait photographer, and afterward he is surprised to see him turn up in Mexico as the country's major brewer. But as with Heinz Schnildknecht, the man is really something else, in this case a Russian spy working to expose Campbell as a U.S. embarrassment. Then there is the business with Lincoln. Nazi propagandist Paul Josef Goebbels, surely one of the worst monsters in history's cartoon gallery of evil figures, is shown to be an admirer of *The Gettysburg Address,* praising its effective audience manipulation. But the person who really cares for the speech, who is literally brought to tears every time he reads it, is Adolf Hitler. Now wait for the third turn of irony: the most gleeful fan of Campbell's vicious anti-Semitic broadcasts is none other than Franklin Delano Roosevelt, aficionado of the whole absurdity.

Playing with threes thus holds the novel together, giving readers the impression that all this narrative action that jumps across boundaries of time and space is actually a coherent statement. It coheres because there is a reasonability to Vonnegut's underlying theme, a theme so complex that it could never have been argued without this supporting technique. Another character with three identities, George Kraft (alias Iona Potapov), becomes at one and the same time Howard Campbell's most sincere friend and the agent who is working most seriously and effectively to arrange his exploitation, torture, and death in Moscow. Simultaneously, Kraft is a genuinely important modern artist, hailed as the first painter to comprehend and adopt the aesthetic of his age. How is such behavior possible? One of Campbell's prison guards is Arpad Kovacs, who as a Jew survived the war by becoming a member of the Hungarian SS. Looking over a transcript of one of Campbell's wartime broadcasts, in which coded information to the Allies was hidden among layers of the most vile propaganda, he expresses disappointment at the document's weakness. As a phony SS man Kovacs was much better. "Goebbels should have fired you and hired me as the radio scourge of the Jews," he boasts. "I would have raised blisters around the world!" (*MN*, 9). As for his work with his German platoon, he is even more enthusiastic:

Arpad beamed, remembering his S.S. days. "What an Aryan I made!" he said.

"Nobody ever suspected you?" I asked.

"How would they dare?" he said. "I was such a pure and terrifying Aryan that they even put me in a special detachment. Its mission was to find out how the Jews always knew what the S.S. was going to do next. There was a leak somewhere, and we were out to stop it." He looked bitter and affronted, remembering it, even though he had been that leak.

"Was the detachment successful in its mission?" I said.

"I'm happy to say," said Arpad, "that fourteen S.S. men were shot on our recommendation. Adolf Eichmann himself congratulated us."

"You met him, did you?" I said.

"Yes—" said Arpad, "and I'm sorry I didn't know at the time how important he was."

"Why?" I said.

"I would have killed him," Arpad said. (9–10)

Such loyalties to the act of the moment, even when the moments are so basically contradictory, reflect Campbell's behavior throughout the novel. It is not just that he has lived a double life. For Vonnegut's purposes it is important to note not only that he was a Nazi propagandist and an

American spy but also that he was *the best* German propagandist and *the best* Allied spy. Campbell admits, "I've always known what I did. I've always been able to live with what I did. How? Through that simple and widespread boon to modern mankind—schizophrenia" (*MN,* 136). Sometimes this style of mental illness is comic, a reduction ad absurdum of behavior that explains such a goofy gang as the White Christian Minutemen, a neo-Nazi group that wants to make a hero of Campbell even as the United States government disclaims him, the Soviets seek to kidnap him, the American Legion wishes to hang him, and Israeli intelligence works for his abduction to Jerusalem for a war crimes trial. Early readings of the Vonnegut canon, such as James Lundquist's *Kurt Vonnegut,* published in 1977, discounted *Mother Night* as the only novel (to date) that used no science-fiction elements, with the lack of fantasy making the action uncharacteristically grim. But there is nothing morbid about the author's understanding of politics and nationalism; for each group, whether it be a country's intelligence system or a motley assortment of fringe extremists, distinctions of belief come across as pure slapstick. How do such programs operate? Like "a system of gears whose teeth have been filed off at random," Campbell advises, with the White Christian Minutemen as his example at hand, but theorizing for all groups whose politics usurp other concerns: "Such a snaggle-toothed thought machine, driven by a standard or even a substandard libido, whirls with the jerky, noisy, gaudy pointlessness of a cuckoo clock in Hell" (168–69). Needless to say, the characters operating within this system are hilarious.

Yet Lundquist and the other early Vonnegut critics are correct in finding a serious purpose for this comedy. In *Mother Night* the author is not simply diagnosing the mental illness peculiar to this modern age. The wish to maintain an integrity of self in a chaotic world—certainly a traditional pursuit of artists of all times—has always been a schizophrenia of sorts. Campbell's retreats to art and love follow this pattern. But crucial to its success is that there be a self to which one can flee, a self that by virtue of one's love and art cannot be penetrated and abused by others. Like any fictive maker of the ages, Campbell offers "lies told for the sake of artistic effect"; deep inside, his self knows that his fictions are "the most beguiling forms of truth" (*MN,* x), despite their surface being given to the effects of art. As Hitler's Reich comes into being, he writes "medieval romances about as political as chocolate *éclairs*" (26), and so when put into American service as a spy against the Nazi war machine he seeks safety in satire and parody. Campbell confesses, "I had hoped, as a broadcaster, to be merely ludicrous" (122). As for seriousness, that comes in the romantic dramas he writes for himself and his wife, a narrative that will show "how a pair of lovers in the world gone mad could survive by being loyal only to a nation composed of themselves—a nation of two" (27).

Art and love should be inviolate. But in the new world of *Mother Night* they are violated at every turn, calling Campbell's refuge of the self into profound question. Toward the war's end he gets a hint of how his strategies have gone wrong when his father-in-law, a Nazi as ardent and die-hard as any in this book, tells Campbell that he was at first suspicious of the broadcaster's motives, as well he should have been, given that the propaganda was being made ludicrous beyond belief as a way of helping its author save his self-respect. "But this is a hard world to be ludicrous in," Campbell learns, "with so many human beings so reluctant to laugh, so incapable of thought, so eager to believe and snarl and hate. So many people wanted to believe me!" (*MN,* 122). The father-in-law has proof. At first suspecting (correctly) that Campbell is a spy, he concludes that it does not matter: "Because you could never have served the enemy as well as you served us" (75). How so? The man has realized, "almost all the ideas that I hold now, that make me unashamed of anything I may have felt or done as a Nazi, came not from Hitler, not from Goebbels, not from Himmler—but from you." Taking his son-in-law's hand in the rubble of Berlin, he confesses propaganda's deepest truth: "You alone kept me from concluding that Germany had gone insane."

So much for Campbell's refuge in art. As for the inviolable security of love, the most private of all emotions, shared with just one other, the beloved who gives the same allegiance in return, Vonnegut's protagonist is even more grossly disillusioned. Meeting with his American spymaster at war's end, he is told that his wife, long missing after an eastern-front tour to entertain the troops, is dead. How do the Allies know this? Campbell has told them! The information, learned by other spies within Germany, is considered crucial, and so it is fed into the material for a broadcast, the best way these agents have of communicating. For Campbell the revelation is devastating:

This news, that I had broadcast the coded announcement of my Helga's disappearance, broadcast it without even knowing what I was doing, somehow upset me more than anything in the whole adventure. It upsets me even now. Why, I do not know.

It represented, I suppose, a wider separation of my several selves than even I can bear to think about.

At that climactic moment in my life, when I had to suppose that my Helga was dead, I would have liked to mourn as an agonized soul, indivisible. But no. One part of me told the world of the tragedy in code. The rest of me did not even know that the announcement was being made. (*MN*, 140)

Hence truth gets turned into lies, love becomes pornography, and the artist of the beautiful becomes a creator of ugly filth. But does Campbell learn from these revelations, taking heed from what his father-in-law and his boss in American intelligence tell him? No, because the subliminal structure of *Mother Night*, the absurdities rebounding in triplets, once again comes into play. As his days of hiding out in New York's Greenwich Village reach their end, with forces from the left and right and lunatic fringes closing in, someone miraculous appears: Helga. Except she is not Helga but rather Helga's younger sister, Resi, pretending to be Campbell's love. For a moment he believes her. But even after he sees through her disguise he accepts her as Helga anyway, so desperate is he for love even under pretense. Yet this does not mean that Campbell finds salvation. Far from it, because Resi is not really a substitute for Helga after all—she is a Russian spy working for Campbell's kidnapping.

How has the modern self been lost? By making it the center of the universe, Vonnegut suggests, in his book a mistake as big as that of those who would act in the name of God's plan. As *The Sirens of Titan* undermines this latter belief, so does *Mother Night* confound the former. Because human beings have abandoned all else and fled to their selves as the romantic center of the universe, when the self collapses, everything, quite literally, is lost. At the novel's end Campbell realizes this. Having been convicted by an Israeli court, the same one that is trying Adolf Eichmann, of crimes against humanity, Vonnegut's protagonist finds himself awaiting execution in the morning. His last day's mail brings him a letter that could save him, a document of exoneration from his American spymaster taking official responsibility for his acts—making Campbell, so to speak, a hero in the eyes of the court, not a villain. The prisoner remarks, "So I am about to be a free man again, to wander as I please. I find the idea nauseating" (*MN*, 201). Therefore, for the first time in the entire novel, he takes matters into his own hands: instead of submitting to execution by the Israel government for crimes against humanity, he elects to "hang Howard

W. Campbell, Jr., for crimes against himself" (202). This closing sentiment completes the thought that Vonnegut, signing the book's front matter as a purported textual editor, expresses as his own judgment: "This book is rededicated to Howard W. Campbell, Jr., a man who served evil too openly and good too secretly, the crime of his times" (xii).

Throughout his narrative Vonnegut has mixed the loftiest of moral thoughts with the most vulgar forms of slapstick comedy. Like the triplets of absurdity, much of it is subliminal: readers have to make a roster of characters, for example—Campbell, his friend Heinz, his friend Kraft— to see how many are named after soups, catsups, and processed cheeses from any contemporary American home's kitchen. A similar sense of humor characterizes *Cat's Cradle,* again as a balance to Vonnegut's heavily moral theme. Indeed, now it is humor itself that serves as the author's technical breakthrough, starting not just with the novel's first chapter but from the table of contents. Here there are even more chapters than in *Mother Night:* 127 for the book's 231 pages. Like its predecessor, chapter titles are self-consciously silly, such as "When Automobiles Had Cut-Glass Vases," "The Last Batch of Brownies," and "Barracuda Capital of the World." As in *Mother Night,* the titles are deliberately off-putting, considering the author's subject, which is named in the first chapter's title: "The Day the World Ended." Even that idea is given a send-up, for although the protagonist has set out to write a book only metaphorically related to Earth's apocalypse—6 August 1945 with the first atomic explosion over Japan—by the end events have led him to the actual demise of this planet. In the process a new religion has been founded and explained: Bokononism. But its lyrical teachings, which in the Judeo-Christian heritage would be expressed as Psalms, are here sung in the rinky-dink rhythms of little ditties called "Calypsoes." Like the texts of a real religion, they are numbered; but when printed out they look as unreligious as what a marimba band would be playing at a Caribbean singles' resort. Which is precisely what Vonnegut intends. If his themes are to have any usefulness at all, it will be because they are self-evident as pieces of artifice, and an undercutting humor keeps that awareness foremost in the reader's mind.

In *Mother Night* texts compete for the authority to exist as truth. In assigning the book a moral, Vonnegut—writing as the self-professed author from his new position as an instructor at the University of Iowa Writers' Workshop—was careful to hedge his bet. "We are what we pretend to be," he proclaimed, but he allowed some latitude for action, adding, "so we must be careful about what we pretend to be" (*MN,* v). His narrative has made clear what are faulty pretenses: self-willed schizophrenia, of course, but also art and love when they are styled to escapist ends. Yet if one is indeed "careful," can there be a valid pretense? In the front matter of *Cat's Cradle* three more texts operate in a mutually self-corrective way. "Nothing in this book is true," reads the conventional disclaimer, followed by an epigraph ascribed to *The Books of Bokonon,* verified by chapter and verse: "Live by the *foma** that make you brave and kind and healthy and happy." It is the asterisk that hedges Vonnegut's bet here, for at the bottom of the page this term is glossed as "*Harmless untruths*" (*CC,* [5]). *Foma* turn out to be the new book's magical elements, assuaging the cruelties and sadness of *Mother Night.* In his spy novel Vonnegut had featured the destructive pretenses that make modern life so terrible; the only untruths played with in *Cat's Cradle* are those that are "harmless." These *foma* are key elements in the novel's religion, Bokononism. But why should religion be a valid pretense when art and love are not? Had not *The Sirens of Titan* clarified Vonnegut's thinking on presumably holy matters?

The problem common to traditional art, love, and religion is that, in Vonnegut's view, they place humankind at the center of meaning. The Bokononism offered in *Cat's Cradle* avoids this egocentricity by showing how people can be comfortable by admitting that the world they live in is not under their own or God's control. The "lies" of this new religion are purgative, yielding happiness, balance, and comfort. They reorder our notion of the finite world so that we may accept it, rather than rebel in fruitless anger. This is the first step toward accommodating oneself to the temporal and spatial notions unveiled in *Slaughterhouse-Five.* Above all, Bokononism is not an opiate. Instead it does what any fiction writer must do, which is fulfilling "a sacred obligation to produce beauty and enlightenment and comfort at top speed" (*CC,* 189). As a system of artifices, a novel by definition must have a central meaning for all the things it introduces, and the novelist must eventually reveal that meaning to be successful—thus someone like Vonnegut is using the methodology of faith in every book he writes. In *Cat's Cradle* he lets Bokononism flesh out the metaphors for novel writing. Novels have characters who, willingly or unwillingly, wittingly or unwittingly, work together to create plots and see them resolved. Bokononism parallels this technique by teaching that "humanity is organized into teams, teams that do God's will without ever discovering what they are doing. Such a team is called a *karass*" (14). Therefore the protagonist who is writing the book that turns out to be *Cat's Cradle* tries to include in his narrative "as many members of my *karass* as possible" and "to examine strong hints as to what on Earth we, collectively, have been up to" (170). As Stanley Schatt notes in his study *Kurt Vonnegut, Jr.* (1976), this cast of characters is notably myopic, none of them able to discern the consequences of their own actions, much less a larger pattern of meaning (57). But that is what Vonnegut as novelist and Bokonon as a religionist intend: "If you find your life entangled with somebody else's life for no very logical reason," the prophet says, "that person may be a member of your *karass*" (*CC*, 14), a reminder that the conditions of life are by definition myopic. The breakthrough in this religion is that now we see that we cannot see. Were an answer needed to explain the twisted life of *Mother Night's* sadly misused protagonist, it could be found in *Cat's Cradle.*

The eschatological imperative behind Bokononism is shared by all religions. What makes Vonnegut's device so innovative is the way it deems such eschatology absurd, as this fable from the prophet teaches:

> In the beginning, God created the earth, and he looked upon it in His cosmic loneliness.
>
> And God said, "Let us make living creatures out of mud, so the mud can see what We have done." And God created every living creature that now moveth, and one was man. Mud as man alone could speak. God leaned close as man sat up, looked around, and spoke. Man blinked. "What is the *purpose* of all this?" he asked politely.
>
> "Everything must have a purpose?" asked God.
>
> "Certainly," said man.
>
> "Then I leave it to you to think of one for all of this," said God. And He went away. (*CC*, 214–15)

The Books of Bokonon read much like the Bible's New Testament, as if to emphasize Vonnegut's parody. But the changes, however slight, are significant. The tone is even more elementary than that of the familiar Christian texts, preparing the way for a simplification of message—another technique the author will use in *Slaughterhouse-Five.* Christianity is far from being thrown out, or even overthrown, for that matter; fundamentalist critics who condemn Vonnegut for being antireligious miss the point, for instead of negating sacred documents he is simply rewriting them to better effect, doing for religion what novelists do for their worlds of fiction—making them work more effectively toward the human goals of beauty, comfort, and enlightenment. This new religion does not change everything. Reading the Twenty-third Psalm, for example, "Bokonon tried to overhaul it" but "found out that he couldn't change a word" (*CC,* 171). In his own public statements on Christian liturgy Vonnegut will show similar reverence for the Sermon on the Mount, a frequent reference in *Palm Sunday,* in which the author characterizes much of his speech-making as the giving of sermons.

Bokononism is not the novel's only eschatological device. Although the protagonist cites it frequently from the start, the other characters in *Cat's Cradle* encounter it only toward the end of the narrative's action, when events have shifted to the tiny Caribbean island of San Lorenzo. Before that there is much to do in Ilium, New York, where the objects of the narrator's study have resided. Chief among them is Dr. Felix Hoenikker, inventor of the atomic bomb. John, as the narrator is named—his book begins, "Call me Jonah. My parents did, or nearly did. They called me John" (*CC,* 13)—travels there to learn all he can about this man, now deceased, who made apocalypse an everyday possibility in modern life. The focus is specific, limited to what happened in the great scientist's household on 6 August 1945, and to find out that John requests interviews with family and friends. In the meetings that follow he learns that almost all those involved had their own sense of purpose. Son Frank made sense of things by building model airplanes, daughter Angela by playing clarinet—each to the exclusion of almost everything else in life. The youngest child, Newt, provides the most information, such as the morning-to-morning routine after his mother died and his big sister Angela took over running the family. He reports, "I can remember cold mornings when Frank, Father, and I would be all in a line in the front hall, and Angela would be bundling us up, treating us all exactly the same. Only I was going to kindergarten; Frank was going to junior high; and Father was going to work on the atom bomb" (23). Not that atomic research provides an eschatology for the famous man. His mind is elsewhere: finishing breakfast one day when leaving for Sweden to receive the Nobel Prize, he absent-mindedly leaves his wife a tip under the plate; on a day much like Newt is describing he gets into the car to find its battery dead, and after sitting there for several minutes he speaks up, but only to say, "I wonder about turtles. . . . When they pull in their heads, do their spines buckle or contract?" (23).

Turtles become, for a time, a satisfying system of meaning for the man. As Newt explains, they and their absence are the closest things he can relate to the atomic bomb's discovery: "Angela was one of the unsung heroines of the atomic bomb, incidentally, and I don't think the story has ever been told. Maybe you can use it. After the turtle incident, Father got so interested in turtles that he stopped working on the atom bomb. Some people from the Manhattan Project finally came out to the house to ask Angela what to do. She told them to take away Father's turtles. So one night they went into his laboratory and stole the turtles and the aquarium. Father never said a word about the disappearance of the turtles. He just came to work the next day and looked for things to play with and think about, and everything there was to play with and think about had something to do with the bomb" (*CC,* 24).

As childish as is the language in *The Books of Bokonon* and as ultimately deflating of great meaning as is the Stonehenge-to-Kremlin historiography in *The Sirens of Titan,* Newt's story makes the novel's first key point: that if anyone insists on an overriding meaning that will make sense of human life, then he or she should be ready to think one up. Not that Dr. Hoenikker's innocence is entirely winsome. Ilium is the same town, albeit in the present and not the future, that Vonnegut featured in *Player Piano.* And the General Forge and Foundry is the same company, its Research Laboratory in *Cat's Cradle* dedicated to the same unrestricted methodology of pure research as was the General Electric facility where Vonnegut's brother worked and for which the author wrote publicity. Research unfettered by commercial concerns would seem a great good, an ideal almost too perfect to be true; but at GE it was. Likewise, as Vonnegut feared at the time and would demonstrate in his first novel, scientific research unfettered by moral concerns—by a simple interest in how its results would be used, to be even simpler—could be a great evil; and the fact that the means for atomic warfare may have been born this way is all the more troubling.

The novel's action is propelled by comedy; just about everything the Hoenikker family does is hilariously self-defeating. But given that it is the world's eventual demise that is at issue, a serious side to the narrative is needed as well. The characters and their doings need to be joined up with the teachings of Bokononism, and for this reason the action leads to the island of San Lorenzo, where Frank has found work in the service of the local dictator. One of his father's last discoveries was of a property called "ice-nine," a molecular restructuring that raises the freezing point of water to well above the normal level of earthly activity. Once loosed upon the world it will freeze everything—and is thus the ultimate doomsday machine, well beyond the threats of nuclear terror. Does this scientific product speak for the ultimate nihilism of human life? Newt may think so. As his brother Frank retreated to a world of model airplanes (now translated into his toying with the politics of San Lorenzo) and as his sister Angela has found solace in the musical artistry of her solo clarinet playing (making her very much a lone performer of what would otherwise be the social symphony of life), Newt tries painting. His works look like "sticky nets of human futility hung up on a moonless night to dry" (*CC*, 137). He can say why, tracing his empty aesthetic to the game of cat's cradle his father played with him as one of their few points of contact. "No wonder kids grow up crazy," he tells the narrator. "A cat's cradle is nothing but a bunch of X's between somebody's hands, and little kids look and look at all those X's." And what do they find, the narrator wonders. "*No damn cat*," Newt responds, "*and no damn cradle.*"

To the empty lives of the Hoenikker children Bokononism offers the same solace as it does to the blighted island of San Lorenzo. Newt's objection is that artfulness of the cat's cradle variety has excluded the finitely real. The artifice that is needed is one able to handle the finite on its own terms, without recourse to "lies." Existence in San Lorenzo is depressingly futile, and so Bokononism can hope to do little with that. It never raises the people's standard of living: "The truth was that life was as short and brutish and mean as ever" (*CC*, 144). But what it offers is a system that allows the truth to exist, yet in a way that people are not forced to pay attention to it. They are instead given roles and are "employed full time as actors in a play they understood, that any human being anywhere could understand and applaud." Bokonon makes himself an artificial scapegoat—always to be chased, never to be caught, letting people delight in the ritual as an end in itself. As for the finitely real, it is just that: an external repository of certain elements, some of which may be evil but none of which is egocentrically identified with humankind.

Hence Bokononism is not an opiate, nor is it irresponsible. It turns away from nothing and in fact accepts the unpleasant facts of reality for what they are, as a part of the whole truth—but never as Truth itself. The single identified saint in *Cat's Cradle*, Julian Castle, does all he can to undercut a simplistic picture of his good. Indeed, as a character, "He forestalled all references to his possible saintliness by talking out of the corner of his mouth like a movie gangster" (*CC*, 138). The man heroically saves countless lives but also appreciates the grotesqueness of his own situation, which is a continuation of his father's work to atone for the Holocaust by this time *saving* six million lives. One of the novel's most shocking moments of grim humor is when Castle's father steps back from his jungle hospital, which is almost buried in the corpses of plague victims, and tells his son that "someday this will be all yours" (135). In *The Fabulators* (1967), the first book on contemporary American fiction to include Vonnegut's work as a subject for study, Robert Scholes argues that such dark comedy is the only antidote to a corresponding excess of horror. If evil is securely located in a coexisting finitude, there is no need for Vonnegut's narrator to be worried about all the satanic things Castle says; his acts of good stand by themselves as an index of his worth. This is what Bokononism teaches: "We do, doodley do, . . . / What we must, muddily must, . . . / . . . / Until we bust, bodily bust" (216) . And as the words of its last rites affirm, "I loved everything I saw" (181). The sentiments that save Billy Pilgrim in *Slaughterhouse-Five,* his belief that everything is beautiful and nothing hurt, are not long to come.

Comedy's role in handling reality is a given in Vonnegut's work, but with *Cat's Cradle* this method comes to the fore as a structuring device. The mixture of good and bad as a frankly hilarious situation becomes an autobiographical element later in the decade as the author puts even more of himself into his works. There is the retrospective preface for *Welcome to the Monkey House,* in which the same duality is found in the words from his brother (who is taking care of a newborn) and from his sister (who in the process of speaking them died of cancer): "Here I am cleaning the shit off of practically everything" and "No pain," sentiments the author describes as "the two main themes of my novels" (*WMH,* xiv). When in *Slaughterhouse-Five* Vonnegut's father says, "you never wrote a story with a villain in it" (*SF,* 7), no reader will fear that the writer has become an irresponsible jokester or blithe optimist. Instead, Vonnegut's public pronouncement has been that he is "a consistent pessimist" (*WFG,* 162) ever since learning about the fate of Hiroshima and Nagasaki. Writing on the fall of Biafra, he admits that "joking was my response to misery that I can't do anything about" (146), but he has also reminded readers, quoting Shakespeare, that "to weep is to make less the depth of grief" (162). The joking in Bokononism is not a palliative; instead it is a fundamental reordering of human values, solving the problem that has made people uncomfortable being the center of the universe, so ill at ease that they claim God's purposes for their own.

Despite their rogues' galleries of unpleasant incidents, both *Mother Night* and *Cat's Cradle* are positive works. Howard W. Campbell, Jr., commits not so many crimes against humanity as crimes against himself, the latter of which, once recognized, can be successfully and personally purged. *Cat's Cradle* goes a step further by relieving humankind of its unbearably egocentric responsibility for the conditions of natural existence. Granted that the world can become absurd and that a good life may be finally unlivable; at this point any Vonnegut character can responsibly bow out, having "the good manners to die" (*CC,* 220)—and with great composure and respectability do as Robert Scholes describes and "turn the humor back on the joker" (*Fabulators,* 44). For this is precisely how *Cat's Cradle* ends.

The dualities of *God Bless You, Mr. Rosewater* are deceptively simple. Rich and poor are the major ones, with happiness and unhappiness as the presumable corollaries. But Vonnegut's structural innovation in retelling a prince-and-the-pauper story reaches well beyond the ironies of simple reversal. Yes, Eliot Rosewater sets aside his riches to live among the poor, part of his program of rescaling the philanthropic efforts of his mighty Rosewater Foundation to the practicalities of human need—for example, he papers the phone booths of dirt-poor regions in Indiana with stickers asking people what is the absolute minimum they would take for not killing themselves, and then he argues them down even further when they call for help. In time readers can see that he is accomplishing far more than individual Band-Aid solutions; by novel's end Rosewater will have stood America's entire social ethic on its head so that there might be some basic worth for humankind. A sense of worth is certainly needed, for in economic terms *God Bless You, Mr. Rosewater* is the author's cruelest work. Written at the worst financial and professional time in Vonnegut's life— when his family magazine market for short fiction had entirely collapsed, when the novels he wrote to cover the lost income were not selling, and before both economic and career matters were ameliorated by an instructorship at the University of Iowa—this novel risks a reductive view of humanity. As its opening sentence states, "A sum of money is a leading character in this tale about people, just as a sum of honey might properly be a leading character in a tale about bees" (*GB,* 15). Eliot Rosewater's test will be whether he can disprove this thesis, just as Vonnegut's challenge as a novelist is to find a redeeming answer in the rags-versus-riches contrasts he inverts.

The world of this novel certainly asks to be inverted, for as encountered it seems particularly vicious. Norman Mushari is one of the first characters introduced and in terms of the thematically driven plot is one of its more important functionaries: he is a lawyer who has learned that just as a good pilot should always be looking for somewhere to land, a person in the legal profession should always be looking for a great amount of money to change hands. But that is just the careerist side of Norman. To make his point Vonnegut adds that in addition to all else—his nickname "the weasel," the fact that his firm has made him a partner because its doings could profit from a touch of mercenary nastiness—"He had an enormous ass, which was luminous when bare" (*GB,* 17). Mushari, although a minor character, is introduced first because he is the one to put the novel's plot into action, having noticed a great amount of money that could be made to change hands if its present holder were declared insane. Is Eliot Rosewater insane? According to Lawrence R. Broer's treatment of the book in *Sanity Plea: Schizophrenia in the Novels of Kurt Vonnegut* (1994), this question has even larger implications than Mushari's financial ones. Is the good that Eliot seeks to do undone by the idiotic simplicities of his remedies, or is his revision of human worth a mentally sound one? Broer finds that Eliot's measures continually undercut themselves, a reminder that Vonnegut is never one to present pat solutions. But the document Mushari presents as initial proof of Eliot's mental illness seems sufficient to have the man judged mad, for its contents—in the form of Eliot's intended advice to his eventual successor as director of the great Rosewater Foundation— paint a picture of America that makes its destruction of human values too ghastly for even the most committed anticapitalist to believe.

In this letter Eliot tells how over the past one hundred years the Rosewater family fortune was acquired. It is not a pretty story, beginning with a draft-dodging Rosewater from Civil War days who makes a fortune manufacturing swords and bayonets. After the war this ancestor moves on to the next stage of American cupidity, organizing a vertical trust and becoming a robber baron. From there come stock swindles, political bribes, and eventually political office. "Thus did a handful of rapacious citizens come to control all that was worth controlling in America" (*GB,* 21), Eliot writes. "Thus was the savage and stupid and entirely inappropriate American class system created. Honest, industrious, peaceful citizens were classed as bloodsuckers, if they asked to be paid a living wage. And they saw that praise was reserved henceforth for those who devised means of getting paid enormously for committing crimes against which no laws had been passed." The result, in Eliot's words, is as vicious as the narrative description of Norman Mushari: "Thus the American dream turned belly up, turned green, bobbed to the scummy surface of cupidity unlimited, filled with gas, went *bang* in the noonday sun."

Eliot's outrage sets the tone for this whole novel, in which characters are either so naively good or grossly bad that they seem figures in a medieval morality play. Given that Vonnegut's subgeneric model this time around is the story of the prince and the pauper, such allegory is fitting. There is even a source for this attitude, an influence from the author's childhood that he was starting to incorporate in his work as it approached the period of its maturity and strength. Kurt Vonnegut grew up in an upper-middle-class home, the library of which was stocked with typical classics loved by popular readers, including works by Rudyard Kipling, Robert Louis Stevenson, and the like. Young Kurt was taught to respond to this litera-ture the way its writers intended: sentimentally. In addition he spent many childhood hours in the company of his family's cook, who had an even more affective literature to share. As Vonnegut recounts in the preface to *Wampeters, Foma & Granfalloons,* the experience was a formative one, cre-ating a mood he would return to in times of stressful need:

> Her name was Ida Young, and I probably spent more time with her than I spent with anybody—until I got married, of course. She knew the *Bible* by heart, and she found plenty of comfort and wisdom in there. She knew a lot of American history, too—things she and other black people had seen and marveled at, and remembered and still talked about, in Indiana and Illinois and Ohio—and Kentucky and Tennessee. She would read to me, too, from an anthology of sentimental poetry about love which would not die, about faithful dogs and humble cot-tages where happiness was, about people growing old, about visits to cemeteries, about babies who died. I remember the name of the book, and I wish I had a copy, since it has so much to do with what I am.
>
> The name of the book was *More Heart Throbs;* and it was an easy jump from that to *The Spoon River Anthology,* by Edgar Lee Masters, to *Main Street,* by Sinclair Lewis, to *U.S.A.,* by John Dos Passos, to my thinking now. There is an almost intolerable sentimentality beneath everything I write. British critics complain about it. And Robert Scholes, the American critic, once said I put bitter coatings on sugar pills.
>
> It's too late to change now. At least I am aware of my origins—in a big, brick dreamhouse designed by my architect father, where nobody was home for long periods of time, except for me and Ida Young. (*WFG,* xxiv–xxv)

From his childhood, then, Vonnegut draws the two elements that define *God Bless You, Mr. Rosewater*'s art: an experience of family wealth gone bad to the taste before it dissipates entirely and a sentimental approach to lit-erature that helps redeem the disappointments of such a life.

Because Eliot has not produced an heir, next in line to direct the foundation is Fred Rosewater, a distant cousin in Rhode Island who sells small-time family life insurance policies. Like Eliot, he deals with indignities of existence that make human aspirations seem small indeed; much of the novel's brilliance lies in Vonnegut's ability to make all stations of life, from the highest to the lowest, look depressingly unattractive. But there is a reason for this sad state of affairs, as Eliot explains in his statements on economics. And when Eliot's arguments run out he has an expert to call on: the science-fiction writer Kilgore Trout.

Trout is much more than a *raisonneur* (reasoner, answerer). Unlike Reverend Lasher in *Player Piano* with his master's degree in anthropology, Trout's education has been in the hard school of life, whose homely lessons on human nature he makes saleable, in a tawdry way, as space opera fantasy. He asks the question What are people for? and is able to answer it because he has the sci-fi writer's understanding of imagination's transforming power. Early in the novel Eliot visits a science-fiction writers' convention—a real one located in Milford, Pennsylvania, that sci-fi fans will recognize as the annual convocation directed by author Damon Knight. Here Vonnegut's protagonist takes the stage and tells the assemblage that despite their hackneyed formulas and ridiculous themes they are the only writers who care about the human predicament and, even more importantly, the only ones who try to do something about it. What's their secret? The same as Vonnegut's: knowing that reality is not an absolute condition but only a human description changeable from describer to describer and completely relative according to culture. Examples for this need not be exotic themes from outer space but rather something as simple as money. To make his point he takes out his checkbook and scribbles drafts for all the writers present, giving them two hundred dollars apiece. "*There's* fantasy for you" (*GB*, 31), he proclaims. "And you go to the bank, tomorrow, and it will all come true. It's insane that I should be able to do such a thing, with money so important." Yet he is able to because of how the economics of America are set up. There is also something that writers can do, which is to "think about the silly ways money gets passed around, and then think up better ways."

The effect is allegorical, much as in a morality play—but it works as a solid proof. In appreciating how reality is just a description of how cultural practices are naturalized into a form of absolute law, both Rosewater and Vonnegut draw on more than social theory. The latter's understanding of money's transformative power comes from his family's experience in the Great Depression, when events on Wall Street changed their way of life in Indianapolis, teaching young Kurt how reality is no more absolute than the terms defining it—just look how the stock market crash had radically altered those terms. Therefore the author will not let his protagonist idealize the poor since idealism is the most absolute standard of all. When Eliot closes down the foundation's lavish Park Avenue offices and moves his headquarters to a shotgun attic walk-up over a liquor store in the long-forsaken ancestral hometown in Indiana, he is doing more than just rechanneling funds otherwise marked for symphonies, ballets, and art museums. He is taking this money that looked so good among the finer things of life and running it though the economic mill of the dead-end lower classes, where his clientele is the group of pathetic unfortunates forever a day late and a dollar short. Some are repulsive; some are borderline insane. The most heroic among them are volunteer firefighters, such as Eliot wishes he can be. But most are as disgusting as Eliot becomes, none of them doing a thing to lift themselves above the devastated, strip-mined countryside the Rosewater wealth has left them as its detritus.

What then can be done for improvement? Kilgore Trout articulates the program that Eliot has been enacting, which is to discard the ethic of the American economic dream. Valid for a new country founded in the wilderness with a desperate need for everyone's work (and with ample resources to reward it), that dream had valued people according to the work they did and value they produced. But when civilization has developed beyond this production stage, with the need for such work removed, a new standard of value needs to be introduced. People must be valued simply for what they *are,* Trout teaches—to be loved uncritically, as indeed they must be, given the poor examples of humanity Eliot has to deal with. As for personal conduct, Eliot has a motto that inverts Howard Campbell's credo from *Mother Night:* "Pretend to be good always, and even God will be fooled" (*GB,* 203). Such frank candor is part of what Trout sees as a new mythology needed for postindustrial America, and it is a new mythology indeed that Eliot invokes in his baptism service: "Hello, babies. Welcome to Earth. It's hot in the summer and cold in the winter. It's round and wet and crowded. At the outside, babies, you've got about a hundred years here. There's only one rule that I know of, babies—: 'God damn it, you've got to be kind'" (110).

Eliot's program may be as sentimental as *More Heart Throbs,* but idealistic it is not—an important distinction in following Vonnegut's practice of avoiding absolutes. His way of resolving the otherwise inexorable economic plot of this novel is equally relative. The charter of the Rosewater Foundation uses direct inheritance as its standard of succession. Because Eliot has sired no heirs, Norman Mushari has sought to take control of its millions from him. But Rosewater foils this by accepting paternity for every child in Rosewater County, thus dispersing his money in the most thorough way imaginable. As in the ending to *Cat's Cradle,* the joke is turned back upon the joker, in this case the avaricious lawyer who has sought to use a letter of the law to his own advantage. By creating this parody of an absolute, Eliot turns it inside out and achieves his more humane purpose of getting the Rosewater millions out of the hands of people who would misuse them and into a form in which they might do some good.

As with *The Sirens of Titan, Mother Night,* and *Cat's Cradle,* Vonnegut's success in *God Bless You, Mr. Rosewater* is founded on his facility with technique. While *Player Piano* speaks straightforwardly with theme, its major innovation being the same as the author's rejected master's thesis, these four successive novels would do even more for fictive experimentation than comparing civilized and primitive groups had done for the anthropological message informing the first work. Choosing easily recognizable subgenres for his basic forms was surely a good idea on Vonnegut's part, for each already let the reader know what the general theme would be: space opera almost always extends philosophical vision; spy thrillers traditionally involve their protagonists' risks of self; apocalyptic narratives have their endings determined from the start; and prince-and-the-pauper tales almost inevitably find the greatest riches to be in the simplest circumstances. With each novel's form taking care of itself the author could use technique to express his deeper concerns. As a novelist Kurt Vonnegut was securely in command of his art, which was by now as serious as anything the trade had to offer.

The problem was that this particular trade could not produce a living income. Paperback originals earn the same pay as *Saturday Evening Post* short stories because their authors are expected to produce them at a similar rate; but Kurt Vonnegut was lavishing two years of work on each effort, worthy enough for seriously regarded fiction but misplaced for the economic formats to which *The Sirens of Titan* and *Mother Night* were consigned. As proper hardcover originals *Cat's Cradle* and *God Bless You, Mr. Rosewater* could have earned more had they sold in good numbers—but they did not. Plus the family magazine market for short fiction had, for Vonnegut's style of work, closed completely. Thus 1964 was for the author a troublesome-looking time. *God Bless You, Mr. Rosewater,* appearing the next year, was unlikely to earn more than its advance; along with a check from the *Post* for Kurt's last story there, a satire of the Kennedy family that could not be run because of the president's assassination, the *Rosewater* advance would have to feed the Vonnegut family until something else could be devised. Fortunately something would: by turning to a new genre entirely, that of the personal essay, Kurt Vonnegut would not only regenerate a steady cash flow but also find a handle on the novel he had wanted to write since coming home from World War II. Each line of endeavor would be a notable success.

Chapter Three

SPEAKING PERSONALLY

Slaughterhouse-Five and the Essays

"THE HYANNIS PORT STORY" is more than Kurt Vonnegut's last piece of fiction for the *Saturday Evening Post*. That it never appeared there, waiting for publication five years later in *Welcome to the Monkey House,* makes it fit into the author's canon all the more comfortably, for in this narrative he looks forward to the next stage in his career. As a short story it uses a formula Vonnegut had exploited from his start with the family magazines, the theme of homely simplicity triumphing over wealth and pretension. But the device is played out with several major differences. The wealth and fame are immensely greater than in "Custom-Made Bride" and any of the other earlier tales. As well they should be, for these trappings belong not to fictive creations but to actual people, the family of President John F. Kennedy living in Hyannis Port. It is the third distinguishing element of this story that shows the method Vonnegut began using at that time and which would bring him his greatest success: the story's events, as richly fabulous yet historically true as they are, get measured from the narrator's highly personal point of view. In "The Hyannis Port Story," President Kennedy is much like the actual sitting president, and the narrator is much like Kurt Vonnegut. In bringing the two together a refreshing perspective is gained, one that the author would exploit for the rest of his career, propelling himself to great fame with *Slaughterhouse-Five* and sustaining his role of public spokesmanship ever after.

In terms of short-story salesmanship this Kennedy piece was surely a last-gasp effort. Already having reduced its fiction, the *Post* would soon go the way of *Collier's,* Vonnegut's other big market, and cease publication. To fill this gap in his income the author turned to something new, writing highly personal essays on current topics for other popular magazines, among them *Esquire, McCall's,* and *Life.* In need of money, he took on book reviews, especially tough ones such as covering the new *Random House Dictionary,* personalizing the experience as best he could. This personalization drew the notice of publisher Seymour Lawrence, who figured that anyone who could write so engagingly about a dictionary would surely be interesting as a novelist. In the meantime Vonnegut had taken an instructorship in creative writing at the University of Iowa, earning less than eight thousand dollars per year. A twenty-five-thousand-dollar advance from Lawrence let him quit and work full time on *Slaughterhouse-Five,* a novel whose structure shows the effects of all this personal essay writing. Yet before the novel and before the first essay stands "The Hyannis Port Story," evidence that Vonnegut was developing in this direction well in advance of economic need. If as a *Saturday Evening Post* story it marked the end of one road, its narrative method signposted a grand new avenue toward the ultimate Vonnegut effect.

The current events of this piece are as solid and as necessary as those in any essay. Its readership in 1963 would not just remember Dwight D. Eisenhower's recent presidency but would also know that this two-time winner had never been accepted by the Republican Right, which made a conservative hero of Sen. Robert Taft from Ohio. They would also know more about Walter Reuther than that he was president of the United Auto Workers, for at the time this man was even more important for his involvement with Kennedy politics. Because the Kennedys had such starlike popularity even *Post* readers could be trusted to know such particulars as the fate of Adlai Stevenson, beaten out for the nomination and given an awkward ambassadorship to the United Nations instead. All of this information would be crucial for an essay, but for his special purposes Vonnegut uses them as key elements in his fiction. Why fiction? Because he has noted that by 1963 the Kennedy fame has become as fabulative as any piece of creative writing, with both legendary narratives and literary references—the PT-109 war story, for example, and the constant comparisons of the Kennedy style to life in King Arthur's Camelot. Why not mix in some fiction of his own, particularly from the plain and simple world outside? This was the world, after all, that was real. The Kennedy hysteria was something else indeed.

"The farthest away from home I ever sold a storm window was in Hyannis Port, Massachusetts, practically in the front yard of President Kennedy's summer home" (*WMH,* 133)—these opening words make reference to the famous scene but measure things from a much more humble source, the narrator's own. Everything in the narrative will be valued from this point of view, which spans the simple and the fabulous. In the process *Post* readers are brought into the equation, for the storyteller's perspective is much closer to their own than to that of the Kennedys. The posture is really Vonnegut's own. The North Crawford, New Hampshire, from which the narrator travels is as homely a place as West Barnstable, Massachusetts, seven miles away from Hyannis Port but light years in distance from the Kennedy glamor. On his humbler part of Cape Cod, Kurt Vonnegut has run his short-story business in the same style as this narrator's trade in storm windows and bathtub enclosures, so it is appropriate that the Kennedy business takes less prominence in his life than simply getting the job done. Having a business matter confused with politics has prompted a Kennedy neighbor, Commodore Rumfoord, to order a full set of storms and screens, rewarding the narrator for right-wing sentiments the man does not have—he has already wisely advised his magazine readers that he has yet to decide between Kennedy and Goldwater for the next year's election. But a sale's a sale, and taking it gets him caught up in the Hyannis Port turmoil.

Dealing with this turmoil constitutes the story's action. For all the Kennedy notoriety, this simple tradesman is the person who faces most of it, but in his reaction is a clue for understanding the president. It is summer 1963, and the Cape is awash with gawkers drawn by the Kennedy fame. In a traffic jam, the narrator finds himself stalled next to Ambassador Stevenson. The two get out and walk around a bit. "I took the opportunity to ask him how the United Nations was getting along. He told me they were getting along about as well as could be expected. That wasn't anything I didn't already know" (*WMH*, 136), readers learn. If this sounds like a good-natured but banal exchange between neighbors, so be it; in the ultimate democracy of a traffic jam the Ambassador's limousine is getting no farther than the narrator's van. For the second time now the standard is affirmed: a job is a job.

When UN ambassador and storm-window salesman meet, it is on the level of the latter. In a similar way Vonnegut's narrator brings the whole Kennedy hullabaloo to his own level, where he can deal with it as an honest workman. He will have to do this to survive the installation, given the determination of these rich folks to drag him into their own stories. But the pattern is clear just from his drive into town. Unsnared from traffic, he finds himself on the commercial strip where everything has become thematic, from the Presidential Motor Inn and the First Family Waffle Shop to the PT-109 Cocktail Lounge and a miniature golf course called the New Frontier. Needing lunch, he stops for a waffle, but he is faced with an equally corny menu with entrees named after Kennedys and their entourage. "A waffle with strawberries and cream was a *Jackie*," he reports, and "a waffle with a scoop of ice cream was a *Caroline*" (*WMH*, 136). And so forth? No, it is even worse, for "they even had a waffle named Arthur Schlesinger, Jr." But here is how he not only makes the best of it but also brings the whole affair into a more reasonable orbit: "I had a thing called a *Teddy*," which mercifully is left undescribed, "and a cup of *Joe*" (137).

The *Post* readership of 1963 could be expected to know how appropriate these menu names were and even that the Harvard historian was a top administration adviser. Such identifications were signs of Kennedy notoriety—everyone at the time knew them, and as a writer Vonnegut was able to manipulate them in narrative play. In a few years literary critics would begin using such terminology, finding that such cultural signs worked together like syntactic forms in a generative grammar—*semiotics* will become fashionable in America about the same time as Kurt Vonnegut's fiction. And popular readers certainly knew what a sign was—perhaps not in deconstructive terms but definitely in the way this story uses the device. For as he approaches his customer's property the narrator notices something to the Rumfoord house besides its towers and parapets. "On a second-floor balcony was a huge portrait of Barry Goldwater" (*WMH*, 137), the conservative Republican likely to face Kennedy in the 1964 election. "It had bicycle reflectors in the pupils of its eyes." Is this not odd for a property right next door to the president's home? Such is the point: "Those eyes stared right through the Kennedy gate. There were floodlights all around, so I could tell it was lit up at night. And the floodlights were rigged with blinkers."

This remarkable line is followed by one in which the narrator pauses to draw a breath. "A man who sells storm windows can never really be sure about what class he belongs to," he tells his readers and reminds himself, "especially if he installs the windows too" (*WMH*, 137). Given the crazy semiology at hand, he judges it best to keep out of the way, getting the job done quickly so that he can return to the calmer world of North Crawford. But his customer, Commodore Rumfoord, insists on chatting with him through the job, in the process drawing the poor man into the rarified world of presidential politics. In the process there is much fun with the contrasts between the old money style of Rumfoord's Republicanism and the Kennedy ambience—one wonders which is worse, their liberal politics or nouveau status in this yacht club community. But a serious theme emerges. Mocked by a guide on a sight-seeing boat as an unproductive member of the idle rich, the commodore begins doubting himself;

after all, with the tradesman quietly observing, he has seen his beloved son fall in love with a Kennedy cousin and plan for marriage into the clan.

Has the old man's life amounted to nothing? Here is where the story begins resembling a classic Vonnegut *Post* composition, as the narrator's quiet example of steady work provides an antidotal example for Rumfoord. He can redeem himself, his wife points out, by simply doing something *useful* (his commodore's title dates from having captained the Hyannis Port yacht club for one year a generation earlier). The entire atmosphere becomes nicer as the house quiets down and everyone can enjoy the peace that lies beyond blustering politics and the pretensions of old money.

But Vonnegut cannot let his story end just yet. This is, after all, his new style of work, in which historical reality becomes integrated with the structure of fiction—and the narrative's most famous figure, President John Fitzgerald Kennedy, has yet to appear. One guesses that he would like to keep out of it, given his neighbor's adversarial politics and flamboyant habits of self-expression. But in the quiet of the story's nightfall a familiar voice comes across the lawn: that of the president asking the commodore why his Goldwater sign is dark—the son-in-law of Soviet premier Nikita Khrushchev is visiting and would like to see it. Khrushchev? Half a day earlier this name would have sent Commodore Rumfoord into fits, but in his new mood he just complies respectfully. "He turned it on," the narrator reports, and "the whole neighborhood was bathed in flashing lights." Especially in the visitor's presence, and right in the president's face, is this not the greatest insult of all? These have been the reader's worries all along, but now the homely truth is revealed. Would the commodore please leave the sign on? the president requests. "That way I can find my way home" (*WMH,* 145). Far from taking it as a sign of political animosity, President Kennedy has been using the display for what it is literally: a sign marking the way to where he lives. What could be more neighborly?

Turning the great and the famous into the comfortably familiar and ordinary would be Kurt Vonnegut's method for the personal essays he would begin writing about this time. With a method much like that of "The Hyannis Port Story," the narratives of these pieces—and they were heavily anecdotal—would approach some currently challenging event and, by measuring it against the author's experience, reduce it to manageable size. A mass murderer on Cape Cod, the Maharishi Mahesh Yogi, genocidal warfare in Biafra, the extravagances of America's space program—these and other topics generated a steady stream of essays that replaced Vonnegut's lost short-story income. More importantly, they deepened an autobiographical strain that began appearing in his fiction at this same time, typified by the prefaces he wrote for the 1966 hardcover edition of *Mother Night* and the 1968 collection of his short stories, *Welcome to the Monkey House,* that implicated his own life in his otherwise creative writing. At this point the Vonnegut effect seems to be as much "Vonnegut" as "effect," especially when integrated into such a major work as *Slaughterhouse-Five.* For the previously unwriteble material of the author's World War II experience at Dresden this new manner proves critically helpful; if there is indeed nothing to say about a massacre, the author would have to talk about something else—namely himself. This is precisely what he does in a book review sufficiently anecdotal to merit inclusion in his short-story collection. What does one say about a dictionary? Lexicology defies popular comment, even when there is a conflict to its story, as Vonnegut finds in the debate between prescriptive and descriptive linguistics. And so he characterizes the argument as it seems to him: "Prescriptive, as nearly as I could tell, was like an honest cop, and descriptive was like a boozed-up war buddy from Mobile, Ala." (*WMH,* 108). This is the style that would not just get the hungry writer more assignments but would also draw publisher Seymour Lawrence to his work.

There is more to this method than the inclusion of self as a point of reference. The nature of Vonnegut's personality also generates a unique structure, one that would be instrumental in getting the difficult matter of Dresden expressed. Here too the essays are a helpful guide for seeing the methodology take shape. "Science Fiction" is an essay written for the *New York Times Book Review* of 5 September 1965 and collected as the lead piece in *Wampeters, Foma & Granfalloons.* Its message is a serious one: that Vonnegut has never liked being called a science-fiction writer because such categorization relegates his work to triviality. For this, science-fiction buffs are partly to blame, given their insistence that everything they like be qualified as sci-fi. More important than this complaint, however, is the way Vonnegut structures it, taking off from readers who find futuristic tendencies in *1984, Invisible Man,* and even *Madame Bovary:* "They are particularly hot for Kafka. Boomers of science fiction might reply, 'Ha! Orwell and Ellison and Flaubert and Kafka are science-fiction writers, too!' They often say things like that. Some are crazy enough to try to capture Tolstoy. It is as though I were to claim that everybody of note belonged fundamentally to Delta Upsilon, my own lodge, incidentally, whether he knew it or not. Kafka would have been a desperately unhappy D.U." (*WFG,* 4). Franz Kafka in a fraternity rush at Cornell University?

The image is preposterous—and funny because of that. But most effective is the way Vonnegut gets such diverse terms together, using the rhetorical fallacy of the excluded middle to suggest that if science fiction is to Franz Kafka as Franz Kafka is to Delta Upsilon fraternity life, then Herr Kafka is suffering as a D.U. brother. Yes, he surely would have. But allowing such an image to discredit the claims of science-fiction buffs involves a deliberate misuse of rhetoric, thus getting Vonnegut's narrative to a point it might not otherwise be able to reach.

This and almost every other essay Kurt Vonnegut would publish in the late 1960s uses his own personality to force a comic issue that seals his otherwise conventionally expressed argument. These instances usually are positioned like a punch line in a joke: after a serious question has been posed, and after the listener has made some serious mental effort to answer it, at which point the joker springs the trap, providing the relief of laughter that comes with the happy dismissal from hard, serious thought. In the science-fiction essay the author has made his point by the time Franz Kafka comes along; the D.U. story is just some icing on the cake, letting readers leave with a happily complicit attitude—they have gotten the joke. Vonnegut's essay on the Maharishi, who was all the rage at the time as a guru to the stars who preached a self-improvement doctrine so easy that anyone could master it in a few quick lessons, forecasts its joke in the title: "Yes, We Have No Nirvanas," a play on the old novelty song "Yes, We Have No Bananas" that joked with linguistic patterns of reason (and of nonreason!). The writer starts off by making fun of himself, mocking his own irritation that his wife and daughter have invested seventy dollars of his money in the Maharishi's program. But the punch line comes when Vonnegut, supposedly a religious skeptic, leaves the flimflam of a transcendental meditation session in search of something quite surprising: "I went outside the hotel after that, liking Jesus better than I had ever before liked Him. I wanted to see a crucifix, so I could say to it, 'You know why You're up there? It's Your own fault. You should have practiced Transcendental Meditation, which is easy as pie. You would also have been a better carpenter'" (*WFG*, 39–40). Appraising the U.S. space program, Vonnegut plays the same trick he does for explaining astrophysics in *The Sirens of Titan*, quoting a children's book on the subject but using the device to make fun of himself: "'We are flying through space. Our craft is the earth, which orbits the sun at a speed of 67,000 miles an hour. As it orbits the sun, it spins on its axis. The sun is a star.' If I were drunk, I might cry about that" (78). The message is that to ignore human needs on earth

while wasting billions on space is even more irresponsible than alco-
holism. "Earth is a pretty blue and pink and white pearl in the pictures
NASA sent me," he writes, adding that on his way down to Cape Cana-
veral he flew over Appalachia. "Life is said to be horrible down there in
many places, but it looked like the Garden of Eden to me," he confesses.
"I was a rich guy, way up in the sky, munching dry-roasted peanuts and
sipping gin" (84).

The space program as a drinker's buzz, the Maharishi teaching transcendental meditation to Christ crucified, Franz Kafka as a terribly unhappy D.U.—these are jokes against logic, using logic's own terms, that
help Kurt Vonnegut find ways to articulate the otherwise unspeakable
aspects of a massacre. Attempting to write a book about Dresden coincides
with the great critical debate over whether a novel could be "about" anything. The 1960s had begun with novelists such as Philip Roth and Stanley Elkin worrying that the personal extravagances and public idiocies of
current life were eclipsing even satirists' abilities to make fun of the American scene—the scene was simply doing too good a job of it itself. At the
same time theorists debated the referentiality of fictive language, or of any
language at all; deconstructionists argued that any linguistic system operated not on identities but on differences.

The currency of these debates registers within *Slaughterhouse-Five* when
during his trip to New York City, Vonnegut's protagonist, Billy Pilgrim,
gets himself involved with a radio show's panel discussion of the presumed
death of the novel. For all of his trouble at making a living with the genre
Kurt Vonnegut might well have agreed; but when Billy ignores the critical
dialogue taking place and just launches into his explanation of life on
Tralfamadore, he is giving hints at how, in the author's hands, the form has
been reinvented. Tralfamadore—the distant world several galaxies away
from which the flying-saucer pilot Salo had come in *The Sirens of Titan*
to determine (through no fault or effort of his own) several thousand years
of world history—is for Billy a parallel universe, where the problematic
aspects of his earthly existence are all nicely resolved. When considered as
a creation of science-fiction writer Kilgore Trout, a significant character in
this novel as well as in *God Bless You, Mr. Rosewater* (and in other Vonnegut narratives afterward), Tralfamadore becomes just as much a resolution of human problems as Trout's social philosophies are in the previous
work. And so it stands to reason that in the Tralfamadorians' world, which
resolves so much trouble, there would be a solution to the death of the
novel.

What are the problems with fiction in Billy Pilgrim's earthly world? Probably the same ones that have frustrated Kurt Vonnegut in his attempt to write the book he has wanted to write since coming home from the war. It is the limitation of temporal and spatial causality that makes it so hard to wrestle the matter of Dresden into the conventional format of a novel, one observing the traditional unities of time, space, and action and the consequences that result when insisting a story have a beginning, a middle, and an end. On Tralfamadore novels have none of these. In fact they do not look like novels at all, as Billy observes to the disembodied voice that is his mentor on the distant planet:

> Billy couldn't read Tralfamadorian, of course, but he could at least see how the books were laid out—in brief clumps of symbols separated by stars. Billy commented that the clumps might be telegrams. "Exactly," said the voice.
>
> "They *are* telegrams?"
>
> "There are no telegrams on Tralfamadore. But you're right: each clump of symbols is a brief, urgent message—describing a situation, a scene. We Tralfamadorians read them all at once, not one after the other. There isn't any particular relationship between all the messages, except that the author has chosen them carefully, so that, when seen all at one time, they produce an image of life that is beautiful and surprising and deep. There is no beginning, no middle, no end, no suspense, no moral, no causes, no effects. What we love in our books are the depths of many marvelous moments seen all at one time." (*SF*, 76)

It is not surprising that Tralfamadorian fiction answers objections from deconstructionists and death-of-the-novel critics alike. There is nothing here of conventional fiction's attempt at a totalizing effect, a fraudulent impression that life is orderly and that unities of character and idea will, by virtue of systematic study, accrete themselves into some conclusive meaning. It is the false rhetoric of such practices, critics argue, that lets the truly important products of fiction—those "marvelous moments" seen in all their depths—slip away, never to be articulated. It is the reason why, in other words, there is nothing intelligent to say about a massacre, just when a witness of such an event is struggling to say everything: to say everything *all at once* because imposing conditions of time and space steal meaning from the event.

In earthly terms, of course, there are reasons why the depths of many moments cannot be seen all at one time. Even single words must be read, and sentences must be read in sequence for them to make sense. Linearity forces its demands on the reader in just one line of print; expand this demand to the length of a page, let alone that of a chapter or several chapters, and the material confines of a printed novel are obvious. But what if an author could devise a way of writing that did not depend on the reader's steady accumulation of data in any progressive sense, a way that instead let items be noted and then held in abeyance from any need for meaning, until one came to the book's end—and at that point everything suddenly became meaningful all at once? This is the strategy Vonnegut uses for *Slaughterhouse-Five*. Similar to what he is accomplishing at this time in his personal essays, the method involves interposing himself between the troublesome nature of his material and the reader's need to have that material explained. There is, of course, no logical reason for such involvement. That is why the images of Kurt Vonnegut's relation to the Maharishi (seventy dollars of his hard-earned money that his wife and daughter have blown on transcendental meditation sessions) and to the space program (with references to his own inebriation) are so funny. They simply do not belong with the otherwise serious subject matter. But by putting himself in, the author at once upsets the logical structure that keeps things so serious (and so unsolvable) and introduces a comic element that yields the relief of a solution. Vonnegut, and his way of making matters humorous, thus opens a crack in the confinements of convention that have withheld the liberating knowledge he and his readers can now celebrate.

"All this happened, more or less"—so begins this novel that really does not look like one. Fiction traditionally asks its readers to suspend their disbelief, but here they are not required to make such a willing act. There is no reason to, as the story to come is factual with no need to pretend that it is real because it actually is. That is the first rule to be broken. The second is that the author identifies himself with the "I" doing the narration—just as the events of this World War II story truly happened, the person talking about them is the real Kurt Vonnegut. A lifetime of instruction that the narrator of a novel is not the author thus flies out the window. But there is more. Just as in his Maharishi and U.S. space program essays, Vonnegut does something else unconventional: he talks about his writing even as he does it. Thus all the objections that might be raised about the novel in the discussion session Billy Pilgrim attends are answered even as *Slaughterhouse-Five* begins. In an age when fiction cannot be "about" something, this novel is not "about" anything other than itself, an object existing quite firmly in the reader's hands.

There are also some practical reasons why Vonnegut begins in this manner. His is by no means the first war story to come out of the events of 1941–45. Indeed by 1969, when *Slaughterhouse-Five* appeared, there had been many thousands in print and on film, with narratives from subsequent wars in Korea and Vietnam making their own contributions to the literature of present-day warfare. As part of his storyteller's autobiography that forms chapter 1, he lets himself be reminded of this fact when visiting the home of his war buddy Bernard O'Hare. O'Hare's wife, Mary, interrupts the old friends' visit to object to all these texts, complaining how the conventions of fiction virtually demand that the soldiers in such narratives be commanding, heroic, adult figures—roles suitable to be played by John Wayne, Frank Sinatra, and the like. In truth, World War II was fought by young persons such as her husband and Kurt, who from her point of view were little more than children at the time. But children make poor actors in war movies and weak images in war novels. Hence workable models for such action become older. Soon the models replace reality, and war gets portrayed as something adults can handle in an adult way—which inspires children to go off and fight in even more wars.

In chapter 1 of *Slaughterhouse-Five*, Mary O'Hare makes Kurt Vonnegut promise that he will not write his novel this way. Another meeting, with its own lesson about the structures of war and peace, also influences the way this novel will be written. The author and his war buddy make a trip to Dresden to see how things look more than two decades after the bombing. A taxi driver named Gerhard Müller shows them the rebuilt city, and they learn his story, from being a prisoner of war (of the Americans) himself to putting together a happy life in Dresden afterward. Amid all the details of this past quarter century comes one more: that his mother was incinerated in the Dresden firestorm. "So it goes," the author notes, the first of one hundred times that he says this in the novel, spoken each time someone or something dies. Afterward, Müller commemorates their meeting with a Christmas card that Vonnegut quotes in full: "I wish you and your family also as to your friend Merry Christmas and a Happy New Year and I hope that we'll meet again in a world of peace and freedom in the taxi cab if the accident will" (*SF,* 2). The grammar is comically if understandably fractured, which Vonnegut appreciates for the way it runs everything together in serial manner, the only qualifier being an open-ended aside, "if the accident will." Müller's syntax is just what the author of this novel needs, for it throws what others try to discern as history's grand plan into undiscriminating chaos so random that the only principle of order is the fact of no order at all.

The text of this postcard is one of several in chapter 1 that argue against conclusive narrative structure. A limerick turns back on itself, mocking any hopes the author has of benefiting from long experience; a song progresses to a last line that is a repeat of its first, generating repetition after repetition with no advancement. Professionals in the entertainment business warn Vonnegut that writing an antiwar book is about as effective as authoring an antiglacier book or as resisting death itself. Yet resisting death is what every living organism does every day right up to the end. And so like life, *Slaughterhouse-Five* goes on, detailing how hard it has been to write *Slaughterhouse-Five*.

The quarter century it took to produce this book had given Vonnegut plenty of stories to tell in this first chapter. There is his experience as a graduate student at the University of Chicago, where any reports about the Dresden atrocity pale in comparison to news of the Holocaust. At the same time in these immediately postwar years the author also works as a pool reporter for Chicago's City News Bureau, where he is confronted with more death and more dispassionate ways of handling it. Readers hear about his attempts to gather facts about the raid and the frustration that it is still considered secret, and they hear also about how detours in his writing career have taken him to the University of Iowa, where as a teacher in the Writers' Workshop he is no better able to get his war book written. Then publisher Seymour Lawrence comes through with a generous contract, Vonnegut takes off for Dresden with Bernie O'Hare, and the novel gets written—but it is such a short and jumbled and jangled affair that the author is apologetic when he turns it in for publication. Why? Because there is nothing intelligent to say about a massacre, at least nothing that adds up in a coherent, conclusive sense of order. That has been the coherent, conclusive message Vonnegut has broken all the rules of novel writing to clarify in this first, atypical chapter.

Yet looking back on it, chapter 1 of *Slaughterhouse-Five* is as jumbled and as jangled as anything that follows in the book, though readers must have their attention called to all the structural deviations to see it because for two dozen pages they have been carried along quite comfortably. Carried by an orderly chronology? Not at all. From a starting point in 1967, when Vonnegut and O'Hare meet Müller, the action jumps back to 1964, when Vonnegut tracks down his old friend via long distance telephone. Their conversation takes the narrative back to 1945 and from there to the author's various postwar experiences. Readers eventually learn about the publishing contract and the fact that the novel has been written, but only to jump back two years to the 1967 Dresden trip—and not even to Dresden but rather to the night before in a fog-bound Boston airport, where the author puts his sleeplessness to use by reading two more texts, a collection of poetry by Theodore Roethke and a critical study of the French novelist Louis-Ferdinand Céline. If time travel becomes a theme later in the novel and if spatial jumps serve as Vonnegut's way of propelling his narrative across such vast distances, the method for each has been demonstrated right off in chapter 1, a chapter that any reader can follow with ease. Why so? Because the organizing principle has not been spatial unity or temporal progression but rather the inviting presence of Kurt Vonnegut.

Any human being is more interesting than physical models. The story Vonnegut tells in his "Address to the American Physical Society," collected in *Wampeters, Foma & Granfalloons,* is about how concerns of humanism overpower all the interests of a zoo, even for the author's pet dog. In this first chapter of *Slaughterhouse-Five,* Kurt Vonnegut has managed to make *himself* more interesting to readers than any compensatory satisfactions with unities of time and space would be, particularly because his own problems with these unities have made his life this past quarter century such an intriguing adventure. Having tried without success to map out a chronological story line, he turns to a different line, that of the long distance telephone, to prompt some action—and from there it weaves in and out, backward and forward, until the novel he wants to write gets written. Along the way readers learn many things about the author that will help shape their understanding of his narrative to come. He is a veteran of the war, a POW at Dresden who saw the city destroyed in a firestorm. But that alone cannot generate a novel. For *Slaughterhouse-Five* to be written, much more must take place in this man's life, from studying anthropology and reporting small tragedies in Chicago to working for GE in the 1940s, living on Cape Cod in the 1950s, and teaching in Iowa for two academic years a decade later. All that will figure in the novel Vonnegut writes, as will the texts he and the reader peruse in this same first chapter: Gerhard Müller's Christmas card, the limerick about the young man from Stamboul, Yon Yonson's song from Wisconsin, Mary O'Hare's synopses of war movies, Charles Mackay's account of the Crusades, a history of Dresden, Ted Roethke's poem, and Erika Ostrovsky's book on Céline.

Thus in the first chapter of *Slaughterhouse-Five,* Kurt Vonnegut manipulates the structure that will let his protagonist, Billy Pilgrim, understand what life means. Trying to write his novel the conventional way has brought the author nowhere, just as Billy's attempts to bring the world into focus fail. To be successful each must find a different way of transcending the limits of conventional time and space in order to comprehend what these factors hide. Just sitting at his writer's desk on Cape Cod using the techniques that the tradition of the novel make available to him is not productive for Vonnegut, just as trying to do his duty in the army (as a hapless chaplain's assistant) and follow a worthwhile profession back home (as an optometrist married to the boss's daughter) has not given poor Billy much of a clue to existence. Granted, Billy's salvation will be a deus ex machina of sorts, a raisonneur's explanation of things delivered from outside the action and above the intelligence of those taking part in it. But Vonnegut has used such devices before—each of his previous novels has them in one form or another—and always with a double proof worked into the narrative. In *Slaughterhouse-Five* the correlation to Billy's time travel and adventures on Tralfamadore is Vonnegut's own experience in wishing to write about his Dresden experience, being frustrated in trying to do so the conventional way and finally breaking those conventions in order to get the job done. For this, chapter 1 is the model as the author transcends time and space with the long distance telephone calls to old friends, transatlantic travel to places from the past, and a library of reading that makes the temporal and spatial leaps of phones and jet seem child's play.

The author ends chapter 1 with another breaking of conventions, telling readers not just how the story begins but also how it ends. Why then should anyone spend time with the book's many pages knowing how things will turn out? The answer lies in the description of a Tralfamadorian novel Billy's mentor provides: not for any sense of progressive, accumulating knowledge (less at the beginning, more in the middle, and complete at the end) but rather for the depth of many beautiful moments seen all at the same time. Throughout the novel Vonnegut will arrange his narrative to provide this sensation; Billy's time travel lets the author juxtapose elements from different times and places in a way that creates the sense of a third time, the reader's, existing independently from the march of events and the confinements of space. Doing so solves Vonnegut's problems as a writer and Billy's as a human being. In structuring his novel the author emphasizes how he and his character are not the same person.

Three times within the novel as Billy goes about his own business Vonnegut distinguishes himself as a different person in the scene: climbing aboard the POW train, relieving himself in the British prisoners' latrine, and remarking on Dresden's architectural beauty as the prison train rolls in. Note how Billy and Kurt are thus different persons but occupying the same time and place. The two are also sympathetic to each other's aims. Billy's response to Dresden is not to write a novel, but he does type letters to the newspaper and speak his piece on talk radio. His subject is Tralfamadore and its different way of viewing reality, a disposition quite similar to the invention of novelistic form; and of course the Tralfamadorian novel Billy Pilgrim is shown appears to be a structural equivalent to the book Kurt Vonnegut is writing and which his readers now read.

Above all, Vonnegut and his protagonist find themselves conventionally speechless in the face of ultimate but unanswerable questions, unanswerable at least within the limits working to confine them. Here is where the frequently cited novels of Kilgore Trout join the two quests together. One of Trout's works, *Maniacs in the Fourth Dimension,* takes the familiar sci-fi theme of an added level of existence to pose a medical possibility: perhaps supposedly incurable diseases are cases of being sick in a fourth dimension where treatments must wait until physicians from our own 3-D world can cross the barrier and do their work to make the patients better. As a sci-fi device this fourth-dimensionality might bring to mind Vonnegut's similar use of time travel. But in fact it pertains even more closely to an experience Billy has had: getting drunk at a party and being unable to find the steering wheel in his car when he tries to drive home. Vonnegut takes pleasure in letting Billy run through every style of test, from randomly windmilling his arms to starting on the left side and working carefully, inch by inch, all the way over to the right. When no steering wheel is discovered anywhere, the poor drunk assumes that someone has stolen it. Is this true? No, the steering wheel exists but in a different dimension; Billy is sitting in the backseat of his car.

A more important question both Kurt and Billy struggle to answer involves death. Billy faces it when visiting his mother in a nursing home. The woman suffers from pneumonia and can speak only with difficulty, but she struggles with a question. Billy is just as eager to answer it until after several promptings she finally gets it out, leaving her son with nothing to say. Her question is, "How did I get so *old*?" (*SF,* 38). How does someone answer a question like this? It poses the same difficulty that Vonnegut, as author of the novel, must face when trying to write about

Dresden: what do you say about a massacre? Billy's example dramatizes this problem, letting readers share the frustration. But being unable to answer it does not discredit the query or lessen the need to respond. That there is no possible answer produces the empty feeling Vonnegut confronts with Dresden, a narrative strategy that manages to articulate an absence without attempting to fill it, as conventional fiction might. Silence is thus empowered with a voice beyond the talents of physical articulation.

In this way author, character, and reader share the same experience. None of it is exotic. Kurt Vonnegut is as simple and straightforward a person as can be: chapter 1 makes his efforts to write a novel as familiar as the task of anyone trying to get a job done. Billy Pilgrim, as almost every critic studying the novel says, is a virtual Everyman; with nothing heroic about him, his fate is simply to have survived World War II and the Dresden firebombing—and to wonder why. As far as what's required of the reader, no more is demanded than the humanism Kurt Vonnegut has found in his pet dog: a simple interest in people and their doings. Readers of this novel do not need the knowledge of science that Thomas Pynchon demands in *Gravity's Rainbow*, the facility with interweaving plots from world mythology that John Barth expects in *Giles Goat-Boy*, or the mastery of stylistics that William H. Gass requires for an appreciation of any of his works. Kurt Vonnegut is not one of critic Tom LeClair's self-confidant practitioners of fictive mastery, a writer of the novel of excess that intentionally smothers the reader in intellectual overkill. Far from it—*Slaughterhouse-Five* reads at times with the simplicity of a primer for early grades' reading. Everything, from the way Billy searches for the steering wheel in the backseat of his car to how American prisoners of war react to their captivity, is explained in simple, follow-the-instructions form. As well these events should be because their author considers them ungraspable in any conventional way and falsified by the earlier attempts of conventional fiction to do the job. Avoiding deep thought and fancy style in favor of speaking plainly is for Vonnegut at least a way to begin.

This simplicity is not a dumbing down or in any sense a pandering to vulgar tastes. Instead there is a common dignity to what author, character, and reader do. Vonnegut portrays himself not as a precious or precocious writer but rather as a familiar, middle-class American with habits no more extreme than any other married men his age (and likely to get in the same type of trouble with his wife when he makes such typical mistakes as staying up too late and drinking too much). In similar manner Billy Pilgrim is a simple, familiar type: no war hero (lest Mary O'Hare object), just as Vonnegut is seen as no great towering success as a writer (something reputationally true at the moment though soon to be remedied by high sales and critical acclaim for the first time in his twenty years in the business). Of equal importance, the novel's readers are not expected to share the mastery needed to fully appreciate something by Pynchon, Barth, or Gass. But neither is their intelligence insulted. Any space opera present comes in the guise of fiction by Kilgore Trout, whom Vonnegut does not have to characterize as a pathetic failure—Trout does so himself. These sci-fi plots can be taken for what they are, oddball but usually insightful musings that are trapped in the humiliating form of science-fiction pulp. No reader is expected to believe in any of Trout's preposterous fictive situations, but everyone sees them played out—not as the novel itself but as part of its larger ongoing action, ways that the readers can be informed of things as if flipping through a magazine or skimming items on a newsstand. Meanwhile, as Vonnegut and Pilgrim do their sincere best to perform their tasks as novelist and soldier respectively, the reader is asked to do no more than can be reasonably expected: to watch the author struggling with the material of Dresden and witness Billy reduced to muteness at his dying mother's bedside, appreciating how no one is immune to such trauma, given how death, whether on a grand scale or so closely personal, is an inevitable fact of life.

As for Billy Pilgrim's situation, it is much more than having witnessed the destruction of Dresden and survived the event. At the beginning of chapter 2 when he is introduced, we learn that he has become "unstuck in time," living in a "constant state of stage fright" because "he never knows what part of his life he is going to have to act in next" (*SF*, 20). Readers of *Cat's Cradle* will recognize Billy's condition as an inversion of the happy state provided by Bokononism, in which the people of San Lorenzo, otherwise so deprived, were given easily performed roles to play in a drama whose purposes they understood. He would seem a perfect candidate for the teachings of the Caribbean holy man, but by this point there are alternatives: not just the Tralfamadorian ethic from *The Sirens of Titan* but Eliot Rosewater and his favorite writer, Kilgore Trout, still in residence from Vonnegut's previous novel. For Eliot, traumatized by World War II, science fiction makes better sense of the world than do either the higher arts or science, and Trout is the perfect source for articulating his problems—and Billy's, too, once the two men meet. To this system of beliefs Billy becomes a convert and acts energetically to proselytize the world. Time, he teaches (in letters to newspaper editors and ramblings to his concerned family), is a spatial, not temporal entity; it exists not from one moment to the next but in a solid continuum, like the full stretch of the Rocky Mountains visible from on high, with the observer able to look at this or that peak at will. Bad moments that cause people so much trouble are just like one particular segment of the mountain range. "When a Tralfamadorian sees a corpse," Billy explains, "all he thinks is that the dead person is in a bad condition in that particular moment, but that the same person is just fine in plenty of other moments" (23). Therefore he can say something about death while other people remain speechless: "I simply shrug and say what the Tralfamadorians say about dead people, which is 'So it goes.'"

The ethic Billy adopts, of course, is one of simple perspective. Ignore the bad moments and concentrate on the good ones—by itself so banal but when voiced as Tralfamadorian physics having the dignity of the anthropological relativism Vonnegut employs in most of his work. As a cultural description these words beg to be taken seriously, just as in their science-fiction trappings they provide entertainment. In Billy's hands these sentiments become a metaphorical extension of his optometrist's work, letting him do "nothing less, now, he thought, than prescribing corrective lenses for Earthling souls. Many of those souls were lost and wretched, Billy believed, because they could not see as well as his little green friends on Tralfamadore" (*SF,* 25). Time, readers may come to believe, is not a physical absolute but just a cultural description. Regarding it as an absolute can be just as self-destructive as regarding religion that way, a point Kilgore Trout makes in one of his many novels quoted as the narrative proceeds. Trout's *The Gospel from Outer Space,* for example, suggests that in Christian liturgy the Crucifixion story is not properly an absolute axiom of belief but rather is something that can be improved on—the notion that gets Kurt Vonnegut in much trouble with religious fundamentalists who have lobbied that *Slaughterhouse-Five* be banned from libraries and school curricula. For Trout the story of Christ's death as presently told is ineffective because all it teaches is that great trouble will result if the person crucified has big-time connections. Far better, the writer suggests, to reshape the tale so that the crucifiers are condemned for having killed a perfectly average guy. If this were the case, Christianity would be more humanely beneficial.

As teachers, however, Billy and Trout are considered laughable (as is Vonnegut at times) and are scorned (as happens with Vonnegut among the fundamentalists). But this is the way they can make their corrections to impaired vision: not as authorities against whom a wary culture's guard will be up but rather as trickster figures who beguile their readers with entertainments that quietly subvert the standards of belief. Vonnegut had introduced this subliminal technique in *Mother Night,* in which absurdities rebound in multiples of three and names of otherwise exotic characters have a kitchen-cupboard familiarity to them, all of which help make an apparently disorganized novel seem to cohere. In *Slaughterhouse-Five* the trick is clinically subliminal as the linkages are thematically unimportant and technically random. There is no reason, for example, why during Billy's childhood visit to Mammoth Cave the otherwise total darkness is pierced by the glowing face of his father's radium watch dial and that then as a POW in Germany the same young man sees Russian prisoners with faces glowing exactly this way. Nor is there a reason why Billy's POW train is painted with the same orange and black stripes that decorate the caterer's tent at a wedding reception. Many other correspondences can be found throughout the novel. Unrelated to plot or theme or character development, and in most cases not even noted consciously by the reader, they nevertheless pull an otherwise diverse narrative together, making discrete events from many different times and places appear unified. When they work best they allow the reader to time travel, the commonality of the stripes or the radium faces letting attention span the many pages in between—a typically Tralfamadorian effect.

Throughout all this Billy remains almost deadeningly simple. With his Ronald Reagan bumper sticker, big suburban house, and lucrative optometry practice (based less on genuine caregiving than on factory orders for safety glasses and overpriced frames), the man is as solidly middle class as can be imagined. He is not a science-fiction nut or an extraterrestrial enthusiast—Rosewater, Trout, and the Tralfamadorians are just new sources of information for him, practicalities that seem to help with his problems relating to life and finding meaning in it. Billy is, after all, an essentially passive person, and so he has been able to absorb all these new ideas without experiencing a violent change. In this same way the novel in which he is the protagonist manages to be thoroughly postmodern while never putting popular readers off, as works by Ronald Sukenick, Steve Katz, or others of the radical experimentalists might do. Like his outer-space creatures who look like plain old plumbers' helpers, Vonnegut's innovative techniques are drawn from common enough sources so that the book he writes seems more a part of everyday life than a revolt against it.

Revolt against convention, especially in terms of commonly overworked themes, is left to Kilgore Trout, a character easily distanced from Billy's guy-next-door familiarity. As Billy's time travels bring readers to a new awareness by forcing juxtapositions of incidents that would otherwise remain safely insulated from each other by conventions of time and space, Trout's somewhat madcap fictive materials expand Vonnegut's narrative from within. Citations of his many books, undertaken in the manner of Jorge Luis Borges drawing on an imaginary library, make *Slaughterhouse-Five* read like something much greater than the sum of its parts. The great Argentine fictionist had fashioned a rich strategy of imagining all of the books he would like to have written and then quoting them as if they existed. This is precisely what Vonnegut does with Kilgore Trout, with the added benefit of putting in some stinkers he would never dream of writing yet that can be cited for the fun of it. Vonnegut's own sentences and paragraphs are disarmingly simple, but when he is quoting Trout an entire universe of references is provided for readers.

Trout's flesh-and-blood appearance in the novel—after all the flashbacks and flashforwards in Billy's life over the five decades of action scrambled together in its time-travel plot—is itself a matter of fictive structure. It comes in chapter 8, which begins with another character from Vonnegut's earlier fiction: Howard W. Campbell, Jr., who visits Billy's POW camp to recruit American volunteers for the war against Russia. That night Dresden is firebombed and Billy (time traveling) dreams of Kilgore Trout. The next scenes, which in a conventional novel would happen in the immediate aftermath of the bombing, take place in 1964, when Billy talks with Trout in Ilium, New York. Thus the sci-fi writer appears within the context of what would be a conventional novel's climax: the bombing of Dresden. His behavior here accomplishes in structural terms what a realistic account of the bombing (not a part of *Slaughterhouse-Five*) would otherwise provide: a portrayal of conclusive theme. How does he behave? For the first time in his life he acts like a novelist, having learned something he had never before known or even imagined: that his work, written for next to nothing and published as pulp, has a reader.

At the anniversary party to which Billy invites him Trout is so giddy with success that he parodies what fictionists do. The guests are gullible, and so he pours it on, suggesting that all the things that happen in novels are omnisciently true, just as at this very minute "God is listening, too. And on Judgment Day he's going to tell you all the things you said and did" (*SF* 147), followed by severe punishments for bad actions. This, of course, is a preposterous view of fiction, but it in fact exaggerates the type of readings given so naively to traditional novels whose conventions are never questioned. Trout's listener is terrified by this news and becomes "petrified" (148), the way Vonnegut has described himself at the end of chapter 1, becoming (like Lot's wife) a pillar of salt for looking back at the destruction of Dresden. It also looks forward to Billy's posture on the next page when, after listening to a barbershop quartet singing at his party, he nearly collapses, having been turned as rigid as a ghost. What has happened is that in Trout's presence Billy has finally been put in touch with the heart of his Dresden experience, the truth of which has been eluding him for this whole novel that Kurt Vonnegut, for similar reasons, has been having a hard time writing. As the quartet pulls together for some close harmony about "that old gang of mine," Billy suddenly sees four of his guards at Dresden grouped tightly with their mouths similarly open— except in their case it is with the speechless horror of having witnessed the apocalyptic destruction of all they have ever known. It is Trout's presence that for the first time articulates this connection and confirms the meaning of connections between disparate points in time. As with his parody of fiction's truthful nature, Trout's description of looking through a time window to see the past comes across as hokey space opera, something only true gulls would believe in. Yet it is just the space opera and not the notion of time that Billy denies, for the same reason he can deny that he has seen a ghost. What *has* happened to him is that by virtue of this specific temporal relation he is able to tell a story, the same talent Vonnegut's efforts with the structure of *Slaughterhouse-Five* have enabled him to do. In this context Trout's own works are given new dignity. He is a fitting guest at the occasion, which now celebrates not just Billy's eighteen years of marriage but also his newfound ability to put together the truth of his life in 1964 and 1945, the two events combining to produce a meaningfulness that it is storytelling's task to accomplish.

Through it all Billy remains thoroughly normal. The device of time travel (which by this point appears nothing more exotic than an ability to adjust one's self to the multidimensionality of life) lets him live on Tralfamadore (with a kidnapped pornographic movie starlet, no less) while still fulfilling his duties as husband, father, civic figure, and optometrist on Earth. In becoming a storyteller of his own life Billy is no more removed from normality than is Kurt Vonnegut, who takes center stage once more in chapter 10 to conclude the novel. Here readers learn that *Slaughterhouse-Five* is being completed at a point in time they have shared: when newscasts announce the assassination of Sen. Robert Kennedy, one of those occurrences that people customarily can associate with where they were when they heard the news. His attempt has paralleled Billy's, and the words for it have come in a similar way. The Dresden book, like Billy's Dresden experience, is articulated by an intimately expressed characterization of silence, the testimony of four prison guards "who, in their astonishment and grief, resembled a barbershop quartet" (*SF,* 154). Like Vonnegut at the start of this book and like Billy Pilgrim through all of it to this point, they are speechless in the face of such enormity. But now the temporal and spatial juxtapositions of the human mind provide the words. Yes, they are sung decades later in a completely different context. But Billy's imagination helps the language of 1964 articulate the meaning of 1945. Imagination is what novels are made of, Vonnegut knows. But he also recognizes the more important fact that imagination is one of the talents that distinguish human beings from other living creatures.

There are good structures that the human imagination can devise and also structures that work less effectively. Mary O'Hare has warned Vonnegut against the ones that falsify, and in the course of his narrative he finds characters facing the war's events who do the same thing. On the one hand, Paul Lazzaro, for example, is an American POW who interprets everything that happens as a call for personal revenge, to the point that his being is consumed by it. On the other hand, British POWs have turned their camp into a fairyland that denies the war's reality—which is fine for them personally but a great cruelty for their neighboring Russian prisoners, whose starvation they ignore. Yet the imagination shows promise for making things better, even wars. At one point long after the events of Dresden, Billy watches a World War II movie on television, his technical abilities with time and space letting it run backward. It is a simple enough procedure, one that the most basic home movie projector of the era could provide; yet it is replete with such wondrous effects that Vonnegut devotes nearly a page to the happy result:

> American planes, full of holes and wounded men and corpses, took off backwards from an airfield in England. Over France, a few German fighter planes flew at them backwards, sucked bullets and shell fragments from some of the planes and crewmen. They did the same for

wrecked American bombers on the ground, and those planes flew up backwards to join the formation.

The formation flew backwards over a German city that was in flames. The bombers opened their bomb bay doors, exerted a miraculous magnetism which shrunk the fires, gathered them into cylindrical steel containers, and lifted the containers into the bellies of the planes. The Germans below had miraculous devices of their own, which were long steel tubes. They used them to suck more fragments from the crewmen and planes. But there were still a few wounded Americans, though, and some of the bombers were in bad repair. Over France, though, German fighters came up again, made everything and everybody as good as new.

When the bombers got back to their bases, the steel cylinders were taken from the racks and shipped back to the United States of America, where factories were operating night and day, dismantling the cylinders, separating the dangerous contents into minerals. Touchingly, it was mainly women who did this work. The minerals were then shipped to specialists in remote areas. It was their business to put them into the ground, to hide them cleverly, so they would never hurt anybody ever again. (*SF*, 63)

Impractical for real life? Certainly, but this is not Vonnegut's point. The idea of bombing raids going the other way, the usual way, is something that had to be devised at some point. The challenge is motivating the human imagination to work in a more beneficial manner. In *Slaughterhouse-Five* this is what the author's method does. As an effect it is as improvisatory as running a war movie backward, yet as practical as the act of the mechanical handyman who first tried reversing the processes of furnaces and air conditioners to produce the heat pump. There are always temptations to be meanly selfish (Paul Lazzaro) and blithely unaware (the British POWs), and there are also easier ways to write war novels (the examples Mary O'Hare abhors). *Slaughterhouse-Five* does not ignore these possibilities. Instead it engages them as models to demonstrate their ineffectiveness. Their failures contrast with Billy's success in life and Vonnegut's achievement in portraying it, a way of articulating the unspeakable by letting silence have its proper voice.

Chapter Four

SPEAKING FAMOUSLY

Happy Birthday, Wanda June; Breakfast of Champions;
Slapstick; Jailbird; and *Deadeye Dick*

SLAUGHTERHOUSE-FIVE is the last book Kurt Vonnegut wrote from
the comforts of anonymity. If in his short stories for the *Saturday Evening
Post* and novels for the paperback racks of America he spoke like the good
neighbor living next door, it is because he was. But in 1970 all that ended.
His first best-seller was being sold to the movies, where it would be directed
with great success by George Roy Hill. Money, the need for which had
driven the author to write book reviews on any subject available, even
about a dictionary if that were all an editor had to offer, was no longer a
problem. But there were other changes as well. Vonnegut marked them by
undertaking a brief shift of genres, writing the play *Happy Birthday,
Wanda June* (1971). Her name is familiar from both *Player Piano* and *The
Sirens of Titan,* in which a nondescript child character by that name is
quickly referred to in passing actions—appropriately so, for in the play she
appears just briefly, as a ghost. For a time the communal nature of theater
provided distraction and amusement, as did watching the filming of
Slaughterhouse-Five and the 1973 production of his *Between Time and
Timbuktu* (published in 1972) as a National Public Television show. Yet in
the preface to this last work, which was eventually dropped from his canon
because he felt uninvolved with the final product, Vonnegut makes a confession: "I have become an enthusiast for the printed word again" (*BTT,*
xv). Part of his motivation was economic. Film and television had proved
too expensive to tinker with, making him feel obliged to let mistakes stand
because they were too expensive to correct; plus the elaborate nature of
productions is inhibiting. But there was a deeper reason for his reemer-
gence as a staunch supporter of printed fiction: "I have to be that, I now
understand, because I want to be a character in all of my works. I can do
that in print. In a movie, somehow, the author always vanishes" (xv). This

is certainly true for *Slaughterhouse-Five,* in which there is no author present at the opening and close and three times in between, and no one to say "so it goes." As Vonnegut judges correctly, "Everything of mine which has been filmed so far is one character short, and the character is me" (xv). And so with *Breakfast of Champions; or, Goodbye Blue Monday!,* published in 1973, a new string of novels begins that carries the author, now an inernationally famous spokesman, through the balance of the century.

For the first group of these works there is an adjustment to be made. *Slaughterhouse-Five* is not just the last book Vonnegut wrote as a little-known, weakly selling author. It is also the last work done on Cape Cod, where he had lived for two decades; it is the final piece of writing he would do while sharing a household with his wife Jane, to whom he had been married for a quarter century; and it was the end of his career as a provider for six children. He considers these changes important enough to mention first in "About This Play," his preface to *Happy Birthday, Wanda June,* the business of which had moved him to a borrowed apartment in New York City:

> This play is what I did when I was forty-seven years old—when my six children were children no more. It was a time of change, of good-bye and good-bye and good-bye. My big house was becoming a museum of vanished childhoods—of my vanished young manhood as well.
>
> This was on Cape Cod. There were widows all around me—in houses like mine.
>
> I was drinking more and arguing a lot, and I had to get out of that house.
>
> I was supposedly a right-handed person, but I found myself using my left hand more and more. It became the hand that did most of the giving and taking for me. I asked my older brother what he knew about this. He said that I had been an ambidextrous infant. I had been *taught* to favor my right hand.
>
> "I'm left-handed now, and I'm through with novels," I told him. "I'm writing a play. It's plays from now on." (*HBWJ,* [vii])

In a few years, of course, the author would be back publishing novels, but there is a continuity. *Happy Birthday, Wanda June* is developed from an earlier script Vonnegut had written and seen produced fifteen years earlier on Cape Cod: *Penelope,* a treatment of Odysseus's homecoming from his wife's point of view. The dynamics of this theme carry over—in modern dress, language, and circumstance—to the new play, just as the main character of an uncompleted Vonnegut novel of the 1950s, "Upstairs and Downstairs," takes a major role in what would be reimagined as *Breakfast of Champions*. But the motivations for both rewrites are different from the author's situation many years before. "I was writing myself a new family and a new manhood," Vonnegut says of the play; "I was going to fool myself, and spooks in a novel couldn't do the job. I had to hire actors—pay them to say what I wished them to say, to dress as I wished them to dress, to laugh, to cry, to come and go when I said so" (*HBWJ*, [vii]). The living nature of this enterprise would make for a different kind of work—one, for example, that would change in production, right down to experiments with different endings even after its run had begun. *Breakfast of Champions* would be written in similar circumstances, with the author no longer isolated on Cape Cod but living literally right around the corner from his publisher, to whom he could dispatch pages on a daily basis, if desired, and change an ending when the courier, who had been stealing glimpses of the ongoing typescript as he carried it down the street, said that the conclusion did not seem right. Such alterations were important because Kurt Vonnegut was now a best-selling author with great investments riding on his presumed success. It would be important that these new projects turn out right—a far cry from trying out story ideas on *Collier's* and writing paperback originals for a market that at times seems as disinterested as Kilgore Trout's. Like Trout at Billy Pilgrim's anniversary party, Vonnegut now knew he had readers: millions of them, some hanging on his every word. The essays he would write from this point on display an easy assumption of public spokesmanship; for his creative work, though, his posture as a famous writer presents a new challenge.

Change is evident in the structure of *Happy Birthday, Wanda June*. Beforehand, Vonnegut's most typical protagonists were in narrative situations that put them ahead of their times. Paul Proteus, Winston Niles Rumfoord, Howard Campbell, John (as empowered by a reading of Bokonon), Eliot Rosewater, and Billy Pilgrim—all are revolutionists in terms of espousing views well in advance of their societies' willingness to follow. Vonnegut's play reverses this condition; while Harold Ryan has been away society has advanced in appreciation of women's rights and the cause for peace, leaving the protagonist behind. In his earlier works Vonnegut—as a lesser-read author—may well have felt that he was a voice crying in the wilderness, with the heroes of his novels preaching forlornly to a world resistant to their messages. From John's "Call me Jonah" to Howard Campbell's "Goodbye, cruel world," the protagonist suffers the same lack of appreciation as does Vonnegut. With *Happy Birthday, Wanda June,* however, the author writes for the first time as someone society has embraced.

The play's action is philosophical, indicated by the way its characters introduce themselves. Penelope comes first, and her words describe the theme: "about men who enjoy killing—and those who don't" (*HBWJ,* [1]). Next come the three adult males who will occupy the stage for much of the next three acts. Each sums himself up concisely and in great contrast to the others. Harold Ryan is a man who kills men in war and "other animals" for sport. Dr. Norbert Woodly calls himself a healer who finds it "disgusting and frightening that a killer should still be a respected member of society"; his program pleads for gentleness to replace violence, without which humankind is doomed. If Ryan speaks like a Hemingway figure while Woodly comes across with the manner of a peace foundation's prospectus, Vonnegut's effect is intentional. Each is a typical response, representative of the contrasting positions on this issue. There is, however, an alternative voice, one the audience would assume deserves attention: that of Col. Looseleaf Harper, a retired air force vet who dropped the atomic bomb on Nagasaki, "killing seventy-four thousand people in a flash" (2). He must be prompted to speak, and when asked if he would like to he replies in a manner quite different from that of either Ryan or Woodly: "Jesus—I dunno. You know. What the heck. Who knows. . . . I dunno, boy." After all, as Vonnegut's readers will recall from *Slaughterhouse-Five,* there is nothing much coherent to say about a massacre.

Happy Birthday, Wanda June dramatizes these three positions as typified by Ryan, Woodly, and Harper. Because Ryan has been missing in the Amazon rain forest for eight years, any and all men who have kept company with his wife are characterized as suitors, while his reappearance is treated like the return of Odysseus. The emphasis in Vonnegut's play, however, is on the society that has endured his absence and changed in the process, as figured by the new attitudes of his wife and twelve-year-old son. They have not moved as far to the Left as Dr. Woodly's feebly expressed pacifism, but their attitudes have deepened and matured to the extent that they now interrogate all positions, including the previously unquestioned ones Ryan espoused as husband and father. To him Penelope was the literal trophy wife, naive and subservient; Paul, his son, served as the worshipful tyke. Now that Ryan is returning, Penelope and her entourage plan a celebration as it is her husband's birthday as well. As the news has come too late for proper preparations they have to make do with a caterer's birthday cake that was not picked up, its decorative message spelling out the play's title. "We can take off the 'Wanda June' with a butter knife" (*HBWJ*, 34), one of them enthuses, inadvertently dramatizing the fate of the little girl who never gets to celebrate her birthday since she has been rubbed out in a senseless accident. In a play replete with references to death, hers is the only one that happens within the action. Yet through the magic of theatrics she will appear to make a speech about it, playing the role of Kilgore Trout or Reverend Lasher, another Vonnegut raisonneur.

"Who the hell is Wanda June?" (*HBWJ*, 52)—this scene-ending question, voiced by Harold Ryan as he roams his empty apartment on the night of his return, sets in motion the deeper plot action that Vonnegut uses to dramatize the three positions on violence. As the lights come up for the next scene here is Wanda June bathed in light and surrounded by music that "indicates happiness, innocence, and weightlessness." As a "lisping eight-year-old in a starched party dress," she is—as the stage directions indicate—"as cute as Shirley Temple," standing pertly to address the audience with her set-piece speech. Her whole manner is that of the "Wanda June" type the author used in his first two novels, the style of child caught up in the doings of adults and surely a character too young and simple to grasp the complexities of dystopia (in *Player Piano*) or chrono-synclastic infundibula (in *The Sirens of Titan*). Here she expostulates, in childish singsong, about the enormities Harold Ryan, Dr. Norbert Woodly, and Col. Looseleaf Harper have proposed in their adult varieties of articulation:

> Hello. I am Wanda June. Today was going to be my birthday, but I was hit by an ice-cream truck before I could have my party. I am dead now. I am in Heaven. That is why my parents did not pick up the cake at the bakery. I am not mad at the ice-cream truck driver, even though he was drunk when he hit me. It *didn't hurt* much. It wasn't even as bad as the sting of a bumblebee. I am really *happy* here! It's so much fun. I am glad the driver was drunk. If he hadn't been, I might not have got to Heaven for years and years and years. I would have had to go to high school first, and then beauty college. I would have had to get married and have babies and everything. Now I can just play and play and play. Any time I want any pink cotton candy I can have some. Everybody up here is happy—the animals and the dead soldiers and people who went to the electric chair and everything. They're all glad for whatever sent them here. Nobody is mad. We're all too busy playing shuffleboard. So if you

think of killing somebody, don't worry about it. Just go ahead and do it. Whoever you do it to should kiss you for doing it. The soldiers up here just love the shrapnel and the tanks and the bayonets and the dum dums that let them play shuffleboard all the time—and drink beer. (53–55)

As Wanda June speaks, carnival music wells up to accompany her effusions about the heavenly life of Ferris wheels, Little League, and par-three golf. Then her presence fades out, to be replaced by the other actor in this scene, Col. Looseleaf Harper, who delivers a similarly spotlit monologue about returning from the bombing of Nagasaki to address a Boy Scout meeting in a church basement. He relates this experience to his own scouting days, when he earned merit badge after merit badge for ridiculous, even absurd activities ("The Boy Scout Manual said I was supposed to find out what my town did about sewage. Jesus, they just dumped it in Sugar Creek"). "It's a very strange kind of kid that makes Eagle Scout," Harper confides, never having reached that rank himself. "They always seem so lonesome, like they'd worked real hard to get a job nobody else cares about" (*HBWJ*, 56). From here his memories wander to all the advice he had been given as a kid. He reflects, "Jesus—I remember my mother used to make me chew bananas for a full minute before I swallowed—so I wouldn't get sick. Makes you wonder what else your parents told you that wasn't *true*" (57).

You've got to be carefully taught—this sentiment from the *South Pacific* show tune currently being reborn as a 1960s protest song motivates Vonnegut's plot turn. One such teaching from a generation earlier is already in the process of being discounted. From his safari dress and habit of addressing young women as "daughter" (*HBWJ*, 59), Harold Ryan is an obvious image of Ernest Hemingway. Hemingway certainly excelled at warfare and violent adventure, from boxing to big-game hunting; but more important for Vonnegut's purposes, he wrote about those activities in a way that made his style of life a compelling example. It bothers Ryan now that Penelope in his absence has earned a master's degree in creative writing: "What a pity! Educating a beautiful woman is like pouring honey into a fine Swiss watch. Everything stops" (69). But working in an M.F.A. program has been Vonnegut's own occupation in recent years, the program a postmodern phenomenon that has replaced the Hemingway figure with a different model of person, one who attends such things as writing seminars (at Johns Hopkins) or the Writers' Workshop (at the University of Iowa, where Vonnegut taught from 1965 to 1967) and develops a different style from the personal enfiguration as Hemingway. It is during this time, in the wake of Carlos Baker's deflationary biography of the man, that Ernest Hemingway's work falls out of style with the times, and *Happy Birthday, Wanda June* functions as a barometer of literary taste.

In doing his part to carry on the diminishing of Hemingway so necessary for society to envision a new type of hero, the newly famous Kurt Vonnegut calls on his own comic vision. In this effort Wanda June is of much assistance. In heaven she accompanies another person glad to be there, a Nazi atrocity-maker whom Ryan has dispatched to the afterlife. He loves it up here less for the cotton candy and carnival rides than for its sense of the ridiculous. "It was almost worth the trip," he admits, "to find out that Jesus Christ in Heaven was just another guy, playing shuffleboard. I liked his sense of humor, though—you know?" (*HBWJ*, 136). In a classic demonstration of the Vonnegut effect the Nazi describes what he loves about our Savior: "He's got a blue-and-gold warm-up jacket he wears. You know what it says on the back? 'Pontius Pilate Athletic Club.' Most people don't get it. Most people think there really is a Pontius Pilate Athletic Club."

Comments such as these take the cruel ironies of Wanda June's speech and turn them into comedy that subverts the Harold Ryan brand of heroism. How can anyone ever again take seriously the bravado of a wartime hero telling his enemy to go meet his Maker when the Son of God to whom he will be introduced is a character like this? Once Ryan's petty violence toward Dr. Woodly loses him the esteem of his sidekick, Col. Harper, the demolition of old models is nearly complete. When Woodly fights back not with a weapon but with words, the resolution is clear. Words such as Wanda June's, written by Vonnegut, have undermined the man's position, to the point that Penelope can agree: her husband is a fake.

With *Breakfast of Champions,* Vonnegut returns to fiction. As a gesture to his newfound fame he brings back novelist Kilgore Trout as a figure who enjoys a similar good, if surprising, fortune. Near the end of *Slaughterhouse-Five,* Trout had discovered his first reader, Billy Pilgrim. In this new book he is brought face-to-face with a reader who has taken him seriously, even literally, interpreting the allegory of a science-fiction plot as the gospel truth of his own life. This second major character, Dwayne Hoover, is everything Trout is not: economically successful (as a Pontiac dealer and investor in various franchises) and solidly established in American middle-class culture. The novel's structure is a simple one, yet it employs simultaneously evolving plots from different times and spaces. Trout has been invited to speak at the local arts festival, and much of *Breakfast of Champions* is given to tracing the long progress of these two figures coming together. Along the way each has ample opportunity to display his developed character and speak his reasoned piece. The strategy brings two raisonneurs together, making this work Vonnegut's most thoroughly developed novel of ideas.

Having made himself an explicit part of his novels since the 1966 hardcover edition of *Mother Night* (with its new introduction that incorporates the author's biography as an element in the fiction that follows), Vonnegut is not about to give up this important dimension, even though he now writes from a position of fame rather than of anonymity. He begins with a preface talking about the Great Depression, an era forty years distant from the prosperous economy of this novel's present narrative action, yet one autobiographically illustrative of the depression that haunts Dwayne Hoover and the possible cures for it. During his adolescence in the 1930s, Vonnegut recalls, he had a high school job writing ad copy for the *Indianapolis Times,* during which time Phoebe Hurty, a columnist for the paper, taught him an irreverent sense of humor that developed into the way he makes his living today. A second story from these years concerns people afflicted with locomotor ataxia (an effect of syphilis) whom he would see on occasion, their spines welded so that they acted like poorly adjusted robots. From there he moves on to a third event, his mother's suicidal depression, which would take her life. A final subject involves the writer celebrating his fiftieth birthday by trying to purge himself of these and other ideas that have built up into a mental clutter. *Breakfast of Champions,* he says, will flush them all out—as it does, turning loose his ideas on depressions, great and small, and on people who do seem as programmed as robots when it comes to working themselves out of depressive conditions. One factor, however, is not purged, which is the Vonnegut effect of subversively impolite humor.

The novel begins with just such irreverence. Before he discards ideas from his consciousness the author gives them a close examination—much closer than would anyone not sorting through the "junk" that has filled up the mind and making sure it has no usefulness left before throwing it out. He starts with that most familiar of texts, the national anthem of the United States, "The Star Spangled Banner"—surely a well-worn object in every U.S. citizen's mental attic—reading it with such unusually close attention that the truth of it becomes clear: that of all the "quadrillion nations in the

Universe," the United States of America "was the only one with a national anthem which was gibberish sprinkled with question marks" (*BC*, 8). Stripping away the buffering mythology from American history yields something equally disarming. Take the founding fathers; in this novel's view they "were aristocrats, and they wished to show off their useless education, which consisted of the study of hocus-pocus from ancient times. They were bum poets as well" (10). Bad poetry makes for weak mythology, such as the myth of this North American continent being "discovered" in 1492. Vonnegut's narrative advises, "Actually, millions of human beings were already living full and imaginative lives on the continent in 1492. That was simply the year in which sea pirates began to cheat and rob and kill them." More bogus mythology involves these pirates establishing the country as a beacon of freedom, replete with a Statue of Liberty torch resembling "an ice-cream cone on fire." To make his point the author provides a felt-pen sketch—like his word-by-word recitation of the National Anthem, an act so obvious that it forces readers to see freshly what they too often dismiss as the overly familiar. Because he has become not only a famous novelist but a spokesperson for humane values as well, Vonnegut considers it appropriate to make a social point. To do it effectively he once again states matters with a painful simplicity:

> Actually, the sea pirates who had the most to do with the creation of the new government owned human slaves. They used human beings for machinery, and, even after slavery was eliminated, because it was so embarrassing, they and their descendants continued to think of ordinary human beings as machines.
>
> The sea pirates were white. The people who were already on the continent when the pirates arrived were copper-colored. When slavery was introduced onto the continent, the slaves were black.
>
> Color was everything. (11)

Felt-pen drawings with boldly simple lines; recitations of texts already known by heart, known since childhood; a prose style almost singsong in its reliance on basics—these are the devices Kurt Vonnegut uses in his novel's first several pages to determine a level of communication and set a rhythm for its revelations. Vonnegut's prose has always been deceptively simple. Since *Cat's Cradle* especially he has proved himself a master of the sentence sometimes as short as a single word, paragraphs as short as one sentence, and chapters sometimes just a page or two long. But the narrative style in *Breakfast of Champions* takes a quantum leap toward an even starker simplicity. There is an antecedent for it within the Vonnegut canon: the works of Kilgore Trout. Their themes are disarmingly plain, working with the same defamiliarizations that Vonnegut has achieved with his drawings and recitations. And the manner of their telling—being cited, as if a more complete narrative exists somewhere else but need be referenced only in synoptic form—corresponds almost exactly with the way *Breakfast of Champions* is written. Recall the author's characterization of America's founding mythology and compare it with his description of another work by the shabby master of science fiction: "Kilgore Trout once wrote a short story which was a dialogue between two pieces of yeast. They were discussing the possible purposes of life as they ate sugar and suffocated in their own excrement. Because of their limited intelligence, they never came close to guessing that they were making champagne" (*BC,* 208–9).

It is appropriate that Vonnegut adopt the imaginary-library style used for discussing Trout's works because the writing of novels and the measure of their effect on readers are two of the most important concerns in *Breakfast of Champions.* Just one page after his summary of the Trout story Vonnegut—who has at this stage introduced himself as a character in the narrative—speaks in the mode of his preface and first-chapter commentary. "As I approached my fiftieth birthday," he confides, "I had become more and more enraged and mystified by the idiot decisions made by my countrymen" (*BC,* 209). This has indeed been his provocation to write *Breakfast of Champions,* but in the process of doing so he has come up with a possible explanation for why the contemporary world has gone so badly. "And then I had come suddenly to pity them," he says of these fellow citizens, "for I understood how innocent and natural it was for them to behave so abominably, and with such abominable results: They were doing their best to live like people invented in story books. This was the reason Americans shot each other so often: it was a convenient literary device for ending short stories and books" (209–10).

Vonnegut here gives a new turn to the innovative fiction debates of his era—turning them backward, so to speak, because theorists and experimentalists had been decrying conventional fiction's enslavement to the imitation of life. That life imitates art, specifically the art of traditional novels, adds the moral dimension that had either been neglected by the innovative camp or ceded to the conservative opposition. What a riposte this is to arguments voiced in John Gardner's *On Moral Fiction* (1978) and Gerald Graff's *Literature against Itself* (1979), in which old-fashioned novels were accorded an ethical superiority because of their concern for standards of human conduct. Not that the author is willing to give the innovators full credit for improving matters, because in this same chapter he takes advantage of his physical presence in the narrative action to play little pranks on his characters, such as making a telephone ring to distract one of them. "I was on a par with the Creator of the Universe there in the dark cocktail lounge" (*BC*, 200), he laughs. In fact his role in this evolving scene will be to serve as his own spokesperson, to be the chief raisonneur in this novel already replete with figures ready, willing, and able to articulate his position. The fact that Vonnegut does it himself speaks for the novel's ultimately metafictive nature.

Vonnegut is motivated to speak because of what has happened in his novel, which is that Dwayne Hoover has read something by Kilgore Trout and taken it the wrong way. As readers know from *God Bless You, Mr. Rosewater,* Trout has spent his entire career being unacknowledged, and from *Slaughterhouse-Five* they see how discovering that he does have an ardent reader (in Billy Pilgrim) has made him giddy with fame. Has Kurt Vonnegut found the same discomfort in the wake of his own great success? *Breakfast of Champions* has begun with a great deal of personal material on depression, and in the novel that evolves from these roots the author presents a character, Dwayne Hoover, who is thoroughly disinfatuated with all aspects of personal, family, and professional life. Much of his depression derives from what can only be called the essential crumminess of his surroundings. Many of the minor characters who share this novel with him are disenfranchised: by poverty, deprived upbringings, or racial prejudice. His son is alienated from him and works as a nondescript cocktail pianist, awash in tasteless music for an audience dulled by alcohol. His wife has committed suicide by drinking Drano—a particularly horrible death but one associated with such a banal household product that it inevitably characterizes her marriage with Dwayne as a pathetic failure. The man conducts business from a dealership called Dwayne Hoover's Exit Eleven Pontiac Village, another insipidly named enterprise that mocks what should be the nurturing aspects of community. Along this same commercial strip he owns various percentages of familiar franchises, all of which testify to the depressingly shabby quality of contemporary life. His city has polluted its one natural resource, and Dwayne seems contaminated by junk food and chemical additives. In these circumstances facing the long dark night of the soul is a daunting prospect, especially when one's only reason to live is to protect a limited partnership in a Kentucky Fried Chicken outlet.

Kilgore Trout's life, always a depressing affair, is presented in even more degrading aspects than Vonnegut's readers have seen before. When contacted by the Midland City Arts Festival with an invitation to appear at its festivities, he is living in disgusting circumstances amid the sexual commercialization of New York's Times Square, circa 1972. The one advantage is that in this neighborhood he can see his work being sold—as pulp texts to bulk up pornographic picture books. Getting out of this world for a trip to Midland City is no more rewarding because the pathetic sci-fi writer knows no other way to travel except by hitchhiking, a cross-country experience that exposes him to even more depressing persons and places. By the time Trout reaches Midland City he is a total mess—which means that he is perfectly suited for his path to cross with the novel's other disaster of a character, Dwayne Hoover.

Among Kilgore Trout's fiction is a work that pretends to explain life by suggesting that it is nothing but an experiment devised by God to test humankind—an extrapolated Book of Job, one might say. The sci-fi variation is to make the experiment's subject just one person, with everyone else in the world this person inhabits being robots designed for the "destructive testing" of this poor soul. Who is this single person? The answer is simple, as any metafictionist would say: the reader of this book!

As a Pontiac dealer Dwayne Hoover is familiar with the destructive testing to which General Motors submits its products, pushing them past the limits of endurance until they crumble into their constituent parts, all as a way of determining how much use they can tolerate. Dwayne feels that life has done much the same to him. Well beyond all capabilities of tolerance, he is a dangerous person to be reading Trout's book. But it is not the testing itself that drives him crazy. Rather it is the idea that everyone else is a robot. Here is the ultimate nihilism, and it prompts him into a rage of destruction, all of which would be made licit if the people he attacks really were machines. To counter this nihilism Vonnegut takes advantage of his own presence to offer a corrective statement. His example comes from the aesthetic of Rabo Karabekian, the abstract expressionist painter introduced here and kept in the canon until fourteen years later he reemerges as the narrator of *Bluebeard.* Karabekian's canvases perplex the locals, who have no taste for nonfigurative art. In his work, however, Vonnegut finds a presence. The narrow band of light that appears in each Karabekian painting (in the manner of the "zips" that characterized painter Barnett Newman's work) is, in the author's estimation, a suggestion of human awareness. As for the expensive Karabekian oil that Midland City owns, Vonnegut assures the townspeople that "it shows everything about life that truly matters, with nothing left out" and is therefore certainly worth the money: "It is a picture of the awareness of every animal. It is the immaterial core of every animal—the 'I am' to which all messages are sent. It is all that is alive in any of us—in a mouse, in a deer, in a cocktail waitress. It is unwavering and pure, no matter what preposterous adventure may befall us. A sacred picture of Saint Anthony alone [the subject of Midland City's acquisition] is one vertical, unwavering band of light. If a cockroach were near him, or a cocktail waitress, the picture would show two such bands of light. Our awareness is all that is alive and maybe sacred in any of us. Everything else about us is dead machinery" (*BC,* 221).

Vonnegut's analysis is a critically accurate one, reflecting the theory that Harold Rosenberg used in *The Tradition of the New* (1959), his explanation of the motive behind abstract expressionism, and again in his specific study, *Barnett Newman* (1978). In the context of *Breakfast of Champions* the theory is important for distinguishing human beings from machines and thus correcting the whimsy of Kilgore Trout that Dwayne Hoover misreads as fact (the same error a naive party guest commits in *Slaughterhouse-Five*). Living creatures *are not* machines; the cocktail waitresses in this novel, with their cackling salute to the "breakfast of champions" every time they serve a flat martini in this hideous lounge, may seem as lowly as cockroaches, but each form of life shares something wonderful.

Vonnegut's art criticism also relates to issues larger than the Midland City debate. There the issue has been one of representation in painting. While the citizens have been demanding that they be able to see what the painting they bought is "about"—in other words, a realistic portrait of Saint Anthony—Vonnegut borrows Harold Rosenberg's method for explaining the similar work of Barnett Newman, a profoundly religious painter whose work relies on a similar band of light. Standing behind all of this is Harold Rosenberg's axiom that, for an abstract expressionist painter, the canvas is not a surface on which to represent but rather an arena within which to act. In the debates about innovative fiction that Vonnegut has entertained, this theory also applies. For *Breakfast of Champions* the case is just as obvious as in *Slaughterhouse-Five:* the novel is not a stage on which the author displays portraits of characters in action but rather is an arena featuring his act of putting words on the page. As Leonard Mustazza indicates in *Forever Pursuing Genesis: The Myth of Eden in the Novels of Kurt Vonnegut* (1990), *Breakfast of Champions* is less a conventional novel and more an exploration of ideas in loose narrative form.

Those ideas, however, are ones of a novelist at work. Much later in his career the author will experiment with having a novel present its own auto-biography, examining the conditions of its making and having these be the action that maintains the reader's interest. In the novel at hand he shows himself at work—not as mechanically distant from the fictive events as in *Slaughterhouse-Five* but just as involved intellectually and aesthetically.

How personally involved is Vonnegut? Enough so that when the courier taking pages from the author to the offices of Seymour Lawrence at Dela-corte Press complained that he did not think the novel's ending fit, Von-negut took this advice seriously. In the conclusion as first written he is committed to the local insane asylum, along with Dwayne Hoover; unsur-prised at winding up here, he admits that the next challenge is to write himself out of it. At the courier's request the real Kurt Vonnegut would do just that, devising a scene in which he frees Kilgore Trout from his servi-tude as a character, who thanks him in an eerily recognizable voice: that of Kurt Vonnegut Sr. Trout's last request, spoken by the author's father, recalls the challenge Billy Pilgrim's mother posed to her son, asking him to explain how she got so old. Here Kurt's father makes a much more daunting demand: "*Make me young, make me young, make me young!*" (*BC*, 295), he pleads. In real life that is impossible. But in a novel, as in any other work of the human imagination, the task is an easy one, needing only the creator's spirit to be right. By the end of *Breakfast of Champions* it is. Trout will be called back for service in later novels, but in one of them Kurt Vonnegut Sr. will indeed be made young. Being a successful novelist means hard work, the author has realized, but the job has its rewards.

Slapstick (1976) elevates the narrative voice to greater social and politi-cal heights. "This is the closest I will ever come to writing an autobiogra-phy" (*S*, 1), Vonnegut states in the novel's prologue, and then he delivers a work narrated by a protagonist he has made the president of the United States. True, Wilbur Swain presides over a country whose future has turned out to be one of weakness and disillusion. And he is not a statesman or even a politician by training but rather a physician. Yet certain lessons from *Breakfast of Champions* should alert Vonnegut's readers to the direc-tions of theme. In that novel, qualities of American life are certainly in decline. But novelists, even one as lowly as Kilgore Trout, can help. As a reward for such service Trout is given the Nobel prize—not in literature but in medicine, for demonstrating how ideas (the stuff of fiction) have a physical impact on the nature of human life. In *Slapstick*, Dr. Swain will have his own ideas for improving human society; such is the program of his presidential administration, whose slogan "Lonesome No More!" promises to solve most problems by providing each citizen with a hugely supportive extended family. In promoting this belief the narrator speaks much like Vonnegut, who has, just two years before, admitted his essays to the canon by means of their collection as *Wampeters, Foma & Granfalloons,* which is subtitled as *Opinions.*

As critic Leonard Mustazza suggests in *Forever Pursuing Genesis,* Kurt Vonnegut may well have used the 1970s to become a full-fledged novelist of ideas. To appreciate the special nature of the author's work, one should notice just what ideas mean to this author. *Breakfast of Champions* demonstrates their medicinal and physiological effects, but *Slapstick* adds the important disclaimer against conceptual content being the catalyzing agent. In this new novel readers are shown how ideas function not by virtue of their meanings but as badges of friendship—as a sociological rather than purely intellectual tool. How could they do anything else, given Vonnegut's popular basis and appeal? He is no Jean-Paul Sartre, after all, writing novels indistinguishable from philosophical treatises; there is nothing in *Breakfast of Champions* or *Slapstick* that would not amuse and instruct readers of *Collier's* and the *Saturday Evening Post.* For them, ideas do operate in ways that determine the relative health or sickness of an entire society—just think of how, from Kurt Vonnegut's point of view, McCarthyism and the anticommunist witch hunts poisoned the atmosphere of the early 1950s while the early 1960s abounded with promise of happy renewal. Dr. Wilbur Swain's idea that extended families do a better job of caring for their own than can any government program is similarly based on feeling: family members alternatively feel obligated to give care or positively enjoy doing so while the recipient feels loved, needed, and nurtured and has a sense of belonging.

The structure of *Slapstick,* like that of *Breakfast of Champions,* derives from the patterns of Vonnegut's autobiographical statements at the beginning. In this novel the provocation to write comes from a death in the family. With his brother Bernard, Kurt flies back to Indianapolis for the funeral of their last immediate relative, Uncle Alex. From now on, he notes, their old hometown will be just another anonymous American city for them, as their living contact with it has been lost. Henceforth any families they are to have must be artificially extended. Uncle Alex's death also reminds Kurt of how he lost his sister (to cancer) and brother-in-law (to the improbable accident of a passenger train running off an open drawbridge)—the two deaths happening in less than two days and leaving four young boys orphans unless their Uncle Kurt and Aunt Jane would adopt them (which they did, creating another extended family). These deaths have a structure to them, that of slapstick humor, crude and cruel but ultimately palliative. Slapstick is what life seems like, with its endless tests of his limited intelligence and agility. But as a test it comes in the form of a joke, which as an idea is easier to deal with than death itself. The whole affair reminds the author of a Laurel and Hardy movie, one of the comedy vehicles that had helped him survive the Great Depression and all of the smaller personal depressions since. They too struggled with misfortune that often threatened to overwhelm their limited resources; yet "they did their best with every test. They never failed to bargain in good faith with their destinies, and were screamingly adorable and funny on that account" (*S*, 1). Their comic reaction is the one Vonnegut adopts to make his own story proportionately adorable and funny.

Making jokes, the author likes to say, is how he earns his living. It is also how he structures *Slapstick,* a novel set in a world gone so bad that laughter is the only workable alternative. In his public speaking Vonnegut is fond of using jokes to show how their structure works. He will ask his audience a question—a real one, such as What is the speed of light, the capital of Bolivia, the dates of Benjamin Franklin's life. While his listeners struggle with the lack of an encyclopedia or desk reference he will ask another question, such as Why is the price of cream so high? He gives them a moment to ponder this query, which intelligence should be able to handle, and then provides an answer: Because the cows really hate squatting over those little bottles. Goofy as the joke is, it gets a laugh, and Vonnegut is eager to explain why. Having to answer a question is hard work, with a bit of anxiety over perhaps not knowing the right answer. Letting the questioner answer it himself with a comic response gives relief from both the hard work and the anxiety—and that relief is expressed in laughter, a physical release that feels good. Such is the structure of the joke: a setting of tension and then a pleasant release from it.

Wilbur Swain's work in *Slapstick* is to play a similar role as joker to the United States. There is not much left to his presidency. War has fractured the former nation into several regional kingdoms, with simple brute power replacing the strengths of an economy now gone to ruin. Other countries elsewhere on Earth have made their own modifications—most notably the Chinese, who have learned to control gravity and who have also miniaturized themselves until an average Chinese person is the size of a microbe. To this there are advantages and disadvantages. Experiments with gravity have turned the skyscrapers of Manhattan into a graveyard, as elevators can sometimes no longer make the journey upward; and Americans sometimes find themselves suffering from odd influenza-like symptoms, the result of inhaling too many Chinese. But at least these citizens of the Far East are less dependent on the world's resources, which are depleted beyond any ability to support a United States of America such as had dominated the twentieth century a generation before.

There is little plot to *Slapstick*. The action it does have mostly pertains to Wilbur's past and present conditions, each of which involves a debility that can be remedied. As children he and his sister suffered from a side effect of being dizygotic twins: by themselves they are little more than idiots, but together they form a single genius. Is this an allusion to Platonic perfection, unattainable as long as beings remain separate? More likely Vonnegut is directing readers in search of allusions back to his prologue, where his late sister Alice appears as the necessary complement to his comic genius, as she was indeed the ideal reader for whom all his works are intended (giving substance to Platonism, but in a new way). There are other possible allusions to this lost state of childhood, including the fall from innocence and the contrast of Dionysian and Apollonian. But the most typical Vonnegut theme that emerges is the unselfish compassion created by the twins' pledge of mutual allegiance and the suffering that results when this same pledge is broken. Without his sister Eliza, Wilbur is creatively impotent, as pathetic as he is when without the medication needed to treat his Tourette's syndrome. The joke is that one debility is as easily treatable as the other and equally painful when not treated. While the Chinese harness gravity and miniaturize themselves, Wilbur and his sister, as mere children, devise simpler plans for a better human existence. Wilbur explains, "Eliza and I believed then what I believe even now. That life can be painless, provided that there is sufficient peacefulness for a dozen or so rituals to be repeated simply endlessly" (*S*, 44). Society has always known this, but its rituals can be detrimental, such as the variation of Idiot's Delight played by the twins' parents, rich people who delight in turning money into power and turning power back into money again, an endless repetition that depletes resources and depresses the economic classes beneath them. Unlike this practice, Wilbur and Eliza's plan for artificially extended families does not exclude the poor, the humble, or the dull but instead gives everyone, even the most forlorn outcast, the dignity and purpose of membership in a common group. The cultural goal is a simple one, letting humans act like "innocent great apes, with limited means of doing mischief"—which, as Wilbur explains from his wise old age, "is all human beings were ever meant to be" (36). Can such a cultural reconfiguration work? The plot of *Slapstick* shows that it can, with adorably funny practicality. At the novel's end Eliza has passed on to the afterlife—no great shakes, as unlike Wanda June she finds it tediously boring. But she and her brother are still able to communicate, putting their heads together to improve the sad state of paradise—much as Kurt Vonnegut says his own sister still inspires him.

Another form of reverse evolution would become a Vonnegut theme nine years later in his novel *Galápagos,* in which heaven is even more insipidly dull (its residents compare it to a turkey farm). But social re-ordering takes more immediate form in *Jailbird* (1979). Here the author features another protagonist of greater than normal prominence, Walter Starbuck, with thematic and structural involvements resulting from his notoriety. As a government functionary, Starbuck has figured in two major social reorganizations: the New Deal of the Roosevelt administration and the Watergate scandal that drove President Richard M. Nixon from office. In between, Starbuck has endured the anticommunist hysteria of the 1950s and seen American culture work to transform its values in the 1960s. *Jailbird* details this protagonist's attempt to reemerge into the world after serving a prison sentence as an unwitting Watergate accomplice. In real life several Watergate felons, including some of the most outspoken, would be reborn as Christian proselytizers, political commentators, and best-selling memoirists. Starbuck is not the only person in this novel whose life is re-created, though—Kilgore Trout, supposedly set free from fictive life at the end of *Breakfast of Champions,* reappears in the person of Robert Fender, a prison mate of Starbuck whose naive romanticism let him blunder into an act of unintended treason two decades before and who has used "Kilgore Trout" as a pen name for his hopeless attempts to reinvent a world in which he can no longer freely live.

Once again Vonnegut chooses a social motivator and a science-fiction novelist to carry the themes and techniques of his novel. Such is the combination needed for a world being reinvented. In *Jailbird* the author tries reconstructing just about everything from capitalism to Christianity. What makes it succeed as a novel is how Vonnegut interrelates all these changes, drawing on economics and religion to create a more livable world. As a jailbird Robert Fender listens to Edith Piaf recordings, regretting nothing and trying his best to do no wrong while performing little acts of kindness as an uncritical friend to all, including Walter Starbuck, who is surely in need of a friend. The Kilgore Trout stories that Fender writes are gently humane. His more caustic tales are reserved for another pen name—a schizoid practice, perhaps, but one that Vonnegut sees as a necessarily human response to the fragmentary pressures of existence. Starbuck feels comfortable with Fender while being repulsed by the Bible-thumping, born-again Christians who use the example of Jesus to chastise him. "Depart from me, you cursed, into the eternal fire prepared for the devil and his angels" (*J*, 38), these evangelists are fond of quoting. "These words appalled me then, and they appall me now," Starbuck complains. "They are surely the inspiration for the notorious cruelty of Christians." Jesus Christ may indeed have made this terrible statement, Starbuck admits, "but it is so unlike most of what else He said that I have to conclude that He was slightly crazy that day," as would be any living being who inhabits the body of a human, subject to the passions and emotions and chemicals that rule us all.

Writing as Kilgore Trout, Robert Fender tells stories that let readers see the world a bit differently, thus changing their world in the process. His subject matter is comprehensive, covering all aspects of life from everyday behavior to the great issues of mercy and mortality. Walter Starbuck looks back across America's history in the twentieth century, the era in which it functions as a powerful modern society, and recounts how social reformers gave him his own ideals for public service. Vonnegut's own prologue tells a similar story of how a privileged man from his Indianapolis childhood, Powers Hapgood, used his socially gained advantages to become not just a friend of working people but also an active worker in the labor union cause. Among other things, Hapgood tells the young Kurt Vonnegut the story of Sacco and Vanzetti, executed as murderers when all they were guilty of was organizing a labor movement. Walter Starbuck will tell this story too and will also react to the evils in his society by drawing on the same inspiration Hapgood suggests in the prologue, taking heart from the principles of the Sermon on the Mount. Simple courtesy and uncritical love—as learned from Jesus Christ, Robert Fender (both as himself and as Kilgore Trout), and Powers Hapgood—become Vonnegut's touchstones in refashioning a postprison life for his protagonist, who on his first day of life as a former jailbird can be entranced by the simple rituals, easily performed, that make life bearable. Walking down a midtown Manhattan street he is comforted by the quotidian surroundings, as he makes his way to the Royalton Hotel's coffee shop (a location familiar to Vonnegut and his readers, for it is the place Billy Pilgrim stayed in *Slaughterhouse-Five* and where the author lodged when coming down from Cape Cod to the city in the 1950s and 1960s):

> By the time I reached the coffee-shop door, however, my self-confidence had collapsed. Panic had taken its place. I believed that I was the ugliest, dirtiest little old bum in Manhattan. If I went into the coffee shop, everybody would be nauseated. They would throw me out and tell me to go to the Bowery, where I belonged.
>
> But I somehow found the courage to go in anyway—and imagine my surprise! It was as though I had died and gone to heaven! A waitress said to me, "Honeybunch, you sit right down, and I'll bring you your coffee right away." I hadn't said anything to her.
>
> So I did sit down, and everywhere I looked I saw customers of every description being received with love. To the waitresses everybody was "honeybunch" and "darling" and "dear." It was like an emergency ward after a great catastrophe. It did not matter what race or class the victims belonged to. They were all given the same miracle drug, which was coffee. The catastrophe in this case, of course, was that the sun had come up again.
>
> I thought to myself, "My goodness—these waitresses and cooks are as unjudgmental as the birds and lizards on the Galápagos Islands, off Ecuador." (*J*, 123)

The reference to Charles Darwin's islands is not gratuitous. In just a few years Vonnegut would write a novel taking their name as its title and Darwin's theory as a basis for its plot. This particular scene in *Jailbird* shares the notion developed in the later novel that living groups either adapt to changing circumstances or do not survive. The Royalton is a real hotel, its coffee shop an actual institution, one providing an important service to guests and other citygoers each morning. Just as real as the Royalton are its waitresses, who in typical New York City manner are practicing the courtesies they know are necessary for them to survive their jobs and their customers to make it onward into another day. In Starbuck's scene both the problem and its solution are reduced to elements so basic as to efface their previously threatening nature. As a structuring method the device is quite simple. However threatening (and in fact however mundane, as happens here), Vonnegut makes the handling of the occasion a comfortable one. In his prologue he has cited a high school student's appraisal of his fiction's meaning, that "Love may fail, but courtesy will prevail" (*J*, x). *Jailbird* bears this out in Walter Starbuck's actions. In the course of this novel he not only handles the present but also comes to terms with his past, including a radical interlude with a young woman, Mary Kathleen O'Looney, whom he now discovers as an apparently vagrant bag lady but who in truth is powerfully rich. With her he learns how the prescription Robert Fender has written for uncritical love can be fulfilled. In the matter of *God Bless You, Mr. Rosewater*'s resolution, the troublesome assets of Ms. O'Looney are redistributed, broken into an infinite number of parts, the wealth from which is deeded back to the country's citizens, just as the love between her and Walter is recovered and reshaped according to the simpler and more achievable goal of common decency. On several occasions Vonnegut has recalled what readers will recognize as Paul and Anita's automatic dialogue from *Player Piano* and complained that the statement "I love you" virtually demands, like a gun pointed to the head, the response of "I love you, too." What is needed, he says in the prologue to *Slapstick*, is a little less love and a lot more common decency. In *Jailbird* his characters demonstrate a way of living in this better way.

Reconstructing the Gospels to make allowances for Jesus' meaner days and reformulating economics so that money can help the broad mass of people rather than harm them, Vonnegut's novel relies on ideas as old as primitive Christianity and as basic to the twentieth century as the idealism that established the labor movement. Neither of these ideas, or any of the others from *Jailbird*, is terribly original, as Vonnegut is fond of reminding his readers. But that does not make them any less true. As a justly famous spokesperson, the author now holds more comfortably the position he had argued for even as an unknown: that of conservator of all that is good in an American society threatening to evolve in a different way. One of the novel's closing scenes presents a metaphor for how practical such work can be. As Mary dies, Walter Starbuck quells his sorrow by making small talk with the paramedics who have come to take her body away. They happen to be Pakistanis who speak to each other in Urdu. As always, Starbuck shows interest in manners and ways, and is rewarded with this knowledge: "I inquired of them, in order to calm the sobs that were welling up inside of me, to tell me a little bit about Urdu. They said it had a literature as great as any in the world, but that it had begun as a spare and ugly artificial language invented in the court of Ghenghis Khan. Its purpose in the beginning was military. It allowed his captains to give orders that were understood in every part of the Mongol Empire. Poets would later make it beautiful" (*J*, 222).

Can Vonnegut's fictive language do the same for the sometimes harsh and ugly realities of current American life? This moment near the end of *Jailbird* suggests so, and with his next novel the author turns from economics to the arts, seeing if they too can benefit from some restructuring. As usual, he begins with a preface relating his own life to the book's theme and techniques. There will be an empty, unappreciated arts center that he relates to his own artistic genius, which he worries may be depleted (a common fear repeated in most works since the onset of fame). *Deadeye Dick* (1982) has its own protagonist, of course—Rudy Waltz—and it will be his fortunes that are profiled against the background of culture and art in both his family and its larger community. But throughout the novel readers find themselves directed back to Kurt Vonnegut's own situation— from wealthy, cultured parents whose values have become awkwardly obsolete in these newer days, to the fate of a son trying to bridge this distance between past and future.

The 1980s would be America's decade of great multiculturalism, as a new awareness of diverse sources and means of expression became apparent in the country's consciousness. *Eurocentric* as a term had its implications shift from the positive to the negative, and Vonnegut anticipates this trend by having Rudy's father be the most offensively Eurocentric character in the author's canon, albeit in an unintentional, almost winsome way. As a self-confessed dilettante he masquerades through the decline and fall of European art as a way of faking an aesthetic reputation. By playing at being a painter he can excuse his fancy living brought back to the United States and used as a museum-like culture in which he raises his son. Family life for the Waltzes is a mélange of outdated claptrap, with Rudy being born in an antique bed shipped home from Vienna over which hangs a painting by a young Austrian met during student days abroad. The painter's name? Adolf Hitler. But the potential evil of this cultural dustbin lies elsewhere in the father's belongings, a collection of antique firearms comprising almost the entire history of such weaponry. Century after century of European wars have their gruesome, deadly history told in this assemblage of killing machines, and it is from them that Rudy draws the making of his own misfortune. Taking a rifle from the collection one day, twelve-year-old Rudy amuses himself by taking a random shot across the city. Inadvertently he kills a young pregnant mother miles away. Hence his cruel nickname, "Deadeye Dick." And hence his association with that other bit of European history, Adolf Hitler, who in this same year of 1944 is also involved in the business of killing. Between Rudy and the German dictator the legacy of European culture fares poorly. If this is the treasure trove from which America is to draw its sustaining art, the prospects look dim indeed.

At the age of puberty Rudy Waltz is introduced into a world so hostile that he takes refuge in being what he calls a "neuter." This status involves being more than sexless, for he is bereft of personality, interests, and desires, all a consequence of being cut off from any nourishing culture. To remedy this he would like to be a creative artist; but his father, depressed at what the arts have brought his family, insists that Rudy be a pharmacist instead. This theme reflects Kurt Vonnegut Sr.'s disenchantment with the rich culture that had supported Vonneguts for generations but which died during the Great Depression that killed off his practice as an architect and depleted the wealth his and his wife's parents and grandparents had built up in the process of making nineteenth-century Indianapolis a finely civilized city. As a result his sons were told to study something useful: for Bernard, physics (with a doctorate from the Massachusetts Institute of Technology), and for Kurt, a program at Cornell University that would have qualified him as a biochemist had not World War II intervened. This same war puts the finish on the senior Waltz's European culture and makes it all the more inevitable that young Rudy forsake a replication of this culture and choose a simpler life instead, as a night pharmacist in downtown Midland City. Yet the very nature of this job, which Rudy performs in the manner of a Dostoyevskian underground man or Kafkaesque clerk, breeds a culture of its own—or, at the very least, the crying need for one.

It is better that Rudy not grow up within his parents' phony culture. Although he does respect his own father and mother's life, Kurt Vonnegut has certainly made great contributions to the postmodern culture that replaced their own heritage in the pantheon of American values. But Rudy is not as prompt a creator as Kurt, even given the latter's digressions into military service, anthropological study, newspaper work, service in corporate public relations, and early experience with family magazine fiction and the writing of paperback originals. For a time young Waltz flees the world's ugliness (and it has surely been ugly to him) by living in the escapist retreat that "neuterism" cannot help but be. In doing so, he reflects his father's irresponsibility in devoting a life to the flippant trivialities of a once-great European culture now in sad decline. As a result Rudy places himself in what he characterizes as dead storage, in the same condition as the worn-out objects of old European culture that constitute his father's life.

Although Rudy eventually works his way beyond these confinements, writing a play that wins a contest and is produced (albeit unsuccessfully) in New York, his greatest success is crafting little imaginary playlets in his head that let him put existence into manageable form. He describes the method near the novel's end: "We all see our lives as stories, it seems to me, and I am convinced that psychologists and sociologists and historians and so on would find it useful to acknowledge that. If a person survives an ordinary span of sixty years or more, there is every chance that his or her life as a shapely story has ended, and all that remains to be experienced is epilogue. Life is not over, but the story is" (*D*, 208). Just as there are good and bad dramas, aesthetic forms for one's life can have varying degrees of success. Rudy's father's story closed, the son now knows, when he insisted on taking responsibility for the accidental shooting and resultant murder—at which point his life should have ended, given the format he had chosen. But it did not. "The remaining years were an epilogue," Rudy explains, "a sort of junk shop of events which were nothing more than random curiosities, boxes and bins of whatchamacallits" (209). Cultures too should know when to end, given their dramatic insistence on beginnings. Just as artists commit suicide when their epilogues do not fit—Ernest Hemingway is described as an example—national cultures too might consider doing so, which is what Rudy Waltz's America flirts with as an end to its own atomic age.

The elements of Rudy Waltz's life do not add up to much, but at least he has taken control of them and re-created himself by means of art. In this act of structuring he has proposed an identity beyond that of Dead-eye Dick, independent of his parents and the culturally depleted life to which their emptiness had almost sentenced him. His life has been traumatic, but from those traumas, when handled artistically, come self-knowledge and self-responsibility, the two of which can heal deep emotional wounds. As his own creator, he writes this narrative from a hotel in Haiti, the same address Kurt Vonnegut uses to sign his preface. Author and character thus meld—not biographically but aesthetically—as each presents restructurings as simple as harmless fantasies, yet as useful as good recipes (which appear from time to time as pacings in the narrative).

The period spanned from *Happy Birthday, Wanda June* to *Deadeye Dick* takes in the American 1970s. After such promise as the 1960s implied, cultural conditions seemed comparatively blighted, taking their cues from the Watergate scandal that began the era to the hostage crisis in Iran that brought the decade to its end. From Dwayne Hoover and Wilbur Swain to Walter Starbuck and Rudy Waltz, Kurt Vonnegut's protagonists reflect this era. Their shattered prominence speaks for the losses incurred: of the American dream in Dwayne's life; of a prosperously united country in Wilbur's; of the decay of FDR's New Deal into the dirty tricks of Richard Nixon's political operatives; and finally of Eurocentric culture and Western humanistic tradition in Rudy's lifetime. But perhaps not all that much of value is lost, Vonnegut's novels of this period suggest. If all a powerful economy can provide is cans of Drano, percentages in banal franchises, and military strength capable of destroying half the world, then people might be better off without it. Walter Starbuck, who has lived through both the promise of a reformed economy and the ultimate perversion of that reform, feels good in seeing Mary's RAMJAC corporation dissolving its wealth in a more egalitarian fashion than the idealistic socialism of their college days ever dreamed possible. Creating alternatives as simple as Rudy Waltz's is an agreeable prospect for Vonnegut, who stays in tune with more immediate sociopolitical issues through his public spokesmanship in the essays of *Wampeters, Foma & Granfalloons* and especially *Palm Sunday*. This latter book assembles his important nonfiction from the 1970s. Written for specific occasions, prompted by particular occasions, and responding to certain issues, these pieces are by themselves necessarily fragmentary. "But as I arranged those fragments in this order and then that one," the author notes in his introduction, "I saw that they formed a sort of autobiography, especially if I felt free to include some pieces not written by me. To give life to such a golem, however, I would have to write much new connective tissue. This I have done" *(PS,* xvii).

From the materials of his own 1970s Kurt Vonnegut assembles "an autobiographical collage" (the book's subtitle) that parallels the concerns voiced in his novels of this same period. He begins with a celebration of the U.S. Constitution's First Amendment, so crucial to the freedom of expression he depends on in his work. Then, to establish how he comes from an essentially freethinking tradition, he reprints a lengthy genealogy of the Vonnegut and Lieber families, German immigrants of the "Forty-Eighter" generation well over a century before. Next come pieces he has done on writing, followed by a self-interview on his method. A section of reviews and tributes that follow seem random, but from their range of subjects readers can see that the author feels a kinship with figures who speak for the most common strains in American life—be they the radio comedians Bob and Ray or novelists such as Joseph Heller (*Something Happened*) and James T. Farrell. Some thoughts on texts that privilege our imaginations—be they books in libraries or the lyrics of country and western songs—lead naturally to a major piece on the most vernacular American writer of all, Mark Twain. Here Vonnegut describes the key not just to Twain's storytelling but also to his own—that although a premise shapes each story, it is up to the author to furnish a language and create a mood. Delivering an address in Twain's home at Hartford, Connecticut, he takes measure of himself as well:

> It seems clear to me, as an American writing one hundred years after this house was built, that we would not be known as a nation with a supple, amusing, and often beautiful language of our own, if it were not for the genius of Mark Twain. Only a genius could have misrepresented our speech and our wittiness and our common sense and our common decency so handsomely to ourselves and the outside world.
>
> He himself was the most enchanting American at the heart of each of his tales. We can forgive this easily, for he managed to imply that the reader was enough like him to be his brother. He did this most strikingly in the personae of the young riverboat pilot and Huckleberry Finn. He did this so well that the newest arrival to these shores, very likely to be a Vietnamese refugee, can, by reading him, begin to imagine that he has some of the idiosyncratically American charm of Mark Twain. (*PS,* 171)

For the balance of the essays in *Palm Sunday,* Kurt Vonnegut expresses himself much in this manner, covering the same issues that occupy his novels from this decade. Although there is unpleasantness in these subjects, readers will find no outright evil—just sometimes hapless human beings striving against the slapstick ironies of life to do their best with every test. Speaking candidly in the front matter of *Happy Birthday, Wanda June,* Vonnegut acknowledges what some critics find an "intolerable balancing of characters and arguments" that stops short of finding villains and assigning guilt. The author admits that such a balance "reflected my true feelings. I felt and still feel that everybody is right, no matter what he says" (*HBWJ,* ix). How thorough is this belief? As he explains in his play's preface, there is no other way:

> I had, in fact, written a book about everybody's being right all the time, *The Sirens of Titan.* And I gave a name in that book to a mathematical point where all opinions, no matter how contradictory, harmonized. I called it a *chrono-synclastic infundibulum.*
>
> I live in one. (ix)

Chapter Five

SPEAKING COSMICALLY

Galápagos, Bluebeard, and *Hocus Pocus*

LIKE HIS CHARACTER Kilgore Trout, Kurt Vonnegut is not daunted by the task of rewriting major texts, even sacred ones. In his novels published between 1985 and 1990—a remarkably strong period yielding a full, complexly developed narrative every two and one-half years—he refashions the nineteenth century's theory of evolution, the twentieth century's understanding of art, and a future twenty-first century's appreciation of the culturally formative events in American history. Flanking this output of novels are two collections of essays, *Palm Sunday* and *Fates Worse Than Death,* the title pieces of both being sermons delivered in two of New York City's major houses of worship, Saint Clement's Episcopal Church and the Cathedral of Saint John the Divine. In these sermons Vonnegut rewrites liturgical stories, beginning with the Sermon on the Mount.

Even more so than Darwinian science, New York School art theory, and the long, glorious history of America and its motivating symbols, Christ's preaching on this occasion would seem untouchable by the revisionist's pen. Vonnegut was already on record, in the prologue to *Jailbird,* that Jesus' text was sufficient inspiration to counter the grimmest hard analysis of earthly life; it and the Twenty-third Psalm, left unrevised by Bokonon in *Cat's Cradle,* are the sole religious texts the author seems perfectly comfortable with. But in his own Palm Sunday sermon Vonnegut feels compelled to do the same type of tinkering that Kilgore Trout does in *Slaughterhouse-Five* with the mechanics of the Crucifixion story. Neither intervention changes a story's essence; instead both Trout and Vonnegut make minor adjustments to make sure that Christ's message is not misunderstood. If anything, their changes make the stories *more* Christian. At least that is the intent, although fundamentalist believers have yet to welcome the effort.

Vonnegut tells his listeners at Saint Clement's, "I am enchanted by the Sermon on the Mount. Being merciful, it seems to me, is the only good idea we have received so far" (*PS*, 325). Its message, though, is sometimes clouded by the complaint Jesus makes on the night before Palm Sunday, when he chides Judas for objecting to the rich oils being used for his anointment: "The poor you always have with you, but you do not always have me." Christians seeking to avoid this primitive religion's early emphasis on practical communism cite this verse, the author claims, as an excuse against being merciful (and economically generous) to those in poverty. The statement does read as if the Lord is placing his own concerns above those of poor people, making poverty seem a natural, inexorable fact of life. At least that is how Vonnegut recalls folks back home in Indiana excusing their own selfishness. "Whenever anybody out that way began to worry a lot about the poor people when I was young," he recalls, "some eminently respectable Hoosier, possibly an uncle or an aunt, would say that Jesus himself had given up on doing much about the poor. He or she might even paraphrase John twelve, Verse eight: 'The poor people are hopeless. We'll always be stuck with them'" (327). This said, "The general company was then free to say that the poor were hopeless because they were so lazy or dumb, that they drank too much and had too many children and kept coal in the bathtub, and so on." When deprecations like these ran out, there would be Kin Hubbard to quote. From the Hoosier humorist came the quip about the man so poor that he owned twenty-two dogs. How does Vonnegut hope to correct all this? By telling these naysayers "that Jesus was only joking, and that he was not even thinking about the poor."

Here is where two factors come together: the belief that jokes have a nobility to them, with laughter being as honorable as tears; and that such insights are best expressed in a personal vernacular. Combine these two elements and you have the Vonnegut effect. The author explains, "Laughter and tears are both responses to frustration and exhaustion, to the futility of thinking and striving anymore. I myself prefer to laugh, since there is less cleaning up to do afterward—and since I can start thinking and striving again that much sooner" (*PS*, 327–28). This is the reason why Jesus makes a joke. He is tired and probably daunted by the fates awaiting him, betrayal and crucifixion. The oils that Martha and Mary bring to him that evening smell wonderful; massaged into his tired feet, they surely feel heavenly.

"This is too much for that envious hypocrite, Judas, who says, trying to be more Catholic than the Pope: 'Hey—this is very un-Christian. Instead of wasting that stuff on your feet, we should have sold it and given the money to poor people" (*PS,* 329). Having set up the occasion for Christ's humor, Vonnegut shows how the punch line is sprung, the effect of it dependent on a vernacular turn of words:

> To which Jesus replies in Aramaic: "Judas, don't worry about it. There will still be plenty of poor people left long after I'm gone." This is about what Mark Twain or Abraham Lincoln would have said under similar circumstances.
>
> If Jesus did in fact say that, it is a divine black joke, well suited to the occasion. It says everything about hypocrisy and nothing about the poor. It is a Christian joke, which allows Jesus to remain civil to Judas, but to chide him about his hypocrisy all the same.
>
> "Judas, don't worry about it. There will still be plenty of poor people left long after I'm gone."
>
> Shall I regarble it for you? "The poor you always have with you, but you do not always have me." (329)

Thus Vonnegut brings this Bible verse from the night before Palm Sunday into harmony with the Sermon on the Mount, keeping that text's wonderful prescription for mercy intact. Revisions along this order are what the author attempts in *Galápagos* (1985), *Bluebeard* (1987), and *Hocus Pocus* (1990). For evolution, abstract expressionism, and the iconographic character of American history his intent is to preserve them; these are works of gentle humor, not destructive satire. As a group they take a brighter view of life than their trio of predecessors *Breakfast of Champions, Slapstick,* and *Jailbird.* Having accommodated himself to the pressures of fame, Vonnegut now makes them work in his favor. His manner is no longer caustically critical (as he was of the sea pirates and slave owners in the prologue to *Breakfast of Champions*) but is gently, humorously instructive instead, as he fixes Jesus' joke for him in *Palm Sunday.* It is at this point in his career that his speeches become gentler, almost grandfatherly, filled with helpful advice about how in northern climes spring is really two seasons, the full bloom of which is preceded by something Vonnegut calls "unlocking," a tedious delay that depresses folks if they have not made an allowance for it—which the speaker here cautions them to do. He also begins lectures by citing the conventional wisdom that a speaker should never apologize—and then, to his listeners' great mirth, he starts voicing regret for a catalog of unspecified offenses, for all of which he is terribly sorry. As a comic device it brings down the house, but it also makes Kurt Vonnegut more comfortable with his stature, for which there need be no apology whatsoever.

In *Understanding Kurt Vonnegut* (1991), critic William Rodney Allen makes an important point about *Galápagos:* that despite its author's use of science-fiction trappings for the first time since *Slaughterhouse-Five* (a period of sixteen years and three major novels in between), this new work employs a serious use of hard science that has nothing in common with the fantasies of sci-fi writing. Its futurology is, in mechanical terms, off the scale of conventional science fiction, which usually stays within a millennium (if not just a few centuries or less) of the present in order to extrapolate on current trends. *Galápagos* considers events in 1986, just one year ahead of its publication, but from a perspective of one million years into the future. This much time is needed for evolution to do its necessary work in making humankind once again a species that is not so harmful to itself and to others. The long distance is also required for the narrative voice to have the proper authority—not so much of superior intellectuality (as would happen in conventional sci-fi) but of the gentle wisdom a kindly older person might use to assure a younger readership that all is well, the posture from which Kurt Vonnegut speaks in the Palm Sunday sermon and to college audiences across the United States.

It is evident that the author wants this voice to be his novel's rather than so identifiably his own, for *Galápagos* is Vonnegut's first book since the 1966 hardcover edition of *Mother Night* to be published without a biographical preface. For two thirds of its narrative this new work's storyteller is not identified other than as having a million years' perspective on the events being recounted. Only at the start of book 2 do readers learn that he is Leon Trout, son of Kilgore and a construction worker who was killed while helping build the ship that has taken the characters in this action to the Galápagos Islands. In other words he is a ghost who has declined to take up residence in the afterlife, preferring instead to stick around for the eventual transformation of the human race into a better biological format. Hence his corrective vision, a million years after present events and a generation beyond that of Kilgore Trout. For Leon the psychological distance seems about the same.

From the start he speaks cosmically. A million years ago, he assures his readers, human beings had much bigger brains, "and so they could be beguiled by mysteries" (*G,* 3). One of these mysteries pertains to the Galápagos Islands and the remarkable stock of animals there, as if freshly disembarked from Noah's Ark. The Ark reference introduces the story of what the narrator considers a second Noah's Ark, a ship named the *Bahía de Darwin*, which carries this novel's cast of characters to Galápagos, where they survive World War III to become the founders of an eventually new structure of life for humans based on smaller brain capacity. This downsizing has its roots in the way people of a futuristic China miniaturized themselves in *Slapstick*. "Truth be told," Leon Trout advises his readers, "the planet's most victorious organisms have always been microscopic. In all the encounters between Davids and Goliaths, was there ever a time when a Goliath won?" (184). That human brains first evolved to take on greater and greater tasks does not impress the narrator; octopi have large brains, too, he notes, as needed to control their arms:

> Their situation, one might think, wasn't all that different from that of human beings, with hands to control. Presumably, their brains could do other things with their arms and brains than catch fish.
>
> But I have yet to see an octopus, or any sort of animal, for that matter, which wasn't entirely content to pass its time on earth as a food gatherer, to shun the experiments with unlimited greed and ambition performed by humankind. (185)

The different approach to this greedy side of human behavior reflects Vonnegut's ease with the 1980s. In *Slapstick*, written during the previous decade that seems to have been far less comfortable for the author, the game was Idiot's Delight, by which wealthy people fought boredom by turning money into power and then back into money again, as the planet's resources were depleted and the human worth of anyone economically below them was ruthlessly squandered. (For a bleaker view of human life, one would have to go all the way back to *God Bless You, Mr. Rosewater*, when Vonnegut's own economic condition was foundering.) The situation in *Galápagos* is happier; a million years of evolution translate, in Vonnegut's case, to getting out of the 1970s and its rudely invasive rush of fame. An octopus shunning experiments with human greed and ambition is a comical idea; rich people playing Idiot's Delight with their planet's future is not the least bit funny. Viewed from a million years afterward, the nuclear war that ends human life everywhere but on Galápagos seems quaintly appropriate to the era's brainpower, especially when applied to devastating weaponry. As Trout (a veteran of the Vietnam War) puts it, "Nature could never have been that predictably destructive in such small spaces without the help of humankind" (*G*, 190).

Throughout the million years of narrative space comprising this novel, a great deal of information is conveyed. As the original characters settle down to founding a whole new way of life (in both social and physiological terms), Leon is able to trace their evolution as would a novelist of manners given the broadest scope imaginable. A handheld computer, devised to translate languages as they are spoken, survives the loss of most else from civilization and is able to deliver quotes from the canon of English literature at the push of a button—indeed, seeming as if at its own volition, letting the last age of human achievement comment on this newly evolving affair. But the major intertextual contribution to *Galápagos* comes from Charles Darwin, whose *On the Origin of Species* is seen as evolutionary in itself. Trout reports, "It did more to stabilize people's volatile opinions of how to identify success or failure than any other tome. Imagine that!" (*G*, 13). Leon's father, readers recall, received a Nobel Prize for Medicine in *Breakfast of Champions* for showing how ideas have a physiological effect. The son now uses Darwin's work as an example of opinion's broader importance:

> Darwin did not change the islands, but only people's opinion of them. That was how important mere opinions used to be back in the era of great big brains.
>
> Mere opinions, in fact, were likely to govern people's actions as hard evidence, and were subject to sudden reversals as hard evidence never could be. So the Galápagos Islands could be hell in one moment and heaven in the next, and Julius Caesar could be a statesman in one moment and a butcher in the next, and Ecuadorian paper money could be traded for food, shelter, and clothing in one moment and line the bottom of a birdcage in the next, and the universe could be created by God Almighty in one moment and by a big explosion in the next—and on and on.
>
> Thanks to their decreased brainpower, people aren't diverted from the main business of life by the hobgoblins of opinion anymore. (16–17)

Hence the million-year reevolution of humankind back toward something closer to an animal state involves more than just diminished capacity for mischief-making. From his perspective at the far end of this development Leon can make an interesting judgment about such intellectualization: that it was not anything of substance at all but was instead "magical" (*G*, 18). This puts his father's Nobel-winning theory in a new light. Ideas do have a great effect on life, but the reason for it owes more to hocus-pocus than any solidly physical properties—they have a real effect on people only because people allow them to. "We are healthy only to the extent that our ideas are humane" (*BC,* 16), reads the epitaph that Vonnegut puts on Kilgore Trout's tombstone in *Breakfast of Champions.* It is left to Trout's son to judge the implications, and to report on the utopia achieved when idea-making becomes an obsolete human function.

As always in his works, Vonnegut uses events in *Galápagos* to provide some convincing double proofs. A worldwide economic recession that gets the action of his novel moving is referred to as "a sudden revision of human opinions as to the value of money and stocks and bonds and mortgages and so on, bits of paper" (*G,* 18–19); on a planet rich with food enough for everyone, famines develop in certain regions—"And this famine was as purely a product of oversize brains as Beethoven's Ninth Symphony" (24). In making the case Leon sounds a bit like his father, propounding a sci-fi thesis about the oddities of life. He writes, "It was all in people's heads. People had simply changed their opinions of paper wealth, but, for all practical purposes, the planet might as well have been knocked out of orbit by a meteor the size of Luxembourg." Things go so badly that a visitor from another planet might reasonably assume "that the environment had gone haywire, and that the people were in such a frenzy because Nature was about to kill them all" (25). But everything is fine with Nature. "All that had changed was people's opinion of the place."

Just as with the potency of ideas, the correction to this situation has its roots in *Breakfast of Champions,* although in that novel the two were not associated and in this novel they are. As one of the characters learns from her dying husband, the human soul is something to treasure. It is what distinguishes people from animals and is valuable because "It's the part of you that knows when your brain isn't working right" (*G,* 44). It is not further intellectualization, then, that guides human reevolution, but rather an impulse of the soul. Mental dysfunction is certainly common enough, and by no means restricted to large-term mischief such as worldwide economic panics and thermonuclear war. Having large brains even makes marriage a problem. "That cumbersome computer could hold so many contradictory opinions on so many different subjects all at once, and switch from one opinion or subject to another so quickly," Leon notes, "that a discussion between a husband and wife under stress could end up like a fight between blindfolded people wearing roller skates" (66). This time the double proof is expressed in a whimsical vernacular—the phraseology is pure Will Rogers, classic Mark Twain. It recalls the tone Vonnegut uses in his Palm Sunday sermon when describing the social occasion that has taxed poor Jesus close to the limits of physical and emotional endurance. Dining with Mary and Martha, Judas and Lazarus, he does not find the occasion restful. Judas, he knows, will soon betray him, and Lazarus is only recently raised from the dead—"so dead that he stunk, the Bible says" (*PS,* 328). What dinner partners on the male end! "Lazarus is surely dazed, and not much of a conversationalist—and not necessarily grateful, either, to be alive again. It is a mixed blessing to be brought back from the dead." There is a crowd outside, clamoring to see not Jesus but the risen man—"Trust a crowd to look at the wrong end of a miracle every time," Vonnegut puts it, in the same spirit as Leon Trout's description of the hazards of intelligent marriage. "Of what possible use was such emotional volatility, not to say craziness," Leon asks with frank practicality, "in the heads of animals who were supposed to stay together long enough, at least, to raise a human child, which took about fourteen years or so?" (*G,* 67).

"Many events which would have repercussions a million years later were taking place in a small space on the planet in a very short time" (*G,* 137)— this formulation makes the novel's structure possible, a major innovation at this point in the author's career. Everything happening worldwide in the futuristic (by one year) world of 1986 works toward bringing a specific cast of characters to this remote Pacific island; once isolated there from a world otherwise destroying itself in what used to be human terms, this handful of people determines the future of their race as tracked for the next million years. By a combination of specific focusing and virtually infinite extrapolation, Vonnegut is able to put much more into a novel than would normally fit, just as in *Slaughterhouse-Five* he found a way to let an Earthling narrative read with the simultaneity of a work on Tralfamadore. In doing so, he speaks cosmically, using the voice of a million-year-old ghost for a generational and biological update of Kilgore Trout. *Galápagos* has as much narrative time travel as the earlier work, but without the thematic devices that have previously enabled such jumps. Here the ability to move across the developments of one million years to make references, as pertinent, to an action taking place in 1986 seems thoroughly natural, given the perspective and talents Leon Trout enjoys. As in the author's Palm Sunday sermon, particulars from that old action are saved for introduction until the right time—"time" in the sense of the re-evolved status humans have acquired, and which now stands in judgment of their ancestors' doings a million years before. Like Leon, the method is a generational advancement.

As *Galápagos* draws to a close, the narrator speaks of his father. The old man has met him at death's door, when Leon's accident in the shipbuilding yard offers him a trip to the afterlife. One accepts such a welcome if life has been enough; if the person wants more, he or she can stick around, as a ghost, for a million years before the next chance to escape will come along. Hence the time span of the novel Leon narrates. Just as Kilgore Trout begged his own creator at the end of *Breakfast of Champions* to make him young, here Leon's biological progenitor is asked to provide his son more time—five more years—to finish his "research" (*G*, 253). Kilgore tells Leon that it is now or a million years later, implying that the greater figure is what it will take to tell the story of human improvement he has undertaken. Which it probably will, given the epigraph Kilgore provides, a favorite quote of Leon's mother: "in spite of everything, I still believe people are really good at heart"—from Anne Frank (1929–44). Kilgore Trout knows it will take a million years of human reevolution before Anne's sentiment can become true. That may be the pessimistic side of Kurt Vonnegut's novel. The optimistic part is that Leon Trout will be able to see it and write about it. Most optimistic of all is the device by which Leon is saved from Vietnam. In Thailand for a rest and recovery leave and treatment by a Swedish physician for syphilis, the young man is shocked to learn that the doctor is a reader of his father's work, the one and only such reader Leon has ever encountered. This fortuitous connection makes possible Leon's escape to neutral Sweden—and his work on the ship, and ultimately his writing of the work at hand. Here is where the true optimism of *Galápagos* comes through, making it one of the most positive works in Vonnegut's canon: Kilgore Trout's vision has been given living confirmation in a million years of improved human history.

Like *Galápagos*, *Bluebeard* appears with minimal front matter from the author—just a disclaimer that the "hoax autobiography" of Rabo Karabekian that follows is a novel and not a history of abstract expressionist painting, "the first major art movement to originate in the United States of America" (*BB*, [v]). Why Vonnegut uncustomarily stands aside is obvious: the novel that follows takes the form of another artist's vision. Yet by mentioning that the style in which this character paints is of great historic importance, a strong link to the world Kurt Vonnegut lives in is forged. The text is delivered as a document, as will happen again with *Hocus Pocus* and as Vonnegut styled the paperback original of *Mother Night*—in each case a presentation of another person's writing. *Bluebeard*'s internal title page marks it as Karabekian's autobiography, complete with dates (1916–88), just as the faux editorial apparatuses of these other works characterize them as the memoirs of Howard Campbell and Eugene Debs Hartke respectively. As with Leon Trout's work, Vonnegut wishes to offer the text as the product of a specific character's labors. In *Galápagos* that work came to fruition thanks to the fatherly presence of Kilgore Trout. *Bluebeard* and *Hocus Pocus* will also draw importance from the spirit that occasions them.

A third item in Vonnegut's prefatory disclaimer concerns the large amounts of money that have come to be paid, during his adult lifetime, for the essential child's play of art—and for the practice of sports and performance of music too, all of which the author feels are products of human playfulness. And so this "Author's Note" becomes less of a disclaimer than an invitation to associate Karabekian's narrative with many real-life elements Vonnegut has shared. There is the location, for example: the former potato fields of Long Island, to which Karabekian and his colleagues such as Jackson Pollock and Willem de Kooning moved in the early 1950s to take advantage of the extremely low property prices. Today, as Karabekian writes his autobiography, his land is worth millions. So too is the quarter share of a professional football team he has inherited from his late wife—the Cincinnati Bengals, he specifies, confident that sports fans will recognize a former American Football League franchise that had been worth next to nothing before its absorption into the NFL. Land was cheap back then, just like rival-league football franchises—and so, too, were abstract expressionist paintings, which in the late 1940s and early 1950s Karabekian picked up from his friends for the change left over from his GI benefits (like Vonnegut, Karabekian is the survivor of the Battle of the Bulge). Finally, there is the great appreciation in value of European art. The Matisses and Cézannes that the narrator has acquired in war-torn Europe, sold for a pittance by their desperate owners, rival the worth of his Pollocks and Rothkos and interest in the Bengals football team, not to mention that of his Long Island estate (the same place where Kurt Vonnegut owns a second home).

What has made land in the Hamptons, paintings by Matisse and Pollock, and 25 percent of the Cincinnati Bengals Football Club worth so much money? The answer is simple: time. Simply indexing the change in fortune for these objects makes Vonnegut's point, as all these objects have accrued such fantastic value within his own lifetime—in just slightly more than half of it, in fact. In writing his autobiography Rabo Karabekian shows his mastery of a similarly transformative period, encompassing his parents' emigration in dire circumstances from a vanquished Armenia, through his own childhood and apprenticeship to illustrator Dan Gregory in the 1930s, to his experiences in World War II, adventures in the company of penniless great-painters-to-be, and eventual triumph as a painter and art collector.

Techniques of painting are what Karabekian learns from Gregory, a fellow Armenian who has become the highest paid illustrator in the world, although as an abstract expressionist young Rabo will be pursuing a diametrically opposite style. The difference between these two ways of painting is the same element that has effected valuation: time. Consider the narrator's critique of Gregory's illustrations, expressed with the care and components customarily reserved for the greatest masterpieces: "They were truthful about material things, but they lied about time. He celebrated moments, anything from a child's first meeting with a department store Santa Claus to the victory of a gladiator at the Circus Maximus, from the driving of the golden spike which completed a transcontinental railroad to a man's going on his knees to ask a woman to marry him. But he lacked the guts or the wisdom, or maybe just the talent, to indicate somehow that time was liquid, that one moment was no more important than any other, and that all moments quickly run away" (*BB*, 83–84). This conception of time will make special sense for the abstract expressionists, but Vonnegut has used it before, as the Tralfamadorian nature of sequentiality. Compared to their joy with relativity, Dan Gregory can only be considered "a taxidermist. He stuffed and mounted and varnished and mothproofed supposedly great moments, all of which turn out to be depressing dust-catchers, like a moosehead bought at a country auction or a sailfish on the wall of a dentist's waiting room" (84). As opposed to the depths of many marvelous moments seen all at one time, Gregory's art is a static museum; the instances he captured cannot be exchanged for others, nor are they evolving themselves.

Rabo Karabekian's aesthetic is much different, as he explains in a theory of art that conforms to the best modern wisdom: "Let me put it yet another way: life, by definition, is never still. Where is it going? From birth to death, with no stops on the way. Even a picture of a bowl of pears, on a checkerboard tablecloth is liquid, if laid on canvas by the brush of a master. Yes, and by some miracle I was surely never able to achieve as a painter, nor was Dan Gregory, but which was achieved by the best of the Abstract Expressionists, in the paintings which have greatness birth and death are always there" (*BB*, 84). It is this aesthetic that characterizes the narrative of *Bluebeard*. From page to page the action skips seamlessly from period to period in the narrator's life. The effect is Tralfamadorian and every bit as fluid as *Slaughterhouse-Five;* the story evolves from an incident in the 1980s back to something in the 1930s, then onward to the early 1950s before moving back to the first years of the century. As with Billy Pilgrim's adventures in time travel, the juxtapositions are illuminative. As one throws light on another, a third will emerge in perspective. Some readers will find the effect spatial, like the pieces of a jigsaw puzzle slowly coming together. There is this but also more to the narrative quality of *Bluebeard,* for in Karabekian's musings there is a fluidity that keeps each moment of his life, even a moment sixty years distant, perfectly alive.

From the standpoint of time, it would seem that Rabo Karabekian is in happy adjustment. But this is simply because his autobiography is written after a last, conclusive event: his friendship with the young adult novelist Circe Berman and her completion of his understanding of art. Their meeting is by pure chance. In the Hamptons to research a new novel on young people who work for the rich and famous, she wanders onto Rabo's private beach. Her manner brings her immediately into the man's life—not for a sexual relationship but for something far less casual, as it involves a full revision of his value system, aesthetic and moral alike. Ethically she feels that Karabekian has both ignored and squandered his own life story. Indeed, it would hardly seem an important element except that her prodding draws it forth, teaching him the value of honest self-appraisal. She also senses his disappointment with life. The millions he possesses seem little comfort, and he judges his art a failure, considering it an empty receptacle of merely technical expertise even before its market value collapses by virtue of his paintings being done with a commercial oil-based product discovered to be a dangerous toxin. Circe Berman's critique is even worse. Not only does she find Karabekian's work empty but she also decries the lack of substance in the full canon of abstract expressionism, paintings she rejects because they are "about absolutely nothing" (*BB*, 36). One of her first acts is to redecorate the foyer of Rabo's home, a room justly famous in art and architecture magazines as one of the best domestic installations of modern art. She covers its stark white walls with kitschy wallpaper and hangs a series of Gilded Age narrative dioramas. When Karabekian objects, she replies with a sentimental rather than intellectual critique: "'You don't call these pictures of little girls on swings serious art?' jeered Mrs. Berman. 'Try thinking what the Victorians thought when they looked at them, which was how sick or unhappy so many of these happy, innocent little girls would be in just a little while—diphtheria, pneumonia, smallpox, miscarriages, violent husbands, poverty, widowhood, prostitution—death and burial in the potter's field'" (128).

This interpretation revolts the abstract expressionist painter and collector, as it does his next set of guests: a trio of writers from the Soviet Union visiting on a State Department tour. Why does their host have "such trashy pictures in the foyer" (*BB*, 157), they want to know. He replies with Circe Berman's lecture on Victorian sentimentality, which has a remarkable effect. The guests are embarrassed, apologizing profusely and agreeing that this claptrap is indeed the finest art in his home. They view the pictures again, supplying their own narratives, before taking leave as the most grateful people Karabekian has ever hosted:

> I was quite a hit, and was hugged and hugged.
>
> Never before had visitors bid me farewell so ardently! Usually they can hardly think of anything to say.
>
> And they called something to me from the driveway, grinning affectionately and shaking their heads. So I asked the man from the State Department what they had said, and he translated: "No more war, no more war." (157).

War turns out to be one of the major events Karabekian has repressed in his life story. To this point, more than halfway through the novel, he has made just a few (very early) comments on his military service, centering on his wounding during the Battle of the Bulge and the fact that his military speciality has been camouflage. Meanwhile he has remained secretive over what he has hidden out in his potato barn. Locked away from view, it has sparked Circe Berman's curiosity, leading Karabekian to nickname himself "Bluebeard." This secret is the only part of her host's privacy that she respects, allowing the narrative suspense to grow. When the barn's content is revealed, Karabekian does it three separate times spaced at wide intervals across the novel's last third: in chapters 25, 30, and 34 (of a thirty-seven-chapter work). The manner fits *Bluebeard*'s larger structure of temporal leaps and juxtapositions. The first time is during the story of Karabekian's full military service, which stretches from his enlistment as a regular during the last years of the Depression through combat on World War II's African and Western European fronts. Here readers learn of the narrator's POW experience, climaxing with his march into a peaceful valley filled with up to ten thousand survivors from all aspects of the war, including civilians, refugees, Gypsies, concentration camp inmates, and soldiers from all forces. It is 8 May 1945, and the panorama Karabekian witnesses is fixed in his mind so dramatically that it sticks with readers as well. Its second appearance comes during the narrator's postwar reunion with Marilee Kemp, Dan Gregory's mistress and his own former lover. He describes the scene for her as an old soldier's memory, which she can evaluate from her own position as a woman misused by both love and war. Finally, the scene is described a third time when Circe Berman sees it as the subject of the huge painting (eight feet high and sixty-four feet long) Karabekian has completed in the barn and then kept hidden from view.

These three scenes add to the secret's suspense, of course, but there are more specifically thematic and technical reasons for the division. "What a sight!" the narrator exclaims in his first telling about it (*BB*, 208). "And, if that weren't enough for a person to see and then marvel about for a lifetime, listen to this: the very last remains of Hitler's armies, their uniforms in tatters but their killing machines still in working order, were also there," sharing space with the refugees and liberated prisoners of war. "Unforgettable!" Karabekian cannot help exclaiming again, and readers have to agree: in the long and detailed story of the man's life this certainly must be the most dramatic moment, a scene etched in memory so as to last forever.

But Karabekian's method reminds readers of another point: how simply fixing a moment in time, as Dan Gregory has done in his finely accurate but ultimately lifeless illustrations, risks losing the essence of any event. Time has been the missing element in Gregory's cold depictions, and in the autobiography he is fashioning, Karabekian is not about to let this key element of life elude him. Hence the scene will appear more than once. At different times and in different lights it will suggest the fluidity this moment has maintained in the painter's life story. It also lets the reader experience his narrative as a living thing, sustained by movement and change.

By the time of the scene's second description it is five years later in the narrator's life, but this is not a period being visited by the reader for the first time. Several times before Karabekian's status in 1950 has been described, including his friendship with the still-unknown abstract expressionist painters, his experience acquiring older European art, and even that in 1950 he happens to meet Marilee during a visit to Florence. By now, however, readers have learned many things about the man, themselves composite elements picked up here and there as the narrative has hopscotched back and forth through his life. That he and Marilee were lovers, for example—but also how she had arranged his apprenticeship so as to have a reader for the letters she wrote him, letters that revealed a growing expressive talent. That Marilee had been taken to Italy in 1940 by the proto-Fascist Gregory and then, after his death, become the wife of an Italian aristocrat as cover for her work as an American spy—but also how her long range of experience has cultured something new to Karabekian, a feminist philosophy. By the time the scene from 8 May 1945, can be described again for Marilee in postwar Florence, it has become subject to this new womanly perspective. "The Peaceable Kingdom" is what she titles it, an irony considering her opinion that war paintings, even of devastation and suffering, "just egg men on to be even more destructive and cruel," making them think that "Ha! We are as powerful as gods. There has never been anything to stop us from doing even the most frightful things, if even the most frightful things are what we *choose* to do" (*BB*, 240). Actually, Marilee's more technical expertise with art lets her see the merit of abstract expressionism, the style Rabo Karabekian tells her about and of which she becomes the first international collector. These works, he explains, are about nothing but themselves:

> When I was all talked out, she sighed, and she shook her head. "It was the last conceivable thing a painter could do to a canvas, so you *did* it," she said. "Leave it to Americans to write, 'The End.'"
>
> "I hope that's not what we're doing," I said.
>
> "I hope very much it is what you're doing," she said. "After all that men have done to the women and children and every other defenseless thing on this planet, it is time that not just every painting, but every piece of music, every statue, every play, every poem and book a man creates, should say only this: "We are much too horrible for this place. We give up. We quit. The end!" (239)

Thus to the initial end-of-the-war scene are added elements of two theories, the aesthetics of abstract expressionism and the ethics of feminist thought. In *Chaos Theory and the Interpretation of Literary Texts* (1997), Kevin A. Boon makes the case with this passage that abstract expressionism is being praised for its refusal to express any sense of totality. Postmodern novelists argue that totalizations only falsify experience, fictive or otherwise. Marilee's praise for abstract expressionism's refusal to present a totalizing vision is therefore sympathetic with theories behind *Bluebeard*. But these theories of painting and novel writing alone do not reflect the importance of the scene Karabekian has rendered into art. This is why it must be given a third treatment. Even though the reader has known for some time what secret the barn holds, Circe Berman does not. Now the suspense is focused not on the painting but on her. For much of the novel she has been objecting to abstract expressionism's lack of depiction, and so one assumes that she will hail this new representational work. But how will her responses compare with Marilee's? Before readers learn them, Karabekian jumps forward to frame the scene with a future reference. He begins the chapter that will describe Circe's discovery by saying, "It is all part of the regular tour of my museum now. First come the doomed little girls on swings in the foyer, and then the earliest works of the first Abstract Expressionists, and then the perfectly tremendous whatchamacallit in the potato barn" (BB, 282). The third part is always the most successful, he admits—but only after clarifying that the viewing is part of a larger experience. One begins with the sentimental illustrations, the ones that provoke narratives. Then come the triumphs of action painting, where the only subject is the movement of the paint, the artist's activity being its own point. Step one has been the favorite of Circe Berman, step two that of Marilee Kemp. Step three, it follows, is the product of Rabo Karabekian's involvement with the viewpoints of these two quite different women. Only from such complex dialogue can the truth of his major painting result.

Tourists visiting Karabekian's painting have their own dialogues with it, readers learn. "There is a war story to go with every figure in the picture, no matter how small" (BB, 283), he insists, recalling Circe's appreciation of Victorian illustrative art. But he also tells viewers to make up their own stories, thus involving them in a rehearsal of the work's construction—a facet of abstract expressionism, as appreciated by Marilee. Circe's viewing of the huge canvas becomes a narrative event as she studies the various figures. At first she wonders why there are no women, and she must be told that half the people from camps and asylums are female—their ordeal has made them no longer recognizable as such. There are no healthy women, then, Circe suggests. No, she is wrong about that too. Rabo points out, "The healthy women are in the cellar with the beets and potatoes and turnips. They are putting off being raped as long as possible, but they have heard the history of other wars in the area, so they know that rape will surely come" (285–86). Asked if the painting has a title, the artist says yes: "Now It's the Women's Turn" (286).

Their turn for what? To be raped? Or, as Marilee has hoped, to have the chance of taking over control of human destiny after thousands of centuries of male dominance? The ambiguity that implies both answers are correct is reminiscent of Anne Frank's epigraph as used in *Galápagos*. In spite of everything, are people still essentially good? An answer from the Holocaust, or from the period initiating this novel's action, would be no. But given a million years for the species to re-evolve, anything is possible, and the picture painted by Leon Trout suggests that the answer to Anne's question is yes. With the brush now in Rabo Karabekian's hands, there is also cause for optimism.

Because the scene depicted is presented to the reader three times and not just once, there is ample space in the narrative for exploring its importance in Karabekian's life. As a factor in his military career, it is left undepicted until two-thirds through his autobiography. Long before readers know anything about his service life, they are told—thanks to one of Circe Berman's first questions—how Rabo's parents lived and died. Central to their survival are the jewels his mother finds hidden in the mouth of a mass-grave corpse. Only when the war-ending scene is described for the third time do these jewels figure in the narrative, thus appropriating the event as key in Karabekian's own life story, the document Circe Berman has been encouraging him to produce. Until the scene is personalized, it is as empty as the painter's self-destructing canvases—one of the cruel jokes of his career, whereby the commercial house paint he has used for his greatest works so far turns out to be not just toxic but also given to decomposition. "Now It's the Women's Turn" is, in fact, painted over the last traces of one of these massive but disappearing productions.

Bluebeard has no autobiographical author's preface, it is true. But as its story evolves, readers will have noticed many correspondences between Karabekian's and Vonnegut's lives. Dan Gregory's studio of the 1930s is in a part of New York called Turtle Bay, the neighborhood that since the early 1970s has been the author's own; Rabo's adult residence in the Hamptons coincides with Vonnegut having a summer home out there in recent decades. In his brief author's note there are comments about the disturbingly high amounts of money that have come to be paid for paintings and other works of the expressive human spirit, a fortune in which Vonnegut has somewhat uncomfortably shared since becoming a best-selling writer. When early in *Bluebeard* it is told how Karabekian was captured in Luxembourg when World War II was just several months away from ending, one thinks of Vonnegut's own experience and of his character Billy Pilgrim's. Finally, the grand scene of 8 May 1945, saved for three distinct treatments in *Bluebeard*'s last third, corresponds to what readers have seen in the last chapter of *Slaughterhouse-Five*.

In this earlier novel the experience of wandering out from the POW camp into the springtime Saxon countryside is Billy's. But in his *Fates Worse Than Death,* Kurt Vonnegut repeats the scene and makes it his own. As Rabo includes the mouthful of jewels in his own artwork, so does the author here include a fortuitously recovered photograph of himself and his fellow prisoners in the horse-drawn wagon that figures centrally in the novel's episode. There is a great distance between an author and any of his characters; this is one reason why Vonnegut has customarily identified the doings of his own life in a novel's preface or prologue rather than letting it weave its way through the narrative with the reader being uninformed as to what corresponds and what does not. The scene from 8 May 1945, however, is a more complex business. In Karabekian's autobiography it is described three times, from the perspectives of 1945, 1950, and 1985 (the novel's present). How appropriate, then, that in Kurt Vonnegut's canon the same event also appears thrice, with new implications each time: in 1969 (*Slaughterhouse-Five*), 1987 (*Bluebeard*), and 1991 (*Fates Worse Than Death*).

That Vonnegut and Karabekian share service in World War II is an important generational marker. During his own narrative Rabo notes that a fellow Long Islander is a veteran too, but of Korea, while the man's son died serving in Vietnam—one war to a customer, the narrator jokes, in a perfect turn of Vonnegut's own humor. But the Vietnam conflict is a factor in the author's life as well—for, like Joseph Heller's *Catch-22*, it was only during the Vietnam era that he could write his World War II novel and see it accepted not just as a best-seller but also as a work of art so indicative of its present age, the American 1960s.

It is not surprising, then, that a Vietnam veteran should appear as the narrator of Kurt Vonnegut's next novel, *Hocus Pocus*. Eugene Debs Hartke is born in 1940—that is the first thing he tells readers in this book that takes the form of his memoir, replete (like *Mother Night*) with an editor's note signed by Vonnegut that foregrounds the narrative voice all the more. A birthdate in 1940 means that Hartke, a West Point graduate, is prime material for command duty in Vietnam, young and able enough to be right in the heart of things. But the rest of his name resonates with history too, as he promptly explains. Eugene Debs, socialist organizer and the greatest vote-getter of any third-party presidential candidate, is remembered for the quote Kurt Vonnegut uses in many of his speeches and as the epigraph and dedication for this novel: "While there is a lower class I am in it. While there is a criminal element I am of it. While there is a soul in prison

I am not free." It will be Eugene Hartke's fate in *Hocus Pocus* to live out the terms of his namesake's motto. His narrative action dates from the year 2001, eleven years ahead of the time but an even more psychologically distant era because of millennial anticipation. Hartke mocks such expectations. "If all had gone the way a lot of people thought it would, Jesus Christ would be among us again," he notes, "and the American flag would have been planted on Mars. No such luck!" (*HP*, 13). Instead the narrator has seen the year 2000 come and go with no cataclysmic events: "From that I conclude that God Almighty is not heavily into Numerology." (In his own speeches of the time Vonnegut would remark that most biblical scholars now date the birth of Christ as 5 B.C., meaning that 1995 was the actual millennial turn. Its cataclysm? Think about it, the speaker would tease his audience. What happened in 1995? O. J. Simpson!)

Hartke's life story is a simple if disappointing one. Hoping to study English, history, and political science in preparation for a journalist's career, he is instead pressured by his father (who needs a boastable success) to attend West Point. For fourteen years after that, from 1961 to 1975, he is an army officer, reaching the rank of lieutenant colonel. After that he lives for the next twenty-five years in Scipio, New York, teaching at Tarkington College and then supervising it as a state reformatory. At the time of writing he is in residence as a prisoner, under charge (but not yet tried) for masterminding a jailbreak at the State Adult Correctional Institute across the lake from Tarkington. All these facts are presented in the novel's first few pages, prompting the reader to ask why Hartke's army career ended before the customary time for honorable retirement, and why, for goodness sake, he was leading a prison escape, especially when he will wind up a warden himself.

To answer these questions Hartke embarks on a memoir that skips about not only through his own experiences but across the full range of American history. Hence readers are given another time-travel novel, with a textual apparatus to explain the form—in his "Editor's Note" that begins the volume Vonnegut explains that Hartke's narrative has been assembled from hundreds of scraps of paper, all different sizes and textures, as if jotted down in a stray moment, yet numbered sequentially to establish an order: "It is equally likely, though, that he began this book impulsively, having no idea it would become a book, scribbling words on a scrap which happened to be right at hand. It could be that he found it congenial, then, to continue from scrap to scrap, as though each were a bottle for him to fill. When he filled one up, possibly, no matter what its size, he could satisfy himself that he had written everything there was to write about this or that" (*HP,* 7).

The conditions for creating this work, then, are similar to those used by the abstract expressionist painters central to Vonnegut's previous novel, *Bluebeard.* Rather than presenting one-to-one correspondences between their vision and outside reality, both Hartke and Karabekian use the surface confines of the page or canvas as an arena within which to act. This surface, and not the great wide world, sets the limits. And vision itself is not without boundaries. Like a poet working within the structure of a sonnet or a composer setting out to write a symphony, the author is meeting his reader halfway by expressing himself within this mutually manageable form—a form for which Vonnegut's prefatory note is the tip-off.

Hartke's first set piece on history derives from the place where he now lives. Lake Mohiga in Scipio, New York, is already famous in the 1830s as home to the Mohiga Wagon Company, makers of the sturdiest and most commonly used pioneer wagons. A Tarkington founds the company; his son becomes an inventor for the military, introducing the field kitchen and recoil machinery for artillery at the Battle of Gettysburg and spending the last years of his life working on a perpetual motion device, examples of which Hartke finds at the college this man established. The school is also famous for its carillon of thirty-two bells cast "from mingled Union and Confederate rifle barrels and cannonballs and bayonets gathered up after the Battle of Gettysburg" (*HP,* 26). These bells and the perpetual motion machines (the best of which runs only fifty-one seconds) figure as objects important to Hartke's life at Tarkington College.

Hired to teach physics, Hartke runs afoul of conservatives who control the college's board of trustees when he ventures opinions on American history, politics, and literature—in other words, for acting like a complete human being instead of a veal calf, an image that will rebound through the novel, along with other repeated associations that unify his narrative in the manner of *Slaughterhouse-Five*'s subliminal links. From the school's novelist-in-residence and from its history professor he picks up notions that upset the apple cart of American mythology. Take the Alamo, for instance. Instead of being the disinterested heroes of Texas independence, Hartke learns that Travis, Bowie, Crockett, and their colleagues were fighting to introduce slavery to the region—something Mexico had outlawed. Thus General Santa Anna should be considered the equivalent of Lincoln, fighting to keep his country together and free. In the world of 2001, when America is subject to the whims of foreign investment and other forms of exploitation, he jokes that the two major currencies of the realm have become the yen and fellatio. For statements like these Hartke is fired, and in order to stay in the area he takes a job teaching at the state penitentiary across the lake. Here he sees foreign investment at work, as a Japanese corporation has contracted the running of this institution for 33 percent less than it had cost the State of New York to operate it. He also becomes friends with the warden, Hiroshi Matsumoto, a Hiroshima survivor who at age eight had bent over to retrieve a soccer ball kicked into a ditch. "When he straightened up, his city was gone. He was alone on a desert, with little spirals of dust dancing here and there" (*HP,* 218). If Matsumoto had been standing, he would have been one of the atomic blast's casualties. But, then, if Hartke had taken a different exit from a high school science fair, where he had been shamed by cheating with his father on a project, he never would have met the army officer who made his military career possible. And if he had not caused a ruckus when insulted by a civilian on the day of his Vietnam War homecoming, he would not have stopped being a soldier and become a college professor. So run the crystalline structures of this novel.

Despite all the roads not taken, there is a strong consistency to Hartke's experience. In 1975 he is the last man off the U.S. Embassy's roof in Saigon, having loaded the final departing helicopter with those qualified to be saved. A quarter century later he is doing much the same thing, helping prison-break hostages onto another chopper. Given the level nature of his various worlds, attention is given to what has changed. In Vietnam, Hartke was a spokesperson for government lies. At Tarkington he speaks the truth, and he does so again in his work as a prison teacher; the first activity gets him fired, the second classified as an insurrectionary mastermind. He beats the second rap, but only because an army officer called in to restore order recognizes him from Vietnam and has the governor appoint him a general in the National Guard, thereby giving Hartke the rank he has always hoped for. Throughout *Hocus Pocus* there are many such full circles. Sixty years after World War II the United States is controlled by a Japanese army of occupation (in business suits), while social conditions have deteriorated to an equivalent of a free-fire zone, the racism of that war now having become civic policy, with everything from military units to prisons strictly segregated. Yet Hartke continues as best he can, using the college founder's perpetual motion machines to give lessons on human folly and playing the school's carillon so that the metalwork of warfare can be made to chime peaceful tunes.

Is Eugene Debs Hartke a spokesperson for Vonnegut's sociopolitical positions, a raisonneur become protagonist himself? Throughout *Hocus Pocus* there are allusions to the key essays of *Wampeters, Foma & Granfalloons,* the volume that inaugurated the author's career as a commentator on public issues. "Teaching the Unteachable" (*HP,* 112), his phrase for writers' conferences, is adopted by the trustees as a motto for the school's mission (which in truth is nothing more than giving degrees to uneducable children of the very rich). Hartke's meditation seems to him like "scuba diving in lukewarm bouillon" (246), Vonnegut's description of the Maharishi's technique. In just a few lines (281–82) Hartke repeats plot elements from *Player Piano* (revolutionists becoming slaves of the machinery they would destroy), *Deadeye Dick* (a neutron bomb), and *Slapstick* (the caregiving of extended families), climaxed with the appearance of a woman named Wanda June. Throughout the book he is fond of presenting mathematical and numerological teasers—clever little demonstrations that mimic a pattern of order for history and the universe—and then dismissing them as poppycock: "So what indeed! The lesson I myself learned over and over again when teaching at the college and then the prison was the uselessness of information to most people, except as entertainment. If facts weren't funny or scary, or couldn't make you rich, the heck with them" (71).

Ideas *as ideas* are what have vexed Gene Hartke at each point in his career. The concept of crystal formation presented at his high school science fair is a correct one; the flaw is that the work has been shared with his father, shaming him before the judges and other competitors. It is his father's idea, not his own, that he attend West Point, and his service career in Vietnam proves to be an exercise in disinformation. At Tarkington College and Athena Prison telling simple truths gets him in trouble. The inmate he befriends, Alton Darwin, is equally tormented by the presumed truths of his country, and he dies leading a fruitless revolt. "Lethal hocus pocus" (*HP,* 148) is what Hartke calls it all, giving the novel its title.

Yet a genuine raisonneur lurks inside the narrative. Although never identified as Kilgore Trout, he writes a story and publishes it in a magazine just as Trout would. "The Protocols of the Elders of Tralfamadore" appears in a copy of *Black Garterbelt* that Gene has put away in his footlocker from Vietnam, a footlocker that is lost for a decade and a half before being returned to him as he is being fired from Tarkington College. The story's narrative premise is that Tralfamadorians, endeavoring to spread life throughout the universe, use germ forms to do it. But to travel such distances these germs must be immensely powerful. To test out the most potent variety, the Elders of Tralfamadore choose Earthlings, whose "extra-large brains" can "invent survival tests for germs which were truly horrible" (*HP,* 189). As Hartke comments, "They saw in us a potential for chemical evils on a cosmic scale. Nor did we disappoint them." These tests perfect the germs but destroy the planet, leaving it as sterile as the moon, waiting for a stray meteor to pick up the bacteria and carry it on. "If the author was right that the whole point of life on Earth was to make germs shape up so that they would be ready to ship out when the time came," Hartke realizes, "then even the greatest human being in history, Shakespeare or Mozart or Lincoln or Voltaire or whoever, was nothing more than a Petri dish in the truly Grand Scheme of Things" (193).

Thus a range of Vonnegut's ideas from *The Sirens of Titan* through *Slaughterhouse-Five* and *Galápagos* are recapitulated in this Trout-like story. Like Dwayne Hoover's reading in *Breakfast of Champions,* it affects Hartke deeply. "What a relief it was, somehow," he notes, "to have somebody else confirm what I had come to suspect" (*HP,* 194). Hartke's nickname in Vietnam had been "The Preacher" because of his refusal to use swear words, obscenities, or even vulgarities in his speech. It is as The Preacher that he is recognized near this novel's end, made a general, and put in charge of the Tarkington Reformatory. But throughout the novel he has been reforming readers' notions of ideas—preaching to the choir, perhaps, given the loyal following Kurt Vonnegut has developed, but nonetheless summing up the author's themes over four decades of writing. This may be why Kilgore Trout is not named as author of the *Black Garterbelt* story; nothing distracts from these notions being Vonnegut's own.

Nor is Gene Hartke fooled by his own ideas. At the novel's end his illegitimate son appears—not that he has ever known he had one. The child is the result of a one-night affair with a woman covering the war in Vietnam for the *Des Moines Register,* and all he knows about his father is what his mother has confided in a letter to him from her deathbed, when he was just four years old, to be read only after his adoptive father has died. This happened last year, and now the young man has sought out the man who sired him.

The letter, it turns out, consists of ideas Hartke fed the young woman, together with a cocktail pitcher of Rob Roys, to mount a successful seduction. The stories about Hartke's family astound even him; in the twenty-four years since he concocted them he has forgotten the extent to which he planted germs so effectively in her mind. Each is a genuine tearjerker, and even Hartke's son has to marvel at their cumulative effect. "You have certainly had some bad luck" (*HP*, 292), he observes. "Your father comes home blind from the war [after shooting down twenty-six German fighters]. Your childhood sweetheart is hit by a car right before the senior prom [and despite her paralysis becomes Hartke's wife]. Your brother dies of spinal meningitis right after he is invited to try out for the New York Yankees [and has his fielder's glove carried through the war as a memento]." What can Hartke say about all this? "Yes, well, all you can do is play the cards they deal you." Hartke has indeed played them like cards, winning the hand that night in the Philippines right after the flight from Saigon. He had bluffed with similar cards as an army information officer, and lost. Reshuffling the deck as a college professor then made him a success until undone by a conservative trustee who wanted the school's teachers to be no more independent than veal calves. And so on, until he is in his final job as warden of a reformatory, reforming the ideas of a region gone almost completely haywire. At which point a long-lost son shows up to straighten out his thinking.

Despite this self-deprecating view of his own ideas, Eugene Debs Hartke survives as an able spokesman for Vonnegut's point of view. How could he be otherwise, given the name his author has chosen for him. *Hocus Pocus* is surely the most immediately political of Vonnegut's novels, responding to social conditions of the late 1980s as directly as any of his essays. Personal greed and economic neglect were certainly letting the country dissipate into a virtual nonexistence of crumbling infrastructure and foreign ownership, not to mention the hideous deterioration of the ecology. This planet did indeed seem at the point of being used up; but the fact of one's own death is hard, if not impossible, to imagine. Far easier to manage is the hocus-pocus of phony ideas meant to accomplish short-term seductions: of a lover for the night, of students for the semester, or of voters for the next election. But eventually each player's hand will be called. The long-lost son will show up; or, as Hartke says of many terminal events in his narrative, the excrement will hit the air-conditioning (his reputation as The Preacher prevents him from using the vernacular Kurt Vonnegut might prefer).

Having nothing to show when the dealer calls leads to a situation as vulnerable as Hartke faced when working as a Vietnam-era army information officer. With the impending social, economic, and ecological dangers of *Hocus Pocus,* the challenge to speak coherently is even greater than in the wake of the massacre that characterizes *Slaughterhouse-Five*. How the new novel articulates the situation without relying on the hocus-pocus of ideas is interesting. Parallel structures do the job; while one may not be comprehensible the other is, and by dealing with what we know, the author helps us confront what is not as intelligible as we would like. Throughout his narrative, for example, Hartke parallels Japan's economic war on America with America's war on Vietnam, hoping that the consequences of the latter will provide warning for the former. In Scipio, New York, the supposedly peaceful place where Gene Hartke hopes to live out his life, there is the bucolic little college on one side of the lake and the terrible, foreboding penitentiary on the other—as opposite as can be until the narrative collapses their distinctions—and not just once, but three times over as Hartke the teacher moves from one to the other, as the prisoners escape one facility and occupy the other, and finally as the college is reconstituted as a penitentiary. On a subliminal level, akin to the associations in *Slaughterhouse-Five,* there are the catchphrases remarkable mostly for their poetry ("in the shadow of Musket Mountain when the sun goes down") that are repeated in radically different circumstances (for a trysting place of lovers, as the burial grounds for executed hostages). Hence the narrative is knit together regardless of the diversity of its ideas, with readers encouraged to make associations beyond the conceptual level—good advice, given the author's suspicion of ideas. They are associations that reason alone would not suggest: trysting lovers and executed hostages, carefree private college students with rich parents, hopeless felons in a grim penitentiary. By this means Vonnegut is able to articulate a subject that defies conventional imagination. Even subliminally inattentive participation can be encouraged, such as when Hartke ends with another numbers game that sends readers back into the text for items they may have overlooked. Working it out builds one more parallel between war-torn Vietnam and an economically subservient America, and it reimmerses the reader in the associative level of the text.

With *Hocus Pocus,* Kurt Vonnegut's steady production of novels comes to an end. His next one, *Timequake* (1997), would appear after a gap of seven years—by far the longest in a forty-five-year career that had yielded fifteen novels, most of them at two- or three-year intervals. And *Timequake* had to be rewritten after he had major difficulties with its shape. No wonder the author announced it as his last such work. Yet Kurt Vonnegut had been threatening to retire from the occupation of novelist almost from the start, when after *Player Piano*'s lack of commercial success he continued with a decade's work as a writer of short fiction for family magazines. His novels of the 1980s had addressed most of the great public issues of the times. Now, in his sole fictive work of the 1990s, he would return to what had always most intrigued him: matters of form.

Chapter Six

THE AUTOBIOGRAPHY OF A NOVEL

Timequake

TIMEQUAKE IS NOT THE FIRST INSTANCE of Kurt Vonnegut taking problems of composition and turning them into a masterpiece of innovation. In the late 1990s simple old age was one of those problems. The man was in his seventies, one should not forget. For ten years he had been complaining that he was well beyond gold-watch time, wondering when his work would be done. Receiving an award for lifetime achievement from the American Academy of Arts and Sciences, he thanked his colleagues, acknowledged the officers, and paid tribute to the audience for attending— and then asked if now he could go home. Simple exhaustion from the hard work of writing plays its part in *Timequake*, ultimately in a constructive manner. But as the author reveals in its prologue, he had been pounding away at the typewriter, publishing novels since 1952, coincidentally the year Ernest Hemingway made a fable of his own exhaustion with the long, hard process by writing *The Old Man and the Sea*. "And then I found myself in the winter of 1996 the creator of a novel which did not work," Vonnegut complains, "which had no point, which had never wanted to be written in the first place" (*T,* xii). He thinks back to the example of Hemingway's novel and sees a correlation with his own work. It makes for a good story, and so he tells it.

In 1952, of course, Kurt Vonnegut was living in West Barnstable, Massachusetts, on Cape Cod. What better place to appreciate a novel about an old fisherman than in a fishing community? A commercial fisherman who lives next door explains the mistake old Santiago makes, neglecting to cut off the best chunks of meat from his huge marlin and leave the rest of its carcass for the sharks. For his part Vonnegut, already a professional novelist, can see the artistic equivalence. He ventures, "It could be that the sharks Hemingway had in mind were critics who hadn't much liked his first novel in ten years, *Across the River and Into the Trees,* published two years earlier. As far as I know, he never said so. But the marlin could have been that novel" (*T,* xi). In his new, shorter book Hemingway does not make the fisherman's mistake, and Vonnegut vows to learn from his example. "I had recently turned seventy-three," he notes (xii). "My mother made it to fifty-two, my father to seventy-two. Hemingway almost made it to sixty-two. I had lived too long! What was I to do?" Simple. Be not like Santiago but like Hemingway. "Answer: Fillet the fish. Throw the rest away."

Trimming down an oversize novel, however, is much simpler than what Vonnegut accomplishes. There is also the pressure of current events. It is a factor of old age that times seem to be changing for the worse, that priceless treasures are being lost, old standards forgotten, and so forth. But in Vonnegut's case the state of the world is part of his writer's business. After adjusting to his fame in *Breakfast of Champions* (another book called back for rewrites) and his other work of the 1970s, he assumed the responsibility of a great public spokesman—in his fiction as well as in his essays. In *Timequake* sociopolitical and cultural matters would seem to intrude on the narrative except that the author finds a way to weave them into the action—not as a raisonneur's commentary (the method of *Hocus Pocus*) but as a function of the text. Vonnegut has certainly faced formal challenges before, from the situation John faces in *Cat's Cradle*—setting out to write a book about the day our world metaphorically ended and winding up seeing the world destruct—to the task in *Slaughterhouse-Five* of having to articulate the meaning of a massacre when there is absolutely nothing to say. In various other novels subgeneric conventions could be used, such as editing the memoirs of a protagonist (Howard Campbell, Eugene Debs Hartke) or relying on the formats of space opera (*The Sirens of Titan*) or fable (*God Bless You, Mr. Rosewater*). It is with *Timequake,* however, that Vonnegut gathers all the constraints on his writing and turns them to productive purpose. Be they the entropy of old age, the annoyances of critical reception, or the demands of current events that call for the author's response, these obstacles to easy writing become the substance of his work. *Timequake* is less a finished work than the record of one in the making. Yet it is not metafiction any more than the self-apparent devices of *Cat's Cradle* or *Slaughterhouse-Five* limited themselves to the writer's reflexive activity. *Timequake* is not a compositional game, reflecting on the work of its author. Instead it is something no writer of Kurt Vonnegut's generation has tried before. It is not a novel per se but rather the autobiography of a novel, and as such it marks as great an advance in method as did *Slaughterhouse-Five* many years before.

Timequake is not metafictive for an obvious reason: its action represents something in a world exterior to itself. But in this case it is representation with a twist. As the author explains in his prologue, the premise is that because of a seismic disruption in the time-space continuum a decade of history is repeated. Specifically, on 13 February 2001 (five years into the future, in terms of writing time), the timequake sends everyone and everything back to 17 February 1991 (about the time Vonnegut's writing of this book began, following the publication of *Hocus Pocus* and *Fates Worse Than Death*). But this second time through the decade is definitely a re-run; fate has already worked its way into being destiny, and so events have to be acted through as if willed by themselves. "We all had to get back to 2001 the hard way," Vonnegut makes clear, "minute by minute, hour by hour, year by year, betting on the wrong horses again, marrying the wrong person again, getting the clap again. You name it!" (*T,* xiii). Only after repeating what were their free-will actions of the first time around can people work their way back to a new opportunity for creative behavior.

The "timequake" device, then, allows the author a metafictive perspective on the action without forcing him into the posture of a metafictionist himself. There is no illusion that his characters are acting freely this time through, but only because they were the arbiters of their own destiny in the decade's first passing. In *Timequake* they are figures on a stage at the same time they are people living lives. Their inability to do anything different forbids any further self-development, but two people are very much in the know about things: the author and his reader.

The first phase of Kurt Vonnegut's development as an author, climaxing with *Slaughterhouse-Five,* was to make autobiography the generating force of his fiction. This was easier to do, of course, when he was virtually unknown as a public figure; writing as just another middle-class American let him take the most complex issues and resolve them in the vernacular style of a Will Rogers, Mark Twain, or Abraham Lincoln, all the more natural because he was a bonafide vernacular creature himself. When he marks the last day of writing his Dresden novel as 6 June 1968, the day that Robert Kennedy dies, he is relating to his readers in a supremely equal way: on that sad date he and they were all just American citizens being deprived of yet another exceptional political leader. In *Timequake*, Vonnegut can no longer write with such comfortable anonymity. But he can relate to readers as a figure they have made famous. By buying and reading his books they have taken who he is and made that figure a notable one. And so the fact that his new text shares an autobiographical existence with himself makes *Timequake* as much the reader's business as his own.

In these circumstances he sees no need to request from his readers a willing suspension of disbelief. But then he never has, assuming that reality exceeds such standards of believability. In this new novel he brings back Kilgore Trout once again and cites one of Trout's plot lines:

> Who, for example, could believe Kilgore Trout when he wrote as follows in *My Ten Years on Automatic Pilot:* "There is a planet in the Solar System where the people are so stupid that they didn't catch on for a million years that there was another half to their planet. They didn't figure that out until five hundred years ago! Only five hundred years ago! And yet they are now calling themselves *Homo sapiens.*
>
> "Dumb? You want to talk dumb? The people in one of the halves were so dumb, they didn't have an alphabet! They hadn't invented the wheel yet!"
>
> Give us a break, Mr. Trout. (*T,* 88)

No warning against conventional realism has ever been so plainspoken. This straightforwardness typifies *Timequake's* narrative. The timequake it describes has plenty of familiar correlatives, such as a ten-year jail sentence or an actor's job in such long-running plays as *The Fantastiks, Cats,* and *The Mousetrap*—one of Trout's wittier asides is his appraisal of the assassination of Abraham Lincoln by John Wilkes Booth as "the sort of thing which is bound to happen whenever an actor creates his own material" (*T,* 197). Another familiar comparison is offered to Vonnegut in the closing days of World War II, when he and his friend Bernie O'Hare wander as liberated prisoners-of-war across the German countryside. There they meet a dying officer, a member of the feared German SS but no longer a danger to anyone. Why not? Because of his deathbed realization: "I have just wasted the past ten years of my life" (120). History, it appears, is full of timequakes.

The greatest point of familiarization comes with the beginning of *Timequake's* first chapter—its invocation, so to speak. "Call me Junior," the author begins, alluding to not just Ishmael of *Moby-Dick* but John of *Cat's Cradle* as well. In the original typescript of this latter book, when John finds his own last name on an ancient tombstone the name appears as "Vonnegut." With so many of the fictive innovations of the American 1960s yet to happen, and with the author still unsuccessful and unknown, his publishers would not let such a violation of Aristotelian convention stand. But by the time of *Timequake* all this has changed and Kurt Vonnegut can do as he pleases, with a full academy of postmodern theory to say he has every right to collapse the distinction between fictive narrator and composing author, trashing the suspension of disbelief in the process. Aesthetic distance is thus replaced with homely familiarity. "Call me Junior," the author says, adding, "My six grown kids do. Three are adopted nephews, three are my own. They call me Junior behind my back. They think I don't know that" (*T,* 1). Hence readers are invited to consider Kurt Vonnegut not just as the living writer of this fiction but also in the way his children do, knocking him back down to size, as it were, as a child himself of Kurt Vonnegut Sr. The author's father, mother, brother, sister, children, deceased ex-wife, and living present wife all have roles in the narrative, mixing with any number of fictive characters, including Kilgore Trout, who is here frankly identified as his creator's alter ego. For years Vonnegut had told interviewers that Kilgore Trout was an image of what he himself feared he might become: a cranky, unread, and alarmingly idiosyncratic science-fiction writer, whose works are no sooner composed than they are consigned to the trash heap. In *Timequake,* Kurt Vonnegut honors him, together with several real-life literary critics (an equally amazing feat, given the author's ill ease with analysis of his work). With the collapse of his short-story market thirty-some years before, Vonnegut had decided to use subsequent short fiction plots that came to mind as Kilgore Trout stories, to be cited in the novels he was now writing for a living. Like "Call me Junior," this is one more identification meant to make the reading of *Timequake* a comfortably familiar affair.

So familiar, in fact, that in the pages that follow, Kurt Vonnegut can be very much himself. After all, *Timequake* is not a novel but rather the autobiography of one. And so its creator has a perfect right to be present at the nativity and maturation of this product. Again from page one he does so in the manner that has filled most of his professional time during the past three decades: as a public speaker. A century earlier Mark Twain had worked the lecture circuit to pay off bad debts, refusing the escape of bankruptcy as a presumed dishonor. With the same appealingly vernacular platform manner Kurt Vonnegut had worked lecture audiences to good effect as well. In the 1960s he had to do it for the money—before the success of *Slaughterhouse-Five* none of his novels produced a writer's living. In his review of this breakthrough novel-to-be for the *Saturday Review* (29 March 1969, p. 25), the eminent critic Granville Hicks admitted that he might not have known how to handle this strange new work had it not been for one key thing: that a year before, at the University of Notre Dame's Literary Festival, he had heard this author deliver "as funny a lecture as I had ever listened to." The folks at Notre Dame had known Vonnegut only as a supposed science-fiction writer, but hearing his speech convinced them, and Hicks, that "what he really is is a sardonic humorist and satirist in the vein of Mark Twain and Jonathan Swift." Reminded of this comment years later, Vonnegut would remark that it really seemed to help the reception of his work if people had heard him speak first.

This would be a quality he strove for in his writing. As he tells composition students in a piece collected in *Palm Sunday,* "I find that I trust my own writing most, and others seem to trust it most, too, when I sound most like a person from Indianapolis, which is what I am." Not that academics agree with this method. "What alternatives do I have?" he wonders. "The one most vehemently recommended by teachers has no doubt been pressed upon you, as well: that I write like a cultivated Englishman of a century or more ago" (*PS,* 79). Public speaking would keep the author in contact with the rhythms of personal communication, letting him not only see his readership but also interact with it. Throughout the 1970s, 1980s, and 1990s, when as a famous figure he could select his venues, he would give between eight and ten major addresses per year, most of them at colleges and universities, where he strove to stay in touch with newly emerging readerships. Therefore, after inviting the readers of *Timequake* to call him Junior, he starts out with a story about what he says in speeches, rehearsing the audience interaction. It does help when people hear him speak first, and beginning with page one of *Timequake,* that happens.

"I say in speeches that a plausible mission of artists is to make people appreciate being alive at least a little bit" (*T,* 1), he begins in the same first chapter that will offer much evidence that life is a "crock of shit" (3). He continues, "I am then asked if I know of any artists who pulled that off. I reply, 'The Beatles did.'" Within a paragraph Mark Twain comes up as well, bracketing the range of Vonnegut's appeal: from the vernacular side of serious American literature to the great cultural contribution made by those popular musical innovators of the 1960s, the era when Vonnegut became famous. Such joys as Mark Twain and the Beatles provide are necessary, given all that can be unpleasant. This is a world, after all, in which the Son of God and Savior of humankind is crucified, in which the president who has saved the Union and freed the slaves is assassinated. Perhaps the best one can do is heed the jazz pianist Fats Waller, who when playing at his joyful best would shout, "Somebody shoot me while I'm happy!" (2).

This shooting quote appears in a generally negative context, one characterized by the author's father, who when old, tired, and defeated was found by the police to be driving on a license twenty years expired. "So shoot me," Kurt Sr. tells the arresting officer—which is funnier than the depressing things his son says here about a crucified Christ, an assassinated Lincoln, and Henry David Thoreau's world of men leading lives of quiet desperation. But *Timequake* is a book of rebounding associations, and through it runs a motif of references not to shooting but to happiness. The example comes from another of Vonnegut's speeches, this one to students at Butler University in his hometown of Indianapolis, where he says he would be happy to be born and grow up all over again at 4365 North Illinois Street (where his father invited the police to shoot him):

> My Uncle Alex Vonnegut, a Harvard-educated life-insurance salesman, who lived at 5033 North Pennsylvania Street, taught me something very important. He said that when things were really going well we should be sure to notice it.
>
> He was talking about simple occasions, not great victories: maybe drinking lemonade on a hot afternoon in the shade, or smelling the aroma of a nearby bakery, or fishing and not caring if we catch anything or not, or hearing somebody all alone playing a piano really well in the house next door.
>
> Uncle Alex urged me to say this out loud during such epiphanies: "If this isn't nice, what is?" (*T*, 12)

If this isn't nice, what is? Throughout *Timequake* this phrase will be repeated, as if on Uncle Alex's instructions. The many different occasions for which it becomes suitable more than balance the unhappy times that threaten to drag Vonnegut's first chapter down. For all of its prologue that complains of working too late and having lived too long, and for its first chapter given over to negative commentaries on the qualities of life, *Timequake* turns out to be a joyful, even festive book. It is so in part because of Uncle Alex's advice, which his nephew passes on in speeches. Its image of summertime lemonade and lazy days of fishing are pleasant ones, as is the encouragement for the piano player. Fats Waller does not need to be shot. He is just feeling so happy about things that even death would not matter. The key is to recognize these moments and recall them in other, less winsome contexts. What better type of novel for a seventy-four-year-old man to be writing?

As with Billy Pilgrim in *Slaughterhouse-Five,* a flexibility with time helps a lot toward making life bearable. In his prologue the author has his own explanation for time. How can it be that sometimes in this novel it is 2001, other times 2010—then 1996 the first time through its action, then 1996 during the timequake's rerun? "I must be nuts" (*T,* xiv), he allows. But the world he has lived in is hardly saner or better organized. Take his graduate school alma mater, the University of Chicago. In a moment of sanity it drops intercollegiate football—and then uses the empty stadium to develop the atomic bomb. Take Andrei Sakharov, the leading Soviet dissident and opponent of nuclear testing—only because he has already successfully tested his own bomb. And what a family life he must have had, married to a pediatrician. "What sort of person could perfect a hydrogen bomb while married to a childcare specialist?" (5), Vonnegut asks. "What sort of physician would stay with a mate that cracked?" He tries to imagine their dinner table small-talk:

"Anything interesting happen at work today, Honeybunch?"
"Yes. My bomb is going to work just great. And how are you doing with that kid with chickenpox?"

Of course the author finds himself in contradictory situations too, including the one where he is expected to deliver Sakharov's message to an audience at Staten Island College, where the scientist has been awarded an honorary doctorate. The message: "Don't give up on nuclear energy" (6). The way Kurt Vonnegut manages to convey this thought? "I spoke it like a robot."

Timequake proceeds in the manner of Vonnegut's public speaking. Not that novelistic form yields to that of a conventional lecture, for this man's way of giving an address is just as innovative as anything he has done in fiction. For twenty years he has used the same title, "How to Get a Job like Mine," as an umbrella for any number of topics shuffled through from year to year, audience to audience, and even from moment to moment during the occasion. He comes to the podium with a loose-leaf binder, and after some opening banter—about the weather, the seasons, or rules for public speaking (which he breaks)—he will flip to one section or another depending on his mood and the audience's. In constructing his autobiography of a novel Vonnegut is sensitive to both himself and his readers. In the prologue, for example, he feels old and tired, and shows it in his complaints. This sense of fatigue carries over into chapter 1, in which the prospect of a long, hard haul with this work puts him in a mood as negative as can be found anywhere in his work. He mentions how Mark Twain never wished even the people nearest and dearest to him to be returned from death, and how Kurt Vonnegut Sr. felt poorly enough about life as not to mind being put out of it. He quotes Fats Waller's exuberant desire to be shot while he was happy but moves at once to cases when shootings are not comical references: those of Abraham Lincoln, John Lennon, and Martin Luther King Jr. Though he does not say it, Vonnegut uses his alter ego to draw a point from all this depressing material, that "being alive is a crock of shit" (*T,* 3).

Can readers be expected to put up with another two hundred pages of this? Of course not. Like judging the mood of his audience from the platform, the author senses the likely dismay and shifts gears. In chapter 2 he and his readers have some fun with the contradictions so evident in the worlds of nuclear armaments, from the University of Chicago's development of the first atomic bomb to Andrei Sakharov's ambivalent position on the matter. Lest these truths be too depressing, Vonnegut tells of one gratifying aspect of the Chernobyl disaster: how firefighters from Schenectady, New York, paid tribute to their colleagues from that Russian city who risked their lives to help save persons and property. Here the author finds something to be happy about. He exclaims, "Hooray for firemen! Scum of the earth as some may be in their daily lives, they can all be saints in emergencies. Hooray for firemen" (*T,* 6). It was in Alplaus, New York, a suburb of Schenectady, that Kurt Vonnegut was a volunteer fireman; his badge number, 155, is included in the author's biographical note to *God Bless You, Mr. Rosewater.*

Timequake continues like the loose-leaf notebook flipped through for a typical Vonnegut speech. Chapter 3 breaks away to summarize a Kilgore Trout story about a third atom bomb not dropped at the end of World War II—not dropped because the pilot guesses his mother would not want him to do it. Why should Paul Tibbets's mother, known to the world by her name placed on his plane, the Enola Gay, have wanted him to drop the first one? As readers ponder this implication, Vonnegut turns another page to begin chapter 4, with nothing about nuclear warfare but instead the charming story of his Uncle Alex's encouragement to acknowledge times of simple happiness.

A rhythm is thus established, alternating between unpleasant and pleasant aspects of life, through which the author moves with loose-leaf binder materials for the makings of a novel. Not until the end of chapter 8 and the start of chapter 9, which is one-sixth of his way into the book, does Vonnegut give a clue to the timequake story's setting or action. The event will be reported from the American Academy of Arts and Letters, "way-the-hell-and-gone up on West 155th Street in Manhattan, two doors west of Broadway" (*T,* 29), another phrase repeated throughout the novel, helping hold it together. It has indeed taken some time to get there, because Vonnegut, good speaker and writer that he is, wants to make his audience and readers comfortably familiar with how this institution figures in his own life and in this country's culture. Working up to this information is the author's story of being charmed by performances of great modern American drama, followed by Kilgore Trout's tale of how television has destroyed the appreciation of these arts that Vonnegut's generation found so nourishing. The academy, suitably enough, was founded by a late-nineteenth-century fortune and had its building designed in the full glory of neoclassic architecture. Today, with equal appropriateness, its location has become a dangerous slum. As befits the autobiography of a novel, readers thus learn of the author's relation to the academy and of its thematic import before the narrative action in which it plays a part commences. It is first mentioned on page 29, when Kilgore Trout takes the manuscript of his TV-versus-the-arts story and drops it into a trash receptacle outside the academy's door. In the meantime Vonnegut has flashed forward to the clambake in 2001 that celebrates the book's ending, where Trout is an honored guest. Here he tells another story, rewriting the Book of Genesis, part of which involves Satan's invention of alcohol, which Vonnegut then associates with writers, some of them members of the American Academy of Arts and Letters. Before the timequake happens, focused on the lives of the academy as it is, readers know all about Kurt Vonnegut's relation to the arts and how he feels that the benefits of these cultural activities are being lost among the deteriorating conditions of current life.

Much is made of the academy's "acculturation," a term the author uses several times to describe the obsolescence of things such as his mother's fancy manners and his generation's love of the arts. He makes its neighborhood even worse than it is, in the process turning Columbia University, many blocks south, into firebombed ruins, all of it a fitting context for a world now dead to such cultural expression:

> To be perfectly frank, the only people who cared what became of the
> Academy were its staff, office workers, cleaning and maintenance people,

and armed guards. Nor were most of them enraptured by old-fashioned art practices. They needed the jobs, no matter how pointless the work might be, and so were reminiscent of people during the Great Depression of the 1930s, who celebrated when they got any kind of work at all.

Trout characterized the sort of work he was able to get back then as "cleaning birdshit out of cuckoo clocks." (*T,* 52)

So described, the academy is the perfect repository for the fiction of Kilgore Trout. He writes these stories next door, at the former Museum of the American Indian that is now a shelter for homeless men like himself. He throws them into the trash can outside the academy, where "Fuck Art" has been spray-painted across the door—camouflaging by the executive director, in fact, to make the building look unoccupied, but a sentiment that Trout shares. A guard, Dudley Prince, fishes them out and brings them in, sure that they are important messages—as they are. Vonnegut's novels could not exist without the riches they provide as an imaginary yet easily accessible library, and he grants Trout the privilege of knowing how good they are. That the world does not agree is no matter; like Vincent Van Gogh, who knew he was doing great work while being unable to sell a painting, they astonish their author with their importance. As nothing more than that matters, he is pleased to throw them away the minute they are finished being written.

What Kilgore Trout accomplishes is to stock the American Academy of Arts and Letters with a literature sufficient to explain the current social malaise, for which the notion of a timequake is metaphor. Lines from these stories pepper the novel, such as Hitler's last words, "I never asked to be born in the first place" (*T,* 71), which Vonnegut can put in the mouths of everyone from a released convict who writes him for advice ("Join a church") to his orphaned nephews (whom Kurt adopts, a second way of providing the benefits of an extended family). Like Trout's stories in earlier novels, they amplify Vonnegut's concerns without the author having to be his own raisonneur. Plus, Trout appears as a character himself, helping tie his ideas into the physical narrative just as he does in *God Bless You, Mr. Rosewater, Slaughterhouse-Five,* and *Breakfast of Champions.*

This stock of notions puts the lie to *Timequake* being essentially about the actual timequake. The event, which Trout characterizes as the universe's momentary loss of confidence and crisis of self-doubt (should it keep on expanding?), is important as a device for getting Trout's material inside the academy. By being read there, by the artistically disinterested staff, it becomes available in turn to *Timequake*'s readers. As far as any well-developed themes, the timequake's effect is rather simple. Mechanically, its plot twist involves what happens to many people afterward. Having lived on automatic pilot (Trout's descriptive phrase for it) so many years, during which they could exercise no free will but simply be carried along by the necessity of time's rerun, the moment this ten-year span completes its recycling, people are left hanging by their recently restored volition, something they have not been able to use in a decade. Many of those standing atop descending escalators forget to hold on. Drivers neglect to steer their cars, which for ten years have steered themselves. Planes fall from the sky.

Through all of it Kilgore Trout simply writes on, finishing the story he had begun long before. How was it that he is one of the few people for whom the transition from timequake to regular existence is seamless? Because as the visionary he is, he has realized that in terms of quality of existence there is little difference between the determinism of life in a timequake and the alternative of trying to get along freely. Take his favorite quote from Shakespeare, a line he claims sums up life completely: "All the world's a stage, and all the men and women merely players" (*T*, 38). Not caring much about what will happen next is a style of apathy equally characteristic of timequakes and times free of such reruns. As for the day-to-day humiliation that life produces, something Trout describes as having one's ass pulled through one knothole after another, how different is this from living in a timequake? "I didn't need a timequake to teach me being alive was a crock of shit," he says. "I already knew that from my childhood and crucifixes and history books" (93).

The relativity that a timequake provides is even more important for the way Kurt Vonnegut constructs his autobiography of a novel. One of the book's constant points of reference, along with motifs, catchphrases, and echoes of Trout's fictions, is the author's habit of dating his manuscript pages. "More news of this day, halfway through the rerun, as another autumn draws near" (*T*, 128), he writes; his brother has come down with cancer. The dimensionality of this single reference (and there are several of them scattered throughout the novel) is complex. For the reader, it is one more reminder that he or she is participating in a timequake, perusing Vonnegut's experience in assembling the work many years before. "Listen: Only three weeks ago at this writing, on September 6th, 1996" (147)— comments like this allow the reader to experience the author's efforts as a rerun, happening again and again at whatever point in the ongoing history of the world they are read. By the end of its run on the *New York Times* best-seller list, the book had surely prompted over 150,000 individual timequakes, every one of them as valid as the process Vonnegut describes.

But there is another dimension to such time pegs, as journalists call them. On page 128 readers learn that Bernard Vonnegut has been stricken with cancer. Then on pages 142–45 they are informed that late in life—but before learning of his fatal illness—the same man had taken up a form of abstract expressionist art, amusing himself with the accidental nature of creativity. By the time readers finish the book they will learn that "My big and only brother Bernard, a widower for over twenty-five years, died after prolonged bouts with cancers, without excruciating pain, on the morning of April 25th, 1997, at the age of eighty-two, now two days ago" (*T,* 215). Bernard Vonnegut, dead and alive, is thus integrated with the evolution of *Timequake*—stricken on page 128, still in clean health on pages 142–45, and then dead from the disease on page 215, just five pages from the novel's end—but not before a practical joke the brothers shared way back in 1947 can be rehearsed with great joy. And so an ever-vital biography of Kurt Vonnegut's brother can be fabricated at the same time the novel is taking shape.

The story of Bernard's late-life action painting turns out to be metafictively fabulous, telling how Kurt has chosen to write this book. The narrative concerns art, a common topic to most of *Timequake*'s chapters. Here it involves an earlier reference to Kurt Sr.'s easy praise for his daughter Alice's creative efforts, making her feel patronized, "lavishly praised for very little effort because she was a pretty girl" (*T,* 86). Bernard may be seeking praise from his brother when he sends along examples of his own new art; but in his wisdom Kurt Jr. does not give it. He advises, "If you really want to know whether your pictures are, as you say, 'art or not,' you must display them in a public space somewhere, and see if strangers like to look at them. That is the way the game is played. Let me know what happens" (144).

There is more to it. Audiences for art can rarely respond to such work without knowing at least something about the maker. Even the cave painters of Lascaux, France, have an identity of sorts. A painting, after all, like any creative work, including a novel, is a conversation between two human beings, and it helps to know the kind of person on the other side of this dialogue. As he writes Bernard:

"I dare to suggest that no picture can attract serious attention without a particular sort of human being being attached to it in the viewer's mind. If you are unwilling to claim credit for your pictures, and to say why you hoped others might find them worth examining, there goes the ball game.

"Pictures are famous for their humanness, not for their pictureness."

I went on: "There is also the matter of craftsmanship. Real picture-lovers like to play along, so to speak, to look closely at the surfaces, to see how the illusion was created. If you are unwilling to say how you made your pictures, there goes the ball game a second time." (*T*, 145)

In writing *Timequake,* Kurt Vonnegut follows his own artistic advice. Never more than a few pages of narrative action can elapse without the author stepping in to reveal something about himself. To those experienced in the Vonnegut canon, the effect is appealing because they have heard many of these things before, from his essays, interviews, and autobiographical prefaces to the novels. The familiarity of these references makes it more comfortable for readers to make their way through the new novel, for a hand they trust is guiding them. *Timequake* seems most alive, to be the autobiography of a novel, because readers see the author constructing it, coming alive in a timequake-inspired rerun of the creative action. Again, this timequake is produced by the act of reading. Here is the sense of "playing along" that the author recommends to his brother for the success of his art.

The stories about himself that Vonnegut puts into *Timequake* are both appealing and revealing. There is much, as veteran readers might expect, about his upbringing in Indianapolis and his father, mother, brother, sister, Uncle Alex, and other relatives. Because Bernard is diagnosed with cancer during the novel's writing, that event is put in; when he dies after the typescript has been completed, an epilogue becomes not only necessary but also fitting. One of the cultural treasures Vonnegut has celebrated in this book is jazz. His own test as a fiction writer is to improvise with what he has; and so when life throws him something new (in this case Bernard's demise), he goes with it, just as a master of jazz will add a new development to his improvised solo if another band member tosses in a provocation.

Throughout the book he has talked about his wives, past and present. There are several references in the narrative, spread about here and there like the catchphrases and various motifs—indeed, it is the function of these phrases and motifs to knit the otherwise disparate references together. Sometimes Jane Cox, Kurt's first wife, is seen as a new bride, giving up her fellowship in Russian at the University of Chicago because she is pregnant with their first child, Mark (who is mentioned several different times—as a child, as an author, and as a physician). Other times the portraits are of her prep school days and college work at Swarthmore. Sometimes she is married to Kurt, other times divorced. Her pet phrase, "I can't wait," becomes one of the novel's many verbal motifs. Like Bernard Vonnegut, she dies—before her husband has begun writing *Timequake,* and thus immune to its rerunning. The stability of this occasion lets Vonnegut give it a chapter, with plenty of time for the author to set the stage for her death. By then (1986) she had married Adam Yarmolinsky, and contact with her previous husband was mostly by phone. Kurt recalls, "The last conversation we had, we two old friends from Indianapolis, was two weeks before she died. It was on the telephone. She was in Washington, D.C., where the Yarmolinskys had their home. I was in Manhattan, and married, as I still am, to the photographer and writer Jill Krementz" (*T,* 116).

Their conversation thus includes elements of two entire lifetimes, started together as schoolchildren back home in Indiana, encompassing a marriage and the raising of six children, a present that incorporates shared interests in the adult lives of these children (their diverse occupations are listed), and a future that involves Kurt continuing in marriage with Jill Krementz in New York while Jane faces death as another man's wife in the nation's capital. These are twelve different worlds, all brought together in a brief phone call. Why is Kurt Vonnegut still involved in them? When Jane asks him, as if he would know, what would determine the exact minute of her death, he is not surprised. For many years he had made all the decisions, determined all the directions, from Indianapolis to Chicago and from there to Schenectady and Cape Cod. She is dying of cancer, with doctors telling her she has approximately so much more time to live. She has used both conventional and alternative medicine to extend her life, submitting to procedures their son Mark (the doctor) said he would never accept himself. Given the cancer and all this intervention, *something* will determine when her time comes. And so she asks. Kurt answers:

> I told her on the phone that a sunburned, raffish, bored but not un-
> happy ten-year-old boy, whom we did not know, would be standing
> on the gravel slope of the boat-launching ramp at the foot of Scudder's

Lane. He would gaze out at nothing in particular, birds, boats, or whatever, in the harbor of Barnstable, Cape Cod.

At the head of Scudder's Lane, on Route 6A, one-tenth of a mile from the boat-launching ramp, is the big old house where we cared for our son and two daughters and three sons of my sister's until they were grownups. Our daughter Edith and her builder husband, John Squibb, and their small sons, Will and Buck, live there now.

I told Jane that this boy, with nothing better to do, would pick up a stone, as boys will. He would arc it over the harbor. When the stone hit the water, she would die. (*T,* 116–17).

Jane believed this, her ex-husband says, because she was forever going along with any type of white magic that made life seem more alive. As her death approaches, he does this for her.

On a more modest level he is able to transform time and space for someone else, thanks to a totally coincidental meeting. Throughout the book Vonnegut has talked about his printmaking with Joe Petro III ("named like a World War"), and at one point in the novel, "Only three weeks ago at this writing, on September 6th, 1996," he and Petro open a show in Denver, Colorado (*T,* 147). To commemorate the event a local microbrewery produces a special beer, "Kurt's Mile-High Malt," using coffee, the secret ingredient of the author's maternal grandfather's prize-winning lager. That in itself is a timequake of sorts, but a much better one transpires from the occasion. The microbrewer is John Hickenlooper, son of Kurt's fraternity brother more than half a century before. Vonnegut confides, "My fraternity brother had died when his son was only seven. I knew more about him than his own son did!" (148). He is able to create a living picture that Hickenlooper has never seen, full of the joys of college life during those years before World War II. "Happy days!" Kurt calls them, adding, "We thought we'd live forever."

The elder Hickenlooper lives again in this portrait drawn for his son, just as Jane comes alive in the story Vonnegut tells about her approaching death. In each case the normal constraints of time are undone, so that something better may happen with the materials. Only after stories like these have familiarized the reader with the kind of person Kurt Vonnegut is does he reveal the climax of his original timequake novel. From the prologue readers remember that the author was convinced from his reading of *The Old Man and the Sea* not to make the mistake Hemingway's fisherman did, leaving the best parts for the sharks. Instead, Vonnegut has said he will fillet out what should be saved, in the process creating an autobiography of the work by detailing what is happening to him as it is rewritten.

The climax to the timequake's action is simple, but it is also remarkable for the role it grants Kilgore Trout. Even more so than his parting comments in *God Bless You, Mr. Rosewater* and *Slaughterhouse-Five,* and certainly more successfully than his plea at the end of *Breakfast of Champions* (that the author make him young), Trout becomes a national hero by restoring order. And more: the sense of order that he restores is better than the one it replaces. The scene in which it happens is clear and direct. In the mayhem and destruction caused by newly freed people not knowing how to handle life in post-timequake conditions, he encourages people not to reclaim their willfulness but rather to heed this advice. He tells them, "You've been very sick! Now you're well again" (*T,* 155). Just as crucially, he urges them to action because there is important work to be done.

The effect of Trout's encouragement is much greater than just getting folks out of the immediate post-timequake period. True, their ability to direct their lives has atrophied during the ten years of time's rerun. But the sci-fi writer has already noted that he has never seen much difference between this and the apathetic way too many people let their lives slip from determination to determination, never caring enough to even try for control. Trout's appraisal of contemporary culture is only slightly more pessimistic than Vonnegut's; as always, it is the alter ego who writes the truely bizarre stories and speaks the most damning lines. But in *Timequake,* as in the earlier novels in which he plays roles, Kilgore Trout speaks up with a solution as well. *You've been very sick, but now you are well again. There is important work to do*—he has adopted this formulation because a simple call to free will has not worked. Indeed, characters in the novel reject it, just as Tralfamadorians teach Billy Pilgrim to do in *Slaughterhouse-Five.* The reformulation allows people to take action without accepting the full responsibility of free will, which in a world of many existing determinations they should not have to do. They are not being called on to account for the nature of the world. All they are being asked is to do something to make an immediate situation better.

One of the catchphrases repeated several times throughout *Timequake* comes from Kurt's son Mark Vonnegut, M.D., a pediatrician but before that the author of a book about his schizophrenic breakdown and recovery, *The Eden Express* (1975). Mark's advice is that whatever life may be, we are all in it together and should be helping each other through it. Kilgore Trout's call to action is what puts Mark Vonnegut's program in order.

In the novel's plot, that program continues under Trout's direction, with such a better life for all that the man becomes nationally honored. In the autobiography of a novel that is *Timequake's* larger dimension, the parts that show Kurt Vonnegut not only metafictively revising the manuscript but also going about day-to-day living, revealing many things about himself, Mark's program and Trout's implementation of it are echoed in the many sentiments the author finds it normal to express. We have heard his lamentations of how television has destroyed so much appreciation of the arts, how the magic of such plays as *Death of a Salesman, A Streetcar Named Desire,* and *Our Town* may be lost on younger audiences. To rekindle the magic for an audience made passive by TV he writes *Timequake,* personalizing the aesthetic as he does in his successful speeches. Plus there are his commentaries on current events and the state of society, which allow him to repeat his son's advice: "For Christ's sake, let's help more of our frightened people get through this thing, whatever it is" (*T,* 163).

Have figures in life ever done that? And have the arts ever captured their process of doing it? Another key point in *Timequake's* narrative action shows how. The climax to the timequake has been Trout's shining moment in the ruins of the American Academy of Arts and Letters, calling people to action in a way that transforms the entire country. The denouement takes place a bit later, in another part rescued from the shredded carcass of Vonnegut's original novel. The occasion is a performance of Robert E. Sherwood's *Abe Lincoln in Illinois* by an amateur theatrical group whose leading actor happens to be (as part of the novel's original plot) the only living (if illegitimate) descendant of John Wilkes Booth (timequake!). The cast party after this performance turns out to be a celebration of the new novel's end, a clambake on the beach to which Vonnegut has invited any number of friends from real life. Kilgore Trout is there, being honored for his service to America and given the job of sound-effects man for the play.

Trout's role is not coincidental. Vonnegut puts him there to underscore important lines in the play, spoken by Lincoln just before the key sound effects are to happen. Sherwood's play is shown in one of those magical moments of drama that have moved Vonnegut earlier in the book, and in *Timequake* he rehearses it so that his readers may share the effect. The part Vonnegut features is Lincoln's address to his fellow citizens in Springfield, Illinois, where he is leaving to assume the presidency. It is more than a lofty office for the job involves leading a country that has fulfilled the ancient dream of shaking off chains and finding freedom "in the brotherhood of life" (*T*, 202). Now, in February 1861, that democratic order is threatening to come apart: "We gained democracy, and now there is the question of whether it is fit to survive." A literal man of the moment, Lincoln ponders the implications:

Perhaps we have come to this dreadful day of awakening, and the dream is ended. If so, I am afraid it must be ended forever. I cannot believe that ever again will men have the opportunity we have had. Perhaps we should admit that, and concede that our ideals of liberty and equality are decadent and doomed. I have heard of an eastern monarch who once charged his wise men to invent him a sentence which would be true and appropriate in all times and situations. They presented him with the words, "And this too shall pass away."

That is a comforting thought in time of affliction—"And this too shall pass away." And yet—let us believe that it is not true! Let us live to prove that we can cultivate the natural world that is about us, and the intellectual and moral world that is within us, so that we may secure an individual, social and political prosperity, whose course shall be forward, and which, while the earth endures, shall not pass away. . . .

I commend you to the care of the Almighty, as I hope that in your prayers you will remember me. . . . Good-bye, my friends and neighbors. (202)

It truly is a magnificent moment in history, one that the playwright and actor make magical in drama. Leaving his home of a quarter century, to which he knows he may never be able to return, Lincoln sets out to do the important work that needs to be done. Offstage, Kilgore Trout does his part as the sound-effects technician, blowing the train whistle that signals Lincoln's departure into the great future that will see him free the slaves and save the Union, at the cost of his own life. That is history, and this has been the drama of it. But for his autobiography of a novel Kurt Vonnegut adds one more note. Throughout he has been attentive to unplanned offstage sounds, and here is another of them: "As the curtain descended, there was a sob backstage. It wasn't in the playbook. It was ad lib. It was about beauty. It came from Kilgore Trout" (203).

Trout, of course, is the toughest audience possible for the Vonnegut effect, yet he cooperates and even adds to it. In the novel's action he performs a hero's role, much like Lincoln's. As the narrative of the timequake's end puts it, "On the afternoon of February 13, 2001, alone, and then during the next two weeks, Kilgore's Creed did as much to save life on Earth as Einstein's *E equals mc squared* had done to end it two generations earlier" (*T,* 170). Now, in the action's aftermath that celebrates the book's completion, Trout gives another lesson, this one slanted not to daily survival but to philosophical integrity. On the starlit beach where the festive clambake has taken place, where many people important to Kurt Vonnegut's life have gathered, the shabby old science-fiction writer gives the author some personal instruction. Looking at the stars, it is indeed possible to feel insignificant. Even such forces as time and light are diminished in such circumstances, demonstrable when one picks a star, then a second one, and realizes that for light to pass from one to the other many thousands or millions of years must elapse. Such is the immensity of the universe, an immensity that might well make a single human being feel like nothing much at all.

But look what that human being can do. Trout asks the author how long it has taken his eye to pass from one star to the other. A second, perhaps. "Even if you'd taken an hour," Trout says, "something would have passed between where those two heavenly bodies used to be, at, conservatively speaking, a million times the speed of light" (*T,* 213). And what is that, Vonnegut asks. "Your awareness," Trout replies. "That is a new quality in the Universe, which exists only because there are human beings." It is just as much a physical reality as anything scientists account for, but it is as yet something they have been hesitant to define. Why so? Because it is more than human awareness. For want of a better word, Trout calls it "*soul*" (214).

As the autobiography of a novel *Timequake* uniquely privileges both author and text. It stands as the record of Kurt Vonnegut's awareness as he spends about a year reconstructing the draft of a novel. In telling much not only about his writing but also about all the other affective things happening to him, he sets the stage for the Vonnegut effect, just as the writers he has admired contrive the magic that accompanies the lines that have moved him—examples are "Attention must be paid," "I have always depended on the kindness of strangers," and the words from Thornton Wilder's *Our Town* that he sees and hears his adopted daughter Lilly speak as a thirteen-year-old actress. In the process—*as the process,* in fact—readers have encountered him comforting his dying wife, Jane; reacting to the death of his brother, Bernard; and simply filling half an hour of an average day in his Manhattan neighborhood buying an envelope and mailing a letter —all because he does not work by computer, which gives him a marvelously enjoyable chance to relax in his community. The text he produces is equally alive. Its author has his metafictive moments but never at the expense of becoming an abstract creator; there is always a very real man at work here. His novel is much like him, as one would suppose it should be but which conventions of fiction too often disguise. Nothing about life is falsified or idealized—between Vonnegut and Trout, some pretty damaging evidence is presented. But like the Beatles, Kurt Vonnegut succeeds at making people feel better about it. Like his son the medical doctor, he has helped his fellow human beings get through this thing, whatever it is.

Is *Timequake,* then, the author's autobiography? Only to the extent that it focuses on those parts of his life when he is writing it. And the sharpest point of that focus is the narrative action of the timequake itself, concise as it is—what could make for a more distinct profile? The materials about Kurt Vonnegut writing it are softer material, but the effect is always to draw the reader's attention back to the novel at hand, the vehicle by which he is not only expressing himself to the world but also living in it at the moment. If he were not rewriting a major novel at the time, the book would not be an autobiography of that work but simply of the author. *Fates Worth Than Death: An Autobiographical Collage,* published in 1991, is what *Timequake* might be like without the timequake—and without Kurt Vonnegut writing a novel about it. It is about the same length and draws a similar portrait of the author. As such, it resembles the soft materials of *Timequake;* the hardness comes not with a developing novel but in the public issues being addressed. Some of them are immediately life-or-death problems, such as the revolution taking place in Mozambique, where Vonnegut visits on behalf of a charity trying to save lives in the middle of it. By writing an article for *Parade* magazine, a Sunday newspaper supplement read by tens of millions, he will draw attention to the plight and encourage its relief. A laughable ideal? Perhaps so. "The photograph at the head of this chapter shows me in action in Mozambique, demonstrating muscular Christianity in an outfit that might have been designed by Ralph Lauren" (*F,* 175), the author mocks. "The aborigines didn't know whether to shit or go blind until I showed up. And I fixed everything." A cruel joke? Only at himself. Readers of *Wampeters, Foma & Granfalloons* will remember the author's similar trip to an embattled Biafra, where another genocide was taking place—and how laughter was his response only to misery he could not do anything about. In truth, the Biafra piece did much to focus attention on these people's plight, and even more so on the general human need for supportive communities in the matter of the Ibos' huge extended families. In *Timequake,* when his own focus is on writing the novel, Vonnegut can still draw on his Biafra experience of a quarter century before to remake this point, helpful as it is to the autobiography of his novel at hand.

Other parts of *Fates Worse Than Death* recall the stories in *Timequake* that Vonnegut tells about himself to let readers know the kind of person he is, the type of human being with whom they are engaging in a creative conversation. The best of these is his essay about the Vonnegut family's group of summer cottages on Lake Maxincuckee, ninety miles north of Indianapolis. "No matter where I am, and even if I have no clear idea of where I am, and no matter how much trouble I may be in," he writes, "I can achieve a blank and shining serenity if only I can reach the edge of a natural body of water. The very edge of anything from a rivulet to an ocean says to me: 'Now you know where you are. Now you know which way to go. You will soon be home now'" (*F,* 49). The rhythms are the same as in Kilgore Trout's creed from *Timequake,* "You were sick, but now you're well again, and there's work to do" (*T,* 200). Each absolves the listener of any terrible responsibilities: of free will, synoptic knowledge, or analytical skill. In Vonnegut's case Lake Maxincuckee is three miles long and two and a half miles wide. As a youngster he could be left to wander freely along its shore since he could not get lost—just keep going straight and he would wind up safe at home. Can there be a better metaphor for human security? As the author would propose in *Galápagos* and elsewhere, people seem happiest when asked to be no more than great apes, performing simple, repetitive tasks and finding reward in that. Yet from *Breakfast of Champions, Bluebeard,* and *Timequake* we know that he also treasures the difference between humankind and their simian ancestors: the sense of awareness, the quality that in this last work Kilgore Trout is so bold as to call "soul." Vonnegut's essay on the lake starts with the secure ease of repetitive action and builds up to a nostalgic yet convincing portrait of childhood that he finds it important to share. "I ask the reader of this piece, my indispensable collaborator," he adds, reflecting the theory of artistic engagement he has urged his brother to heed in *Timequake:* "Isn't your deepest understanding of time and space and, for that matter, destiny shaped like mine by your earliest experiences with geography, by the rules you learned about how to get home again? What is it that can make you feel, no matter how mistakenly, that you are on the right track, that you will soon be safe and sound at home again?" (*F,* 50).

Much wisdom like this appears in *Timequake.* What does it have to do with the autobiography of a novel? One must remember Jorge Luis Borges's demonstration that if *Don Quixote* were rewritten in the twentieth century in a word-by-word facsimile of the original, it would be a completely new work thanks to the different historical, philosophical, and cultural context in which it reappeared. Thus if Vonnegut had used the occasion of *Timequake* to reproduce his original draft, word for word, it would still be different. It is known that he had been loath to write it in the first place—feeling in old age like Melville's ancient whaling captains who said nothing anymore because they had already said everything. To continue speaking (or writing) is just as great a challenge as that faced in *Slaughterhouse-Five* when he knew that there was nothing intelligent about a massacre. Thus he takes one draft of *Timequake,* with which he feels uncomfortable, and rewrites it: like Hemingway's fisherman should have done, saving the good parts, not to rewrite them but to put them in a new Borgesian context, that of the novel's autobiography. In this latter state it can accommodate the full context of its creation, which is the story of Kurt Vonnegut's life writing it. Hence it becomes a work of much larger dimensions.

At the novel's end the author lets his work find closure by showing how any kind of art can add to life. Throughout *Timequake* there have been examples of human futility and reasons for despair. All is refuted, however, when it is shown how human comprehension, surpassing the speed of light and spanning distances beyond physical measure, provides an ability beyond reason to comprehend the world. Such capability lets people communicate when other methods fail, lets them make something worthwhile of what would otherwise lack redeeming worth. It allows them, in other words, to be artists, a talent even the most insidious forces of modern life cannot kill off. Although both Kilgore Trout and the author's father are fond of quoting Shakespeare, here in *Timequake,* and elsewhere in the author's canon, the novel ends with no mention of the obvious analogue for what Kurt Vonnegut conveys: the magic and also the instructive wisdom of Prospero in *The Tempest.* One thinks of that character's epilogue, which voices many of Vonnegut's own complaints from this work but which also begs the reader's assistance in giving gentle breath to his sails, "or else my project fails." By the end of *Timequake* the author's readers know his faults but also his attributes, especially those he has grown into with advancing age, an important aspect shared throughout this novel. Each has been important in creating the work as shared with his readers. As they are pardoned, so is he.

CONCLUSION

Vonnegut in Fiction

KURT VONNEGUT'S PLACE in literary history has been assured since 1969, when not only did *Slaughterhouse-Five* become a best-seller but also his college underground reputation of the previous decade blossomed into a full-fledged canonical presence. Similar reputations had been built by Joseph Heller's *Catch-22* (1961) and Ken Kesey's *One Flew Over the Cuckoo's Nest* (1962)—neither making much impression at first publication but both becoming paperback bibles of the emerging cultural and sociopolitical transformation known as the American 1960s. It was to this countercultural readership that paperback editions of *Cat's Cradle* and *The Sirens of Titan* appealed. When Vonnegut happened to come along with a new novel in 1969 that summed up many of his previous themes and techniques, he and the times were in precisely the right place for maximum cultural impact. Like Heller's and Kesey's novels, *Slaughterhouse-Five* could talk about classic midcentury events (World War II, the power of the institution) in a peculiarly contemporary way—compared to them, Norman Mailer's *The Naked and the Dead* (1948) shows its age, even though Vonnegut, Heller, and Mailer were born within nine months of one another. But Vonnegut had an advantage over Heller and Kesey as well. Unlike them, he had a string of previously published works ready to be reissued, every one of them seeming to speak to current times, even though the first, *Player Piano,* dated from 1952.

Just as the 1960s came to a close, America had found a prolific author to represent this exciting era. That Kurt Vonnegut was old enough to be most of his readers' father was not a distraction but rather a benefit. The new times were challenging and somewhat intimidating, to participants in the counterculture as well as to observers. Here was someone from the older generation who could be trusted by both sides, who could put apparently destabilizing recent events in a more reassuring context. He had seen the Great Depression and World War II, after all, and been a bemused commentator on the establishment of middle-class postwar life. He championed the social changes of this new era, but he could also see them in perspective. One of his favorite lines in interviews and essays was that he had learned all of his presumed radicalism in high school civics classes taught with the full approval of the board of education in Indianapolis, Indiana, in the heart of the country during the 1930s.

Slaughterhouse-Five and Vonnegut's five earlier novels thus joined *Catch-22* and *One Flew Over the Cuckoo's Nest* in articulating the sensibility of countercultural revolt. The messages of all three are firmly antiwar, anti-institution, and antiestablishment, and their manner of expressing these themes is appealingly vernacular. Heller's parody of military language and corporate talk is hilarious; Kesey's use of Chief Broom as his narrator, caught psychologically within the action yet striving to rise above it, is compelling in its manner of direct address; and Vonnegut, telling readers that "All this happened, more or less," shares the trust of readers already pledged to the honesties of Kesey and Heller. This tone of personal speech, honest and frank and unstylized, stands in contrast to the manneristic prose of John Updike, the moral probity of Saul Bellow and James Baldwin, and the psychological slant to the fiction of Joyce Carol Oates. For a sense of personal voice there were the rhythms and tonal shadings in the works of Bernard Malamud and Grace Paley. But each of these spoke in the vernacular of a time and place no less regional than Walker Percy's South or Edward Abbey's West. Only in Heller, Kesey, and Vonnegut did one find the voice of a new generation, controlled for artistic effect by authors as much as half a generation older but coming into their own with this new sensibility.

With the success of *Slaughterhouse-Five*, Vonnegut was embraced by a second identifiable readership: that of the newly emergent innovative fiction. Some of it, most notably by Thomas Pynchon, would make the bestseller list, but as a rule this style of work was most effective among an academic readership. Vonnegut, of course, would outsell even Pynchon, making him the leading example of this new type of writer who either discarded or radically transformed the conventions of traditional fiction. Close behind him, at least in terms of accessibility to the public, was Donald Barthelme, whose stories in the *New Yorker* stood the style of that venerable magazine on its head. Another occasional strong seller was Jerzy Kosinski; his pseudo-autobiographical novel *The Painted Bird* (1965) broke new ground by containing almost unimaginable horrors from World War II within a deftly controlled prose, while his next fictive work, *Steps* (1968), set a new standard for National Book Award winners with its elliptical sections of narrative presented in almost fragmentary form. "Fragments are the only form I trust," a character says in an early Barthelme story, and the readership for innovative fiction heartily agreed, flocking to *Slaughter-house-Five* as a key example of how the Aristotelian unities and traditional demands for the suspension of disbelief need no longer constrain a novelist reaching out in new directions.

The innovative fiction movement, particularly in its avant-gardist examples, proceeded well beyond the experiments of *Slaughterhouse-Five,* and it is important to understand which of fiction's traditions Kurt Vonnegut was unwilling to leave behind. But by fitting in with the general development of work by authors such as Thomas Pynchon, Donald Barthelme, Jerzy Kosinski, and also William H. Gass, Clarence Major, Ishmael Reed, Kathy Acker, Raymond Federman, and Ronald Sukenick, the author was distinguishing himself from the earlier style of fiction with which he was at first associated, that of black humor. Made famous by Terry Southern, Bruce Jay Friedman, and Stanley Elkin, black humor won its notoriety from theme alone. Its topics and interests were deliberately shocking. But shock effect removed any need for technical innovation. As a revolt against 1950s conformity, its posture was one of rudeness, giving a Bronx cheer to the homely values of the Eisenhower era. As such, black humor looked backward. Kurt Vonnegut's fiction was forward looking, and his argument was never against the values of America in its midcentury stability. Instead he worried about threats to such values, among them institutional power and corporate anonymity. These, he had learned, were best attacked on an artistic basis. It is *how we imagine things* that determines our position toward the world, not whether we wear three-piece suits or barbeque our meals on the patio. While Terry Southern attacked conventional manners, most notably in *Candy* (1958), Vonnegut took on the conventions of fiction—getting to the heart of the matter, addressing not the symptoms of behavior but the causes.

Yet throughout it all Kurt Vonnegut was somewhat old-fashioned, and proud of it. Coming to prominence only in the later 1960s, when his writer's career was already twenty years old, he was linked with novelists born ten years after him; although their novels had similarities, the authors were quite another type of crowd. Barthelme, Kosinski, Pynchon, Sukenick, Reed, and most of the others were born in the Great Depression, but none of them remembered it. Kurt Vonnegut most certainly did, and as an artistically formative experience teaching him how not just economic but also social and cultural values, long assumed to be stable realities, could be transformed almost overnight into an entirely new world. During World War II these other writers were children; true, Jerzy Kosinski suffered its horrors firsthand in Poland, and Thomas Pynchon feasted on its journalism and popular literature, but of this entire innovative fiction cohort only Kurt Vonnegut and Joseph Heller fought in the war, each of them bringing a special perspective to a generation whose own war was in Vietnam. Finally, the typical innovative fictionist of the 1960s was an academic professional. Several had Ph.D.s, and nearly all had been employed since the beginning as professors of creative writing. Vonnegut's educational situation was different. The war had interrupted his undergraduate studies, and his attraction to graduate school was not a careerist move but simply an opportunity offered by the GI Bill. Most important, his training had been in the hard sciences and social sciences, not literature. Leaving graduate school without an M.A. (because his thesis had been rejected) was not an immediate problem since he had never intended to be a professional anthropologist. Studying humankind, he believed, would be helpful for what he wanted to do, which was to develop as a journalist.

It is in this last regard that Vonnegut differs most from other contemporary writers of serious fiction, and it is the way in which he resembles literary figures of an earlier time. Like Mark Twain, Theodore Dreiser, Ernest Hemingway, and any number of others from the middle of the nineteenth century to the first decades of the twentieth, his preparation for being a novelist came from working as a journalist. Kurt Vonnegut may have been destined to be a maker of great literature, but circumstances dictated that he not become so by studying the subject. Although his family was an artistic one, his architect father, humiliated by the collapse of his practice during the Great Depression, insisted that Kurt and his brother, Bernard, study something useful. Hence his majors at Cornell University were biology and chemistry for preparation as a biochemist. For Bernard, nine years older, the father's plan worked, producing a world-famous atmospheric physicist who, among other discoveries, developed the principle of cloud seeding to produce rain. World War II interrupted Kurt's studies; but, as he likes to recall, he was flunking out anyway (a bout with pneumonia during his junior year had put him irrecoverably behind in his class work). Yet by this time the young man already had a profession, with excellent credentials: journalism.

As he had come to fiction from journalism, Vonnegut approached journalism not as an academic subject but as an extracurricular activity. These two factors distinguish his career from those of the innovationists with whom he is stylistically associated. While others would approach writing as work, for Kurt Vonnegut it was fun. The combination of his formal education in the sciences and his avocational love of writing sets him apart from others, especially the increasing number trained by and then working in M.F.A. programs. For these latter people challenges faced by fiction would be theoretical. In Kurt Vonnegut's case they were immediately practical, based not on the study of literature but on participation in daily life. When at the age of forty-three economic circumstances forced him to seek work in such a program, at the University of Iowa Writers' Workshop, he was entranced by the idea that a state institution could be so generous to the arts and also put off by the abstract nature of many of the local projects. Though he loved living in Iowa City and was impressed with the talent of his students, the professional model impressed him as one big pinball game, all effects with little real substance. His teaching career was brief, saved by a contract to write *Slaughterhouse-Five*. Afterward he would teach for short periods at Harvard, the City University of New York, and Smith College—doing his best to coach students but insisting that the ability to write good fiction was a natural talent. It could be refined by practice and instruction but never created from those sources alone. As for successful student writers, Vonnegut encouraged them to get out into the world. Otherwise all they would have to write about would be love and death in the English department.

Kurt Vonnegut's journalism was avocational in inception but thoroughly professional in nature, thanks to the unique character of this activity at the schools he attended. Shortridge High in Indianapolis was one of just two seats of secondary education that boasted a daily student paper. By his senior year Kurt was Tuesday editor and was spending summers writing advertising copy for the *Indianapolis Times*. At Cornell University he worked as a reporter and eventually became managing editor of the *Sun*—a student paper but owned and operated independently of the university. Instead of being subject to the control of faculty advisers and administrative censors, students such as Kurt found themselves publishing what served as Ithaca, New York's morning newspaper, again in a daily format. National and international news was covered, not just school or local issues. And as the author likes to recall, this was a serious era, with the Depression struggling to an end and the pressures of World War II building around him. Putting out the morning daily was serious business.

During his graduate school days in anthropology at the University of Chicago following the war, Vonnegut was once again doing journalism on the side—gritty, nuts-and-bolts writing as a pool reporter for the City News Bureau. He considers this experience important enough to be a scene in the first chapter of *Slaughterhouse-Five*. Soon after this he was working in the public relations department of General Electric's Research Laboratory, hired not as a publicist but as a journalist to improve the bureau's writing and reporting style. From this experience would come *Player Piano* and any number of short stories—some scientific in nature, others focused on the lives of regular people being buffeted by new technologies and corporate concerns. The author would be into middle age and with five novels and two story collections to his name before he would begin learning about love and death in the English department—and then it would be for so briefly as to make little impression on his work.

Yet Vonnegut would become just as much a favorite of the innovative fiction crowd as would Pynchon, Sukenick, or any of the others. Indeed, he would outsell them all and generate more interviews, reviews, and critical essays. The reason is clear and has its roots in his journalism as well as in his practical experience. Some novels of this school are heavily theoretical in nature—most of Ronald Sukenick's work qualifies this way. Others are dauntingly erudite, such as typical works by Thomas Pynchon and William H. Gass. Only one other of the innovative fictionists approaches Vonnegut's richness of everyday life references: Donald Barthelme. Not coincidentally he is the only other member of the group with formative experience in journalism, of a variety quite similar to Kurt's.

Donald Barthelme (1931–89) was nine years Vonnegut's junior, the same age difference that separated Kurt from his older brother, Bernard. Because Don was the son of a famous architect and a "Junior" as well, Vonnegut found an easy and comfortable friendship with him. Though coming from distant regions of the country (Indiana, Texas), each had settled into parts of New York City distinctive for their integral surroundings: Turtle Bay for Vonnegut, a gathering of townhouses in the East 40s, while Barthelme lived in the West Village, on 11th Street between Sixth and Seventh Avenue. As Vonnegut likes to recall, each of them made his neighborhood the focus of his life, a nourishing situation anywhere but particularly so in a great city where invisibility is too often the norm. What made them most similar was not just that in addition to all this each wrote a nonconventional style of fiction appealing to the same readership, but rather that the two of them had also been extremely prolific student journalists and then writers in publicity departments for scientific and educational institutions. Like Kurt, Don was managing editor of his school paper, the University of Houston *Cougar*. He also worked during student years and afterward for the *Houston Post*, writing reviews of films, night club acts, and variety shows. No deeper immersion in the popular culture of America could be imagined—the same popular culture Kurt Vonnegut was contributing to as a writer for the *Saturday Evening Post* and *Collier's* during this same 1950s period. Each experience would give the writer a solid grounding not just in that culture but also in its symbols and signs. Seeing how the culture was indeed an operation of signs was something Vonnegut would perfect in his *Post* stories and Barthelme would adopt, in a more stylishly hip 1960s way, in his own short fiction.

How signs function as a language in the grammar of culture would become known as *semiology*, a form of study being applied to fiction (by the first wave of deconstructionists) just as Vonnegut's and Barthelme's work became well known. Immersion in their culture's signs had taken place with their journalism, but their critical views are probably products of these two writers' experiences in publicity bureaus. Neither was a directly commercial concern. Vonnegut worked not for GE's Products Division (which made everything from toasters to jet engines) but rather for its Research Laboratory, where "Progress Is Our Most Important Product," a slogan he helped demonstrate and which is a classic example of semiology in action. Barthelme, having finished work at the University of Houston (but, like Vonnegut, never graduating thanks to an army call-up, in his case for Korea, where he served as an information specialist), returned to work in its News Bureau. News about a university can consist of football scores, but Barthelme's specialities were the finest activities of the knowledge industry: ideas and aesthetics. As such he became founding editor of the *University of Houston Forum*, a quarterly journal devoted to intellectual commentary and the arts. From this perspective he reviewed the transformation in progress that came to be known as the American 1960s. Writers such as William H. Gass and painters such as Richard Diebenkorn, each of them a leading-edge innovator in his field, placed work in Barthelme's pages. Soon Don was directing the city's Contemporary Arts Museum. This and his *Forum* work brought him to the attention of art critics Harold Rosenberg and Thomas Hess, who invited Barthelme to edit their new journal of art and ideas, *Location*. The magazine only lasted two issues (in 1964), but by then Donald Barthelme was not only settled in New York but was also beginning to publish regularly in the *New Yorker*. Meanwhile a midtown hotel, the Royalton, was a regular stop for Kurt Vonnegut when he came down from Cape Cod, first to meet editors for his stories and then to sell his novels along publishers' row. From different directions the two writers would become famous as pioneers of a new style of unconventional fiction. Their common start in journalism, however, would make their works among the most popular and accessible in this style of literature.

The difference between the *Saturday Evening Post* and the *New Yorker* is largely one of class, augmented by the presumed sophistication that goes with the higher reaches of social distinction. In truth, average Americans have read both magazines quite happily—but with different expectations. The one thing in common between the two is the traditional nature of fiction chosen by the editors. For the *Post,* with its Norman Rockwell covers and feature stories geared toward middle-class interests, a Vonnegut story would be pushing the extremes. Only because his plot resolutions favored homely values and unpretentious behavior could the author slip in such subtle inversions as teenage dysfunction becoming an index to adult issues ("The No-Talent Kid") and the Kennedy mystique decodable in a syntax of signs ("The Hyannis Port Story"). For his part Barthelme seized the *New Yorker*'s fascination with social manners and transformed it into a kind of linguistic vaudeville, in which his very apparency of method became its own subject ("Report" and "The Indian Uprising" plus most of the other early *New Yorker* stories collected in 1968 as *Unspeakable Practices, Unnatural Acts*). Barthelme could even do the Kennedys as semiotics in "Robert Kennedy Saved from Drowning" (published in the *New American Review* but collected in the same volume as his first *New Yorker* work). Real people, famous ones, used as fictive characters; fictive plots that not so much reflected life as mocked life's artifice; an unassuming approach to events that lets their absurdity tumble forth as the storyteller just shrugs it off with vernacular insouciance—all these were unconventional ways to write fiction for any magazine, let alone such bearers of tradition as the *Saturday Evening Post* and the *New Yorker.* Between them Kurt Vonnegut and Donald Barthelme were showing that innovative fiction was not just for literary quarterlies and a readership among the professorate.

Vonnegut's solid experience in the real world also made for a difference in his novels. *Player Piano*'s appearance in 1952 was hardly startling; as dystopian fiction it joined a strong and currently popular tradition supported most famously by the success of George Orwell's *1984,* published in 1949 and, during the Korean War, at its peak of American popularity for its presumed anticommunist theme. Orwell was a man of experience, but in most cases he had to seek it out as a journalist's adventure. Although he was a British Imperial police officer for a time in Burma, he had never worked for a large, postwar corporation as Vonnegut had done with General Electric. Vonnegut's practical experience shows through in *Player Piano*'s resolution. Yes, as in *1984*'s ending there is a failure of the revolution, but not in the individual terms Orwell uses to convey his personal theme of the individual beaten down by the institution. Instead, *Player Piano* closes with the workers absentmindedly tinkering with the machines that have been so destructive of their life ethic, putting them back together out of a simple fascination with gadget-making. Here, the author shows, is the cause for all this trouble in the first place. And he manages to show it in a comically understanding way.

As for the conventions of science fiction, Vonnegut inverts them as well. Typically, invasions from outer space are the doings of alien creatures with superior intelligence. In *The Sirens of Titan* the so-called invasion from Mars is actually an operation staged by kidnapped Earthlings and effected with all the incompetence of a Laurel and Hardy film. As for the mechanics of his science fiction, the author makes it equally laughable, for a very good reason. Traditional sci-fi takes its science seriously—too seriously for Vonnegut's purposes since the points he wants to make are not about machinery but about people. Science fiction of the Harlan Ellison/ Theodore Sturgeon variety is not widely read by mainstream audiences, who may be put off by the brainy science. There is also an intellectual arrogance that sometimes characterizes such work. In contrast, Kurt Vonnegut speaks humbly. In later novels he will create a sci-fi writer named for Sturgeon, Kilgore Trout, a character who is surely the least successful practitioner in the entire subgenre—not for Vonnegut to mock it but rather so that Trout's good ideas can show through in spite of himself, just as the great themes of *The Sirens of Titan* (against religious presumption, in favor of personal usefulness) rise far above its deliberate space-opera claptrap. Like dystopia, science fiction is simply a convention Vonnegut can use, sometimes against itself, for his larger purposes.

The greater scope Kurt Vonnegut has in mind first becomes evident in *Mother Night*. Again he employs a familiar format, here that of a spy thriller. It is no accident that the author chooses popular subgenres for his first three novels, for he is emerging from the world of family magazine fiction and doing it, after *Player Piano*, via paperback originals. Doing so provides a comfortable meeting ground with his readers, with Vonnegut knowing what to do and they what to expect. To a point, that is, for with his protagonist Howard Campbell readers may find more than they bargained for. Campbell is a double agent, a presumably turncoat American work-ing for the Nazis as an extremely effective propagandist while using his anti-Semitic broadcasts to send out coded information to the Allies. But is his true loyalty to the American cause? That is the first atypical question Vonnegut's readers have to ponder. Not that there is an easy answer, for Campbell does not know himself. Ironies abound: Campbell is not only the best American spy; he is also the best Nazi propagandist, with his efforts simultaneously ending the war sooner and making it last longer. Is he a hero or a villain? Spy-novel aficionados are fond of seeing how the contesting sides in a conflict see things differently, but Campbell's situa-tion eclipses this distinction completely. By novel's end he is celebrated by neo-Nazis, of course, but in ways that can only hurt him. Ready to harm him outright are agents from the Soviet Union and Israel. His own native land, America, has disavowed him, as it must for security reasons. But when at the end a U.S. agent breaks all the rules to save Campbell's life, the protagonist refuses this help. The only reason Howard Campbell is not executed by the Israelis for crimes against humanity is that he executes himself, for crimes against himself.

Brilliantly complex and deep as they are, nothing like this happens in the spy novels of Graham Greene, serious literature's other major contri-bution to this sometimes maligned subgenre. Even farther off the scale of tradition are Vonnegut's examples of humor. In this novel and in his next, *Cat's Cradle,* he would show what affinities he had with black humor by presenting characters and scenes that suggested the ridiculous. The dif-ference is that while a black humorist such as Terry Southern may well have been ridiculous, Vonnegut was introducing simple, plain, and true elements into the action, the only thing strange being that such banali-ties were not usually associated with such subjects. Paul Josef Goebbels enthusing over Abraham Lincoln's populist wit? Adolf Hitler shedding sentimental tears over *The Gettysburg Address*? A whole carload of Nazis racking up scores—not of prisoners dispatched to concentration camps but of sets in an intramural Ping-Pong tournament? *Cat's Cradle* would use a similar approach, reducing another larger-than-life figure, this time a scientist who helped invent the atomic bomb, into a naive dabbler who would just as soon play with dime-store turtles. There is some of Hannah Arendt's theory of "the banality of evil" in this technique, but in Vonnegut's case the practice more properly reflects his belief that if we know such characters only through the immensity of their evil we forget that they are human beings, and that any of us is capable of similar monstrosities.

Cat's Cradle and *God Bless You, Mr. Rosewater* combine this offbeat humor with another destabilizing technique, one that would become the author's trademark: short sentences, sometimes just a word or two long, that sometimes serve as entire paragraphs as well. Together with the humor, which was often underscored this way, the technique made Vonnegut's delivery seem colloquial, even conversational. With autobiographical prefaces beginning to appear in his novels about this same time, it all made the narrative seem personal. Like a conversation with a neighbor across the backyard fence, the reading of a Kurt Vonnegut novel was as familiar as talking with the guy next door, yet as exciting as when this friend would present some surprising news. No other American fictionists was writing this way: not Philip Roth (whose personal revelations were meant to amuse and shock), not John Updike (whose autobiographies were of aesthetic stylings), and not Norman Mailer (whose advertisements for himself were dressed in great existential seriousness).

As Vonnegut approached the time when he would write *Slaughterhouse-Five*, then, he appeared strongly sui generis. Where he came from was obvious: the solid middle-class experience of the American midcentury. But what he was making of this material was unique. There were touches of black humor to it, but in a deeper vein that suggested not simple irreverence but rather a wry pleasure in his country's most characteristic foibles—not Terry Southern in nature, but more like Mark Twain. In an age of great stylists, from Updike to Bellow, with all of them raised in the shadow of even greater prose masters from Hemingway to Faulkner, he was being exceptional by speaking unexceptionally—in a simple vernacular unheard in serious fiction for almost one hundred years.

"All this happened, more or less"—with a shrug of the shoulders and shuffle of his feet this spokesperson for the traits of common Americans not only undertakes the narrative of *Slaughterhouse-Five* but also moves his own fiction into the camp of literary postmodernism. No more subgenres, no more generally accepted formats, no more familiar conventions, even if they are used with an eye toward subtle subversion—this new novel about World War II is anything but a typical war novel. Yet neither is it an antiwar novel, something that might have been expected given the cultural climate of the late 1960s that set itself so dramatically against the war in Vietnam. Yes, plenty of antiwar books existed, so there were models aplenty. But as a friend tells the author in *Slaughterhouse-Five*'s first chapter, taking this route is about as promising as writing an antiglacier book. Frank and simple honesty about this predicament helps Vonnegut set a

course of similar candor throughout the novel: no peace movement hero-
ics and no willing suspension of disbelief either. As Samuel Beckett fore-
saw as a postmodern possibility in the work of his mentor James Joyce, a
novel could not so much be about something as be that something itself.
Or as Gertrude Stein hinted about the style of fiction that would succeed
modernism's ponderous engagement with meaning, what you see is what
there is. From the tone of candid personal address to the rejection of subgenre and peacenik theatrics and aesthetic illusion, Vonnegut's choices
come together to make *Slaughterhouse-Five* a novel on the leading edge of
innovation.

Yet even among the postmodernist innovators, so distinctive in their
revolt against both cultural and literary conformity, Kurt Vonnegut's new
novel would stand out for its special approach. Most apparently it is a
small, even modest book; in the first chapter the author apologizes to his
publisher for turning in something so jumbled and jangled and short.
That, of course, is part of the writer's honesty: there is nothing intelligent
to say about a massacre. His method will involve instead a figuration of
silence—not just as a form of inarticulation but because in realistic terms
that is exactly what happened in the immediate aftermath of Dresden's
bombing. No other novel, innovative or traditional, had taken this approach. A big subject demands a big work, writers implied, whether they
be Norman Mailer with *The Naked and the Dead* or Joseph Heller with
Catch-22. As innovation took hold in the 1960s and 1970s, what critic
Tom LeClair in *The Art of Excess* called the "meganovel" or "novel of excess"
became the norm for such seriousness. It better be good, LeClair implied,
and to do so it better be big if any novelist were to portray the war, or history's reaction to it, or the corporate institutionalism that came in its
wake. The classic example is Thomas Pynchon's *Gravity's Rainbow* (1973),
although this author had paved the way with *V.* (1963) in making the
encyclopedic a postmodern norm. To this style William H. Gass, William
Gaddis, and others would make their weighty contributions. The effect
broadened to include what critic Linda Hutcheon in *A Poetics of Postmodernism* called "historiographic metafiction," ranging from E. L. Doctorow's
more historiographic *Ragtime* (1975) to Robert Coover's *The Public Burning* (1977), in which the record of public acts was treated in the same
terms as products of the imagination, equally malleable and subject to
interrogation.

Vonnegut interrogates the war as well, but in a much more offhand
manner. There is no heavy probity that could be mistaken for an arrogance

of intelligence in *Slaughterhouse-Five*. Billy Pilgrim is quiet and unassuming, physically awkward and mentally naive. Although Kurt Vonnegut stands apart from him in the text, the author quickly shows himself to be no great shakes in the panorama of life—it has taken him twenty years to get this book in shape, being talked down along the way by everyone from intellectuals at the University of Chicago to his old war buddy's wife. He has stayed up late at night, drinking too much and using the long distance telephone to settle old scores. Unlike the flamboyant characters in Pynchon and the imposing ones in Gass, both Billy and Kurt are just regular people, as normal and nondescript as the folks who will read their story. The difference is that the two of them have been in Dresden for the firebombing, and that is what motivates their narrative: not informational overkill and aesthetic high pressure, but a simple act of witnessing presence.

That presence has a metafictive aspect as strong as anything in the other wing of fictive postmodernism, the one inhabited by Ronald Sukenick, Ishmael Reed, Grace Paley, and other innovators who have placed themselves squarely at the heart of their work. But once again Vonnegut's effort remains firmly anchored in middle-class life, as opposed to the artistic posture these other writers find it helpful to strike. Fiction is not about experience; it is more experience—this dictum from Ronald Sukenick's *In Form: Digressions on the Act of Fiction* (1985) indicates an element that *Slaughterhouse-Five* shares with more radically experimental fiction such as Sukenick's *Up* (1968), *Out* (1973), and *98.6* (1975). Both authors are pledged to avoid the purely literary, Vonnegut by avoiding the commonly accepted style of war stories and Sukenick by refusing the pieties of an academic canon. Yet no novelist writes in a vacuum, and there is an interesting distinction between these two writers' habitats. Where Vonnegut looks back to vernacular spokespersons such as Abraham Lincoln and Mark Twain, Sukenick admires the example of Henry Miller's fusion of life and art. There is an energy to existence evident in the work of both camps; but in social terms Miller acts as an outlaw while Lincoln is the mender and Twain the critically reforming commentator. Each writer seeks a vibrant, vital relation to reality, something more personally exuberant than the leaden manner of social realism would allow. But Sukenick's motivation is intellectual, aesthetic, and even philosophical. His first example, studied ahead of his first published fiction, is that most thoughtful and self-studied of poets Wallace Stevens. A Brandeis doctoral dissertation supervised by J. V. Cunningham and Irving Howe became Sukenick's first book, *Wallace*

Stevens: Musing the Obscure (1967), setting a program for his fiction that would follow. Here he admires in Stevens the posture he would take in *Up* and his other novels, that relating to reality is possible only by attaining ever fresh perceptions of it. From his early work readers can see how Vonnegut feels this way too; *Player Piano* and many of his stories from *Collier's* and the *Saturday Evening Post* make sense of the brave new world of scientific and corporate forces by seeing them from the unexpected perspective of homely, human foibles. The most obvious trait Kurt Vonnegut displays is originality of imagination, and like Sukenick (with Stevens as his model), he uses this most personally human talent to organize the strange aspects of existence into something a mind can handle. As Sukenick emphasizes, this is not idealism, for the mind in such cases is ordering reality not by imposing ideas on it but by discovering significant relations within it. If anything, the approach is egotistic, for by reconciling reality with their own needs the authors find the formerly hostile landscape more relevant and therefore more real.

The difference within this larger sense of agreement is that Sukenick has pursued this fictive inclination in the English department while Vonnegut has picked it up in the school of hard knocks—some very hard ones, including the Great Depression, World War II, and the transformation of postwar America into a corporate mold that was not to fracture until the disruptions of the 1960s, disruptions of which *Slaughterhouse-Five* is a part. Sukenick finds his own inclinations articulated by Wallace Stevens, and in the first chapter of *Slaughterhouse-Five* Vonnegut can be found tracing affinities with Theodore Roethke and Louis-Ferdinand Céline. But in the latter case readers sense that these are authors who have proved responsive to Vonnegut's experience, helping him face a life with which he has already struggled. Though his own achievement is considerable, Sukenick's struggle has been with intellectual issues—applicable to life, certainly, but pursued as an essentially aesthetic problem.

The case of Ishmael Reed's work offers an equally instructive contrast within an overall sense of artistic agreement. With *The Free-Lance Pallbearers* (1967), *Yellow Back Radio Broke-Down* (1968), and *Mumbo Jumbo* (1973), Reed accompanied Vonnegut, Sukenick, and many other innovators in the literary disruption of tradition that constituted the first major development in American fiction since the modernist breakthroughs of Fitzgerald, Hemingway, and Faulkner. As Vonnegut learned from real life and as Sukenick was discovering in the English departments at Cornell and Brandeis, available models did not always provide good forms for the imaginative work they wished to express. As an African American, Reed had the problematic nature of his own literary history to add to this sense of frustration. Marginalized for so long and only allowed into the mainstream by what some critics decried as tokenism—the tradition of "one black author at a time," from Jean Toomer and Langston Hughes in the 1920s and 1930s to Richard Wright in the 1940s, Ralph Ellison in the 1950s, and James Baldwin in the early 1960s—African American writing was faced with the task of literally inventing itself. Literature arises from life, but many aspects of African American existence had been altered or effaced by pressures of slavery, then of segregation, and even in more enlightened times by a simple lack of retrievable record. Toni Morrison would build a career on the imaginative reconstruction of such lost history. Like Sukenick, Reed (as an academic) would have to combine his street knowledge with library research; after crafting his first novel as a response to countercultural life in New York City's East Village he spent time researching Americana in the University of California's Bancroft Library for his second and in the folklore repositories of New Orleans for his third. *Yellow Back Radio Broke-Down* provides a hilarious mixture of anachronistic elements, while *Mumbo Jumbo* opens eyes with its interpolation of Egyptian mythology and New World hoodoo. Each novel runs amok with fractured literary conventions, no less than any work by Vonnegut, Barthelme, or other of the innovationists. But it is Reed's fate that he has had to recover many of these elements by diligent research. Vonnegut's opportunity to work with the semiotic elements of a culture unsuppressed and unfettered saves him a big step in reaching an informed readership, since the icons and images he plays with are those of the mainstream narrative, however much the writer questions it.

Looking back to Lincoln and Twain and working profitably within the widely shared culture of his era, Kurt Vonnegut becomes the writer who places innovation within the main channel of evolving literary history. Those following in his wake are similarly directed toward not so much rejecting tradition as rerouting it. During the author's brief tenure at the University of Iowa Writers' Workshop one of his more promising students was John Irving. A portion of Irving's first novel, *Setting Free the Bears* (1968), was submitted for his M.F.A. degree, awarded in 1967, but the work that most obviously shows the effect of Vonnegut's mentorship is his second novel, *The Water-Method Man* (1972). Its protagonist is a younger generation Billy Pilgrim, not because of any easy allusions of characters but so that Irving can let the action of the novel's many plots wash over him in a way that lets such pressures of the world take on a character of their own, just as Billy Pilgrim makes possible in *Slaughterhouse-Five*. Although Irving eschews the device of time travel, he does shift locations constantly between four different times in the protagonist's life taking place in the distinct locations of Austria, New York, New England, and Iowa City. There is a quasi-metafictive element that anchors all these times and places: as a graduate student the protagonist is translating an ancient epic written in Old Low Norse, a language so dead that even his dissertation director cannot read it. Realizing this, Irving's writer-protagonist decides to save himself the trouble of laborious translation by reinventing the epic himself, just making it up as he goes along. Its themes become those of his own life, which are the themes of *The Water-Method Man*. Had Kurt Vonnegut been born in 1942 instead of 1922, this is the kind of novel he would be writing.

In his subsequent career Irving has anticipated larger cultural developments, just as Vonnegut has. Irving's next novel, *The 158-Pound Marriage* (1974), takes its name from a weight class in college wrestling, but in substance it rejects the excesses of intellectualism and particularly innovations in fiction that become, in his view, too avant-gardist. The plot involves an experimental novelist named Helmbart, an inverted spelling of "Barthelme" in its occasional (if incorrect) two-syllable pronunciation. It is as if Irving, enamored of similar innovations in his first two works, were saying that by the time of *City Life* (1970) and *Sadness* (1972) Donald Barthelme had gone too far. The density and obscurantism of such stories as "Bone Bubbles" and "Sentence" made some readers feel that Barthelme had become self-indulgent, a *Finnegans Wake* absorption following a more gregarious *Ulysses* period. Much 1960s exuberance was being rejected, including experimentalist extravagances, and Irving's new work reflects this mood. Vonnegut had drawn back with *Breakfast of Champions,* and in subsequent work he fashioned a new style of protagonist above events rather than being determined by them. Irving's direction was to extend his teacher's wish that literature comfort and nurture by recovering a respectable sentimentality, evident in novels from *The World According to Garp* (1978) onward through works into the twenty-first century.

Letting reader reaction be directed by emotions as well as by intellect is one major development in late-twentieth-century American fiction. Another trend traceable to Vonnegut's influence is the dominance of the comic. By adopting a humorous outlook toward their materials a great number of novelists were able to write about the real needs of real people without surrendering to the self-seriousness of conventional realism. One of the first novelists to show this ability was Tom Robbins, whose *Another Roadside Attraction* (1971) extends the Kesey-Heller-Vonnegut style to include close detail from the era's counterculture. Rob Swigart's *Little America* (1977) does much the same, adding an appreciation of how all of America, from the age of Manifest Destiny to the present, has been in thrall to the notion of travel. In subsequent novels Swigart would extend this notion to include space exploration and the afterlife, each of which has its nature formed in the model of Earth's insipidly comic image, right down to motel chains and fast-food franchises. *A.K.A.: A Cosmic Fable* (1978) and *The Time Trip* (1979) work such punch lines not as points by themselves (as black-humor fiction might) but rather in the Vonnegut model of many simultaneous actions, all of them portrayed in a seemingly effortless transition between different regions of time and space. As for jokes, their ability to propel a narrative is demonstrated by Gerald Rosen, whose *The Carmen Miranda Memorial Flagpole* (1977) proceeds by virtue of its stand-up comic howlers, the only art form its characters, kids from the Bronx in the 1940s, have. In this novel Rosen's protagonist does as Swigart's characters do and travels west, taking his jokes with him. What he transports is not a content but a form, and exercising this form lets him structure the new California life of the 1960s that he will encounter—an approach Vonnegut takes in using the classic comedy of the Great Depression to help him survive all of the smaller depressions, personal and public, that have come along since.

Kurt Vonnegut's 1930s and 1940s, encompassing the Depression and World War II, were times he participated in as a young man. At a comparable age Max Apple encountered the 1960s and 1970s, and in his novels and stories he uses many of the older writer's tools to come to grips with this new reality. Like Vonnegut, he starts with short stories; in *The Oranging of America* (1976) readers find the decades of Apple's young manhood treated with the same eye for signs and symbols as Vonnegut used in his *Welcome to the Monkey House* materials of the immediately previous era. The title piece does for franchising what Vonnegut's institutional and scientific stories of the 1950s did for the emerging corporate nature of American life. The title's formulation suggests the change being wrought to the symbolic nature of this country, that it was becoming as trademarked as an orange-roofed motel chain. Like Swigart's characters, Apple's protagonist travels. But he also knows, as if by magic, where to stop; at each of these points he decrees the building of a Howard Johnson's motel, and the rest is history. In his novel *Zip* (1978) Apple extends this talent for semiology to political figures by means of an international boxing match whose opposing fighters are backed by Fidel Castro and J. Edgar Hoover. A second collection of stories, *Free Agents* (1984), combines similar ritualization with a closely textual reading of cultural institutions, such as Disneyland, an approach expanded and extended in Apple's novel *The Propheteers* (1987). Yet also like Vonnegut, this author does not leave readers without an antidote to cultural outrages and sellouts. His prescription for a better style of life is the same as the older writer's: extended family, as demonstrated by the memoirs of how his grandparents contributed to the well-being of his own life, *Roommates* (1994) and *I Love Gootie* (1998).

From John Irving's legitimization of sentiment to Gerald Rosen's propulsive talent with comedy and Max Apple's resolution of the tyrannies of semiotic culture with the benefits of a nurturing larger family, Kurt Vonnegut's themes and methods carry on more than half a century after he gave them first expression. And Vonnegut has continued to write. In a world in which multicultural expression flourishes he delights in the popularization of a notion he saw come into being during his lifetime: that reality is not a naturally existing absolute but rather a cultural description, any number of which can exist simultaneously. In literary terms this appreciation makes possible both the innovative fictions of writers such as Ronald Sukenick, Raymond Federman, and Steve Katz, whose accounts harness creative energy for their persuasiveness, and those of Leslie Marmon Silko, Sandra Cisneros, Maxine Hong Kingston, and Rudolfo Anaya, whose fictive visions emerge from their respective cultures to create new currents in the American stream.

In this newly expanded world Vonnegut writes happily of even broader perspectives, such as the one he takes in *God Bless You, Dr. Kevorkian* (1999). In this series of scripts for WNYC, New York City's public radio station, the author serves as a reporter from the afterlife having used the talents of the famous suicide-assisting physician and the facilities of the State of Texas Bureau of Corrections (currently leading the nation in executions) to take a series of glimpses at the hereafter and then return to tell all about it. Like a budding journalist back on the *Shortridge Echo* or the *Cornell Sun*, Vonnegut finds himself using the basic methods of who, what, where, when, and why to give his listeners and readers the news. Like Mark Twain, he may feel that by living and working into a new century he has been drafted into a second lifetime of service. Yet he performs it cheerfully, and why not? He even gets to interview Adolf Hitler, who sends his sincere apologies for any part he may have played, inadvertently, in the event known as World War II but who also wishes to be acknowledged as a victim too.

Sixty years earlier, filing his last column for the high school paper in Indianapolis and heading off to write more copy at Cornell, young Kurt Vonnegut knew that the German dictator was the biggest news item going. Now, at the start of the new century, Hitler is in the news again. Historians and cultural analysts would say he has never left. But it takes a writer with the talents of Kurt Vonnegut to cover just this type of story, with time travel, irreverent humor, fresh perspective, and all.

BIBLIOGRAPHY

Works by Kurt Vonnegut

Novels

Player Piano. New York: Charles Scribner's Sons, 1952.

The Sirens of Titan. New York: Dell, 1959.

Mother Night. Greenwich, Conn.: Fawcett, 1962 [copyright 1961]. New York: Harper & Row, 1966 (second edition, first hardcover publication, with a new introduction by the author).

Cat's Cradle. New York: Holt, Rinehart & Winston, 1963.

God Bless You, Mr. Rosewater; or, Pearls before Swine. New York: Holt, Rinehart & Winston, 1965.

Slaughterhouse-Five; or, The Children's Crusade. New York: Delacorte Press/Seymour Lawrence, 1969.

Breakfast of Champions; or, Goodbye Blue Monday! New York: Delacorte Press/Seymour Lawrence, 1973.

Slapstick; or, Lonesome No More! New York: Delacorte Press/Seymour Lawrence, 1976.

Jailbird. New York: Delacorte Press/Seymour Lawrence, 1979.

Deadeye Dick. New York: Delacorte Press/Seymour Lawrence, 1982.

Galápagos. New York: Delacorte Press/Seymour Lawrence, 1985.

Bluebeard. New York: Delacorte Press, 1987.

Hocus Pocus. New York: Putnam, 1990.

Timequake. New York: Putnam, 1997.

Collections of Short Fiction [* *indicates a nonfiction work*]

Canary in a Cat House. Greenwich, Conn.: Fawcett, 1961.

    Contents and original publication:

    "Report on the Barnhouse Effect." *Collier's* 125 (11 February 1950): 18–19, 63–65.

    "All the King's Horses." *Collier's* 127 (10 February 1951): 46–48, 50.

Materials published before 1976 included the "Jr." as part of his name.

"D. P." *Ladies' Home Journal* 70 (August 1953): 42–43, 80–81, 84.

"The Manned Missiles." *Cosmopolitan* 145 (July 1958): 83–88.

"The Euphio Question." *Collier's* 127 (12 May 1951): 22–23, 53–54.

"More Stately Mansions." *Collier's* 128 (22 December 1951): 24–25, 62–63.

"The Foster Portfolio." *Collier's* 128 (8 September 1951): 18–19, 72–73.

"Deer in the Works." *Esquire* 43 (April 1955): 78–79, 112, 114, 116, 118.

"Hal Irwin's Magic Lamp." *Cosmopolitan* 142 (June 1957): 92– 95 (with the omission of its final sentence).

"Tom Edison's Shaggy Dog." *Collier's* 131 (14 March 1953): 46, 48–49.

"Unready to Wear." *Galaxy Science Fiction* 6 (April 1953): 98–111.

"Tomorrow and Tomorrow and Tomorrow." *Galaxy Science Fiction* 7 (January 1954): 100–110, as "The Big Trip Up Yonder."

Welcome to the Monkey House. New York: Delacorte Press/Seymour Lawrence, 1968.

Contents and original publication:

All stories from *Canary in a Cat House* with the exception of "Hal Irwin's Magic Lamp"; "Tom Edison's Shaggy Dog" is reprinted with the absence of its last line.

*"Preface." Previously unpublished.

*"Where I Live." *Venture—Traveler's World* 1 (October 1964): 145, 147–49, as "You've Never Been to Barnstable?"

"Harrison Bergeron." *Magazine of Fantasy and Science Fiction* 21 (October 1961): 5–10.

"Who Am I This Time?" *Saturday Evening Post* 234 (16 December 1961): 20–21, 62, 64, 66–67, as "My Name Is Everyone."

"Welcome to the Monkey House." *Playboy* 15 (January 1968): 95, 156, 196, 198, 200–201.

"Long Walk to Forever." *Ladies' Home Journal* 77 (August 1960): 42–43, 108.

"Miss Temptation." *Saturday Evening Post* 228 (21 April 1956): 30, 57, 60, 62, 64.

*"New Dictionary." *New York Times Book Review,* 30 October 1966, 1, 56, as "The Latest Word."

"Next Door." *Cosmopolitan* 138 (April 1955): 80–85.

"The Hyannis Port Story." Purchased by *Saturday Evening Post* in 1963 but not published (because of President Kennedy's assassination).

"Go Back to Your Precious Wife and Son." *Ladies' Home Journal* 79 (July 1962): 54–55, 108, 110.

"The Lie." *Saturday Evening Post* 235 (24 February 1962): 46–47, 51, 56.

"Unready to Wear." *Galaxy Science Fiction* 6 (April 1953): 98–111.

"The Kid Nobody Could Handle." *Saturday Evening Post* 228 (24 September 1955): 37, 136–37.

"EPICAC." *Collier's* 126 (25 November 1950): 36–37.

"Adam." *Cosmopolitan* 136 (April 1954): 34–39.

Bagombo Snuff Box. New York: Putnam, 1999.
   Contents and original publication:
   *"Preface by Peter Reed." Previously unpublished.
   *"Introduction." Previously unpublished.
   "Thanasphere." *Collier's* 126 (2 September 1950): 18–19, 60, 62.
   "Mnemonics." *Collier's* 127 (28 April 1951): 38.
   "Any Reasonable Offer." *Collier's* 129 (19 January 1952): 32, 46–47.
   "The Package." *Collier's* 130 (26 July 1952): 48–53.
   "The No-Talent Kid." *Saturday Evening Post* 225 (25 October 1952): 28, 109–10, 112, 114.
   "Poor Little Rich Town." *Collier's* 130 (25 October 1952): 90–95.
   "Souvenir." *Argosy,* December 1952, 28–29, 76–79.
   "The Cruise of the *Jolly Roger.*" *Cape Cod Compass* 8 (April 1953): 7–14.
   "Custom-Made Bride." *Saturday Evening Post* 226 (27 March 1954): 30, 81–82, 86–87.
   "Ambitious Sophomore." *Saturday Evening Post* 226 (1 May 1954): 31, 88, 92, 94.
   "Bagombo Snuff Box." *Cosmopolitan* 137 (October 1954): 34–39.
   "The Powder-Blue Dragon." *Cosmopolitan* 139 (November 1954): 46–48, 50–53.
   "A Present for Big Saint Nick." *Argosy,* December 1954, 42–45, 72–73.
   "Unpaid Consultant." *Cosmopolitan* 138 (March 1955): 52–57.
   *"Der Arme Dolmetscher." *Atlantic Monthly* 196 (July 1955): 86–88.
   "The Boy Who Hated Girls." *Saturday Evening Post* 228 (31 March 1956): 28–29, 58, 60, 62.
   "This Son of Mine." *Saturday Evening Post* 229 (13 August 1956): 24, 74, 76–78, as "This Son of Mine. . . ."
   "A Night for Love." *Saturday Evening Post* 230 (23 November 1957): 40–41, 73, 76–77, 80–81, 84.
   "Find Me a Dream." *Cosmopolitan* 150 (February 1961): 108–11.
   "Runaways." *Saturday Evening Post* 234 (15 April 1961): 26–27, 52, 54, 56.
   "2BR02B." *Worlds of If,* January 1962, 59–65.
   "Lovers Anonymous." *Redbook* 121 (October 1963): 70–71, 146–48.
   "Hal Irwin's Magic Lamp." *Cosmopolitan* 142 (June 1957): 92–95 (with its ending rewritten).
   *"Coda to My Career as a Writer for Periodicals." Previously unpublished.

Dramatic Works

Happy Birthday, Wanda June. New York: Delacorte Press/Seymour Lawrence, 1971.

Between Time and Timbuktu. New York: Delacorte Press/Seymour Lawrence, 1972.

Work for Children

Sun/Star/Moon. New York: Harper & Row, 1980 (with illustrations by Ivan Chermayeff).

Collections of Nonfiction [* *indicates a fictive work,* ** *an interview*]

Wampeters, Foma & Granfalloons. New York: Delacorte Press/Seymour Lawrence, 1974.

Contents and original publication:

"Preface." Previously unpublished.

"Science Fiction." *New York Times Book Review,* 5 September 1965, 2.

"Brief Encounters on the Inland Waterway." *Venture—Traveler's World* 3 (October/November 1966): 135–38, 140, 142.

"Hello, Star Vega" [review of I. S. Shklovskii and Carl Sagan's *Intelligent Life in the Universe*]. *Life* 61 (9 December 1965): R3, as "Hello, Star Vega, Do You Read Our Gomer Pyle?"

"Teaching the Unteachable." *New York Times Book Review,* 6 August 1967, 1, 20 (with several paragraphs, including the ending, omitted).

"Yes, We Have No Nirvanas." *Esquire* 69 (June 1968): 78–79, 176, 178–79, 182.

*"Fortitude." *Playboy* 15 (September 1968): 99–100, 102, 106, 217–18.

"There's a Maniac Loose Out There." *Life* 67 (15 July 1969): 53–56.

"Excelsior! We're Going to the Moon! Excelsior!" *New York Times Magazine,* 13 July 1969, 9–11.

"Address to the American Physical Society." *Chicago Tribune Magazine,* 22 June 1969, 44, 48–50, 52, 56, as "Physicist, Purge Thyself."

"Good Missiles, Good Manners, Good Night." *New York Times,* 13 September 1969, 29, as "Topics: Good Missiles, Good Manners, Good Night."

"Why They Read Hesse." *Horizon* 12 (Spring 1970): 28–31.

"Oversexed in Indianapolis" [review of Dan Wakefield's *Going All the Way*]. *Life* 69 (17 July 1970): 10.

"The Mysterious Madame Blavatsky." *McCall's* 97 (March 1970): 66–67, 142–44.

"Biafra: A People Betrayed." *McCall's* 97 (April 1970): 68–69, 134–38.

"Address to the Graduating Class at Bennington College, 1970." *Vogue* 156 (August 1970): 54, 144–45, as "Up Is Better Than Down."

"Torture and Blubber." *New York Times,* 30 June 1971, 41.

"Address to the National Institute of Arts and Letters, 1971." *Vogue* 160 (15 August 1972): 56–57, 93, as "What Women Really Want Is. . . ."

"Reflections on My Own Death." *Rotarian,* May 1972, 24.

"In a Manner That Must Shame God Himself." *Harper's* 245 (November 1972): 60–63, 65–66, 68.

"Thinking Unthinkable, Speaking Unspeakable." *New York Times,* 13 January 1973, 31.

"Invite Rita Rait to America!" *New York Times Book Review,* 28 January 1973, 31.

"Address at Rededication of Wheaton College Library." *Wheaton College Alumnae Magazine* 60 (February 1973): 15–17.

"Address to P.E.N. Conference in Stockholm, 1973." *Ramparts* 12 (July 1974): 43–44, as ". . . But Words Can Never Hurt Me."

"A Political Disease" [review of Hunter S. Thompson's *Fear and Loathing: On the Campaign Trail '72*]. *Harper's* 246 (July 1973): 92, 94.

**"Playboy Interview." *Playboy* 20 (July 1973): 57–60, 62, 66, 68, 70, 72, 74, 214, 216, conducted by David Standish.

Palm Sunday: An Autobiographical Collage. New York: Delacorte Press/Seymour Lawrence, 1981.

Contents and original publication (not including the new framing and bridging commentary written by Vonnegut, and not including materials written by others):

"Dear Mr. McCarthy." Previously unpublished.

"Un-American Nonsense." *New York Times Long Island Weekly,* 28 March 1976, sec. 21, p. 16, as "Banned Authors Answer Back."

"God's Law." Previously unpublished.

"Dear Felix." Previously unpublished.

"What I Liked about Cornell." Previously unpublished.

"When I Lost My Innocence." Submitted to *Aftonbladet* (Sweden), previously unpublished.

"I Am Embarrassed." Previously unpublished.

"How to Write with Style." International Paper Company, May 1980, as a handout in their "Power of the Printed Word" program; also featured as a national advertisement in many magazines.

**"Self-Interview." *Paris Review* no. 69 (Spring 1977): 56–103, as "Kurt Vonnegut: The Art of Fiction LXIV."

"Who in America Is Truly Happy?" [review of William F. Buckley, Jr.'s *A Hymnal*]. *Politics Today,* January/February 1979, 60, as "The Happy Conservative."

"Something Happened" [review of Joseph Heller's *Something Happened*]. *New York Times Book Review,* 6 October 1974, 1–2, as "Joseph Heller's Extraordinary Novel about an Ordinary Man."

"The Rocky Graziano of American Letters." Previously unpublished.

"The Best of Bob and Ray." Foreword to *Write If You Get Work: The Best of Bob and Ray,* by Bob Elliott and Ray Goulding, vi–vii. New York: Random House, 1975.

"James T. Farrell." Previously unpublished.

"Lavinia Lyon." Previously unpublished.

"The Noodle Factory." *Connecticut College Alumni Magazine* (Fall 1977): 3–5, 42–43; *Mademoiselle* (August 1977): 96, 104–5, as "On Reading/Writing/Freedom."

"Mark Twain." *Nation* 229 (7 July 1979): 21–22, as "The Necessary Miracle."

"How Jokes Work." Previously unpublished.

"Thoughts of a Free Thinker." Previously unpublished.

"William Ellery Channing." Previously unpublished.

*"The Big Space Fuck." In *Again, Dangerous Visions,* edited by Harlan Ellison, 246–50. Garden City, N.Y.: Doubleday, 1972.

"Fear and Loathing in Morristown, N.J." Previously unpublished.

"Jonathan Swift." Previously unpublished.

*"The Chemistry Professor." Previously unpublished.

"Louis-Ferdinand Céline." Introductions to *Castle to Castle, Rigadoon,* and *North,* by Louis-Ferdinand Céline, xiii–xx. Harmondsworth, U.K. and New York: Penguin, 1975.

"Dresden Revisited." In his *Slaughterhouse-Five.* Franklin Center, Pa.: Franklin Library, 1978, as "A Special Message to Subscribers from Kurt Vonnegut."

"Palm Sunday." *Nation* 230 (19 April 1980): 469–70, as "Hypocrites You Always Have with You."

Fates Worse Than Death: An Autobiographical Collage of the 1980s. New York: Putnam, 1991.

Contents and original publication (not including the new framing and bridging commentary written by Vonnegut, and not including materials written by others):

"Preface." Includes a questionnaire submitted to the *Weekly Guardian* (Great Britain) but previously unpublished in the United States.

Untitled comments on his father. *Architectural Digest* 41 (June 1984): 30, 34, 36, as "Sleeping Beauty."

"Address to the American Psychiatric Association." Previously unpublished.

Untitled comments on his sister, art, and interruptions. *Architectural Digest*

43 (May 1986): 170–75, as "Art/Great Beginnings: In Praise of the Incomplete."

Untitled essay on Jackson Pollock. *Esquire* 100 (December 1983): 549–54, as "Jack the Dripper."

Untitled comments. *Bluebeard*. Franklin Center, Pa.: Franklin Library, 1987, as "A Special Message to Subscribers from Kurt Vonnegut."

Untitled essay on Lake Maxincuckee. *Architectural Digest* 45 (June 1988): 27, 29, 31, as "The Lake."

"Introduction." In *Never Come Morning*, by Nelson Algren. New York: Four Walls Eight Windows, 1987.

Remarks to Hemingway Conference in Boise, Idaho. In *Blowing the Bridge: Essays on Hemingway and For Whom the Bell Tolls*, edited by Rena Sanderson, 19–25. Westport, Conn.: Greenwood Press, 1992, as "Kurt Vonnegut on Ernest Hemingway."

Comments on his "Requiem." Adapted from "The Hocus Pocus Laundromat," *North American Review* 271 (December 1986): 29–35.

Proposed testimony to the Attorney General's Commission on Pornography. *Nation* 242 (23 January 1986): 65, 81–82, as "God Bless You, Edwin Meese."

"Address to the Graduating Class at the University of Rhode Island." Previously unpublished.

"Preface." In *A Very Young Author and Photographer: Jill Krementz at Fifty*. New York: Privately printed, 1990.

Lecture on strategic bombing and its victims. *Smart* (June 1990): 73–79, as "Tough Question, Tough Answer."

Comments to an audience in the year 2088. Advertisement for Volkswagen Corporation in issues of *Time* magazine, 1988.

Essay on relative freedoms. *Lear's* 1 (November/December 1988): 106–15, as "Light at the End of the Tunnel?"

Lecture on science and technology at Massachusetts Institute of Technology. Previously unpublished.

Comments on New York City as a folk society. *Architectural Digest* 44 (November 1987): 76, 78, 80, as "Skyscraper National Park."

Untitled comments. In his *Hocus Pocus*. Franklin Center, Pa.: Franklin Library, 1990, as "A Special Message to Subscribers from Kurt Vonnegut."

Essay on war preparations. *Nation* 237 (31 December 1983/7 January 1984): 681, 698–99, as "The Worst Addiction of Them All."

Sermon on threats to human life. In *Fates Worse Than Death*. Nottingham, U.K.: Bertrand Russell Peace Foundation Spokesman Pamphlet No. 80; "Fates Worse than Death," *North American Review* 267 (December 1982): 46–49.

Address to Unitarian congregation in Rochester, N.Y. *The World: Journal of the Unitarian Universalist Association* 1 (January/February 1987): 4, 6–8, as "Love Is Too Strong a Word."

Essay on Mozambique. *Parade,* 7 January 1990, 16–17, as "My Visit to Hell."

Address to translators at Columbia University. Previously unpublished.

Essay on humor. *New York Times Book Review,* 22 April 1990, 14, as "Notes from My Bed of Gloom: Or, Why the Joking Had to Stop."

Essay on reading. *Kroch & Brentano Christmas Book Catalogue* (1990).

"Mass Promulgated by Me in 1985." *North American Review* 271 (December 1986): 29–35, as "Requiem: The "Hocus Pocus Laundromat."

"My Reply to a Letter from the Dean of the Chapel at Transylvania University about a Speech I Gave There." Previously unpublished.

Transcribed Commentary

Like Shaking Hands with God: A Conversation about Writing. New York: Seven Stories Press, 1999 (with Lee Stringer).

Comedy

God Bless You, Dr. Kevorkian. New York: Seven Stories Press, 1999.

Selected Criticism and Commentary on Kurt Vonnegut

Allen, William Rodney. *Understanding Kurt Vonnegut.* Columbia: University of South Carolina Press, 1991.

Boon, Kevin A. *Chaos Theory and the Interpretation of Literary Texts: The Case of Kurt Vonnegut.* Lewiston, N.Y.: Edwin Mellen Press, 1997.

———, ed. *At Millenium's End: New Essays on the Work of Kurt Vonnegut.* Albany: State University of New York Press, 2001.

Broer, Lawrence R. *Sanity Plea: Schizophrenia in the Novels of Kurt Vonnegut.* Ann Arbor, Mich.: UMI Research Press, 1989. Second edition, expanded, Tuscaloosa: University of Alabama Press, 1994.

Gardner, John. *On Moral Fiction.* New York: Basic Books, 1978.

Graff, Gerald. *Literature against Itself.* Chicago: University of Chicago Press, 1977.

Hicks, Granville. "Literary Horizons." *Saturday Review* 52 (29 March 1969): 25.

Hutcheon, Linda. *A Poetics of Postmodernism.* London: Routledge, 1988.

Klinkowitz, Jerome. *Keeping Literary Company: Working with Writers since the Sixties.* Albany: State University of New York Press, 1998.

———. *Kurt Vonnegut.* London: Methuen, 1982.

———. *Vonnegut in Fact: The Public Spokesmanship of Personal Fiction.* Columbia: University of South Carolina Press, 1998.

Klinkowitz, Jerome, and John Somer, eds. *The Vonnegut Statement.* New York: Delacorte Press/Seymour Lawrence, 1973.

LeClair, Tom. *The Art of Excess: Mastery in Contemporary American Fiction.* Urbana: University of Illinois Press, 1989.

Leeds, Marc. *The Vonnegut Encyclopedia.* Westport, Conn.: Greenwood Press, 1995.

Leeds, Marc, and Peter J. Reed. *Kurt Vonnegut: Images and Representations.* Westport, Conn.: Greenwood Press, 2000.

Lundquist, James. *Kurt Vonnegut.* New York: Ungar, 1977.

Merrill, Robert, ed. *Critical Essays on Kurt Vonnegut.* Boston: G. K. Hall, 1990.

Mustazza, Leonard. *Forever Pursuing Genesis: The Myth of Eden in the Novels of Kurt Vonnegut.* Lewisburg, Pa.: Bucknell University Press, 1990.

————, ed. *The Critical Response to Kurt Vonnegut.* Westport, Conn.: Greenwood Press, 1994.

Pieratt, Asa B. Jr., Julie Huffman-klinkowitz, and Jerome Klinkowitz. *Kurt Vonnegut: A Comprehensive Bibliography.* Hamden, Conn.: Shoe String Press/Archon Books, 1987.

Reed, Peter J. *Kurt Vonnegut, Jr.* New York: Warner, 1972.

————. *The Short Fiction of Kurt Vonnegut.* Westport, Conn.: Greenwood Press, 1997.

Reed, Peter J., and Marc Leeds, eds. *The Vonnegut Chronicles.* Westport, Conn.: Greenwood Press, 1996.

Schatt, Stanley. *Kurt Vonnegut, Jr.* Boston: Twayne, 1976.

Scholes, Robert. *The Fabulators.* New York: Oxford University Press, 1967.

Vonnegut, Mark. *The Eden Express: A Personal Account of Schizophrenia.* New York: Praeger, 1975.

Yarmolinsky, Jane Vonnegut. *Angels without Wings: A Courageous Family's Triumph over Tragedy.* Boston: Houghton Mifflin, 1987.

INDEX

Maharishi, 79, 81, 82, 84, 146
Mailer, Norman, 175, 185, 186
Major, Clarence, 177
Malamud, Bernard, 176
"Manned Missiles, The," 25
Maxincuckee, Lake, 14, 172
McCall's, 75
Melville, Herman, 173
Miller, Henry, 187
"Miss Temptation," 25
"Mnemonics," 20
Moby-Dick, 154
"Money Talks to the New Man," 18
"More Stately Mansions," 25
Morrison, Toni, 189
Mother Night, 10–11, 47, 52–61,
    62, 63, 67, 72, 73, 80, 93, 100,
    105, 128, 133, 142, 152,
    183–84
Mozambique, 171
Müller, Gerhard, 85–86
Mumbo Jumbo, 188, 189
Mustazza, Leonard, 110, 112

Naked and the Dead, The, 175, 186
"New England Enters the Space
    Age," 2–5
New York Times Book Review, 80
New Yorker, 16, 176, 181, 182
Newman, Barnett, 109, 110
"Next Door," 25
1984, 182–83
98.6, 187
Nixon, Richard M., 115, 122
"No-Talent Kid, The," 32, 182

Oates, Joyce Carol, 176
O'Hare, Bernard, 85, 86–87, 154,
    187
O'Hare, Mary, 85, 87, 91, 96, 97,
    187
Old Man and the Sea, The, 151, 166

One Flew Over the Cuckoo's Nest,
    175, 176
158-Pound Marriage, The, 190
Oranging of America, The, 191
Orwell, George, 182–83
Our Town, 168, 170, 186
Out, 187

Painted Bird, The, 176
Paley, Grace, 176, 187
Palm Sunday, 8, 9–10, 19, 63,
    122–23, 125–27, 128, 132, 156
Parade, 171
Parise, Goffredo, 19
Penelope, 99
Percy, Walker, 176
Petro, Joe, III, 166
Player Piano, 1, 17, 20, 37–45, 48,
    65, 71, 73, 98, 100, 102, 118,
    146, 150, 175, 180, 182–83,
    188
Pollock, Jackson, 134
Propheteers, The, 192
Public Burning, The, 186
Pynchon, Thomas, ix, 90, 91, 176,
    177, 178, 180, 186, 187

Ragtime, 186
Random House Dictionary, 75, 80,
    98
Reagan, Ronald, 93
Redbook, 16, 37, 39
Redfield, Robert, 17
Reed, Ishmael, ix, 177, 187, 188–89
Reed, Peter J., xiii, 22, 24, 177
"Report," 182
"Report on the Barnhouse Effect,"
    19, 21–22, 23–24, 25, 41
Reuther, Walter, 76
Robbins, Tom, 191
"Robert Kennedy Saved from
    Drowning," 182